It's Not Like That Here

Teaching Academic Writing and Reading to Novice Writers

Marcia Dickson

Boynton/Cook Publishers
HEINEMANN
Portsmouth, NH

Boynton/Cook Publishers, Inc.
A subsidiary of Reed Elsevier Inc.
361 Hanover Street
Portsmouth, NH 03801-3912
Offices and agents throughout the world

Copyright 1995 by Marcia Dickson.

Every effort has been made to contact the copyright holders and students for permission to reprint borrowed material. We regret any oversights that may have occurred and would be happy to rectify them in future printings of this work.

Excerpts from *Women's Ways of Knowing* by **Mary Field Belenky et al.** Copyright © 1986 by Basic Books, Inc. Reprinted by permission of BasicBooks, a division of HarperCollins Publishers, Inc.

Excerpts from *Literacy as Involvement: The Acts of Writers, Readers, and Texts* by **Deborah Brandt**. Copyright © 1990 by the Board of Trustees, Southern Illinois University. Reprinted by permission.

Excerpt from "Writing Critical Ethnographic Narratives," by **Linda Brodkey** in *Anthropology and Education Quarterly*, Volume 18, Number 2, June 1987. Reproduced by permission of the American Anthropological Association. Not for further reproduction.

Excerpt from **Linda Brodkey**, "Writing Ethnograph Narratives," *Written Communication*, 4.1 (January 1987), pp 25–50. Reprinted by permission of Sage Publications, Inc.

Excerpts from "Remedial Writers: The Teacher's Job as Corrector of Papers" by **John F. Butler**. From *College Composition and Communication* (vol. 31, October 1981). Reprinted by permission of National Council of Teachers of English.

Excerpts from "Ranking, Evaluating, and Liking" by **Peter Elbow** in *College English* 55.2 (February, 1993, pp. 187–206). Reprinted by permission of the National Council of Teachers of English.

Credits continued on page iv.

Editor: Peter R. Stillman
Production: J. B. Tranchemontagne
Cover design: Phillip Augusta

Library of Congress Cataloging-in-Publication Data
Dickson, Marcia.
    It's not like that here : Teaching academic writing and reading to novice
writers / Marcia Dickson.
       p. cm.
    Includes bibliographical references.
    ISBN 0-86709-351-X
    1. English language—Rhetoric—Study and teaching. 2. English language—
Grammar—Study and teaching. 3. Critical thinking—Study and teaching.
I. Title.
PE1404.D45 1995
808'.042'07—dc20   94-36421
                                                 CIP

Printed in the United States of America on acid-free paper.
99 98 97 96 95 EB 1 2 3 4 5 6 7 8 9

For my friend and colleague
Lynda Barry
in grateful recognition of all the times
she's said "What?"
when she probably wanted to say "Go away!"

Contents

Chapter 6
The Horror, the Horror
Assessment and Grading
153

Afterword
183

Appendix
English 053 Course Packet
191

Notes
203

Works Cited
207

Introduction

Pedagogical Theory, Real People

Once, while presenting a paper at a conference held by the American Association of Semiotics, I was accused of privileging "common sense." The accusation has some merit. My attitude toward pedagogy reflects my attitude toward child rearing: read everything you can on raising children, but trust your instincts above anything you read. This position, in turn, reflects my family heritage. When I was an infant, my mother, a modern woman of twenty-five, admonished my grandfather for picking me up when I cried. According to the books she had been reading, picking up a baby would keep it from learning to be independent. "Trudy," my grandfather warned, "the baby might not have read the book."

None of the novice writers I've ever taught have read the book.

This fact often leaves me frustrated, but not defeated. Not having all the answers forces me, and other teachers like me, to see these novice writers for their individual strengths and weakness rather than as group of people who act and react in prescribed ways. The students who are the focus of this book are seldom inherently less intelligent or poorer critical thinkers than their better-trained peers. I have struggled to find a terminology to describe these students that would indicate their potential rather than label them as deficient. After rejecting potentially loaded terms like *developmental* or *basic* writers, I decided to identify my students as *novice* readers and writers because many of the problems I discuss in this book affect *all* readers and writers who find themselves faced with comprehending and producing new and more difficult forms of written discourse. I, too, sometimes find myself in the position of being a novice writer, and I think it's wise to acknowledge this uncomfortable position. In *Declining Grammar,* Dennis Baron offers the following insight about being a novice: "Each time we enter a new part of the education cycle we become beginners who need to learn the ropes and master the conventions before we make the grade" (54). Recognizing the fact that our students are novices at academic reading and writing affects everything from how we read their papers to how they interpret our assignments.

Few teachers can fully understand the dynamics of novice writing classes before they enter the classroom; no book can prepare them for the faces they meet. Teachers encounter a group of students who are resentful of their placement, suspicious of school or downright school-phobic, or convinced that this class will only bring what most of them have suffered through for their entire academic lives: failure. Smarter than they look on paper, these students have only themselves and their families (and sometimes not even those people) to support their right to be in college. They've hurdled emotional, educational, or economic barriers to gain entry to the academy, but they still find themselves set apart because, to varying degrees, they cannot write or read adequately. These novice writers can't be lumped into a group, but they can be placed on a continuum according to their ability to handle written language. At one end, students cannot spell, create complete sentences, or tell the difference between "weather" and "whether." Many cannot generate more than a sentence or two on any topic without feeling that they repeat themselves. Somewhere in the middle, there are students who read novels and newspapers rather eagerly but fail to find the main point in a textbook, and students who can solve any problem, mathematical or scientific, but who can't work through writing tasks posed in the humanities. On the other end of the continuum, we find students who can produce the correct prose that their high school teachers drummed into them but do not think or read critically for nuances, implications, or abstract notions. Lacking those skills, they cannot write critically either.

Placing novice writers on a continuum has appeal. But even as I write these descriptions of students, I grow uncomfortable with this sort of classification system. Such a positioning of writers/problems on a continuous line implies not only that students' abilities are easily identifiable, do not overlap in substantial ways, and can be measured adequately, but also that good teaching is merely a matter of applying the proper theory at the proper time. The object is to move the students as rapidly as possible to a more proficient place on the continuum. Unfortunately, real people can be real problems when you're trying to turn writing theory to classroom practice. Teachers can't find the answer to every instructional problem in a single book. From year to year, the individual needs of students will change the dynamics of teaching and learning so greatly that almost any pedagogy can be rendered null and void. Because they have different backgrounds, skills, expectations, and even different attitudes toward learning, the novice writers who sit in class during the current quarter will not necessarily respond to the same theories that were so successful the quarter before.

This book is one of many that attempt to make teaching, learning, and academic life easier for the teachers who must somehow instruct all the disparate novice writers assigned to them. It tries to take into consideration the fact that most teachers of novice writers have not been trained as composition specialists and that many times these teachers find themselves completely on their own without the advice and support of fellow faculty members. More often than not, the teachers that are working with novice writers are new or part-time faculty brought into their English departments to teach students with severe writing and reading problems. As part of the large group of what is euphemistically called *temporary* faculty, they do not receive release time, developmental funds, or even a break in course load that many (certainly not all) full-time, tenure-track faculty members can count on. Yet these same teachers are expected to turn poorly prepared students into competent writers in one quarter or semester.

No theory or practice, I would argue, can accomplish this turnabout in so little time, not even the one you're about to read. However, I do believe that great strides can be made toward introducing students to survival skills that will serve them in the academy. In my experience, knowing how to read a text and how to explain its meaning *as it applies to your personal experience* is more valuable than the grammar and paragraph instruction that has, with few exceptions, occupied those whom Mike Rose refers to as *underprepared* students. The curricular approach, the Distanced/Personal, outlined in this book connects the academic community with the local community so that the student can make sense of and reflect upon the common problems of both worlds. The object is to develop a literacy that integrates the world of abstract and theoretical knowledge with the practical wisdom learned from friends and relatives.

The Distanced/Personal represents the way most academics construct knowledge, liberally mixing the theory of the journals and texts in their fields with the observations they make of people engaged in the activities of living. This book reflects such a construction. The theorists I draw upon are diverse, selected for their awareness of classroom practice as well as for their intellectual insight. For issues of literacy and learning, I've consulted such works as Shirley Brice Heath's *Ways with Words;* Mary Field Belenky, Blythe McVicker Clinchy, Nancy Rule Goldberger, and Jill Mattuck Tarule's *Women's Ways of Knowing;* Jerome Bruner's *Toward a Theory of Instruction;* Deborah Brandt's *Literacy as Involvement;* Eliot Wigginton's *Sometimes a Shining Moment;* and Carole Gilligan's *In a Different Voice.* The pedagogical theories and practices that influence my thinking are equally diverse: Marie Ponsot and Rosemary Deen, Andrea Lunsford and Lisa Ede, David Bartholomae and Anthony Petrosky, and Peter Elbow and Pat Belanoff. This mixture of composition theorists, only a partial list of the authors, books, and articles that inform my thinking and my classroom practice, dips into both expressivist and formalist composition theory. Like other teachers, I use what I need regardless of who wrote it. Those works represent the Distanced, or academic aspects of my work. For the Personal, I continue to rely upon teachers, not only in English, but also in other disciplines who talk to my students and me about writing and learning. Friends from outside the academy also participate in our studies so that, as often as possible, my students are exposed to all manner of real people using writing and reading strategies to solve real problems. There is no division between the academy and "the real world" in our classrooms. The objective of the Distanced/Personal curriculum is to demonstrate to novice readers and writers how the academy can be just another larger, somewhat confused, but terribly *interesting* community group, absorbed with solving problems that frequently have something to do with the world at large.

In writing this book, I've had to ask myself repeatedly how I can explain the difference between working in a Distanced/Personal classroom and in a more traditional pedagogical environment. Many of the writing activities we use—freewriting, peer assessment, multiple revision, and close work on proofreading—do not necessarily differ from those used by other teachers in other types of classrooms. The difference, I believe, can be found in the collaborative nature of our classrooms and in our department. Students and teachers work together to better understand not only the writing process but also a topic, and teachers collaborate in the risk taking that grows from the pedagogy—new heuristics, new methodologies. In the classroom, the teachers may know more about writing by virtue of training, experience, and age; however, they do not use this knowledge to test the students' ability to construct sentences or to use words with absolute clarity and style. Teachers use their knowledge to help the students learn to search out answers to the latter's own questions—grammatical and critical—and to introduce the latter to the pleasure of learning merely for the sake of learning. Teachers do not set their agenda for teaching above the students' agenda for learning; teachers realize that students often have goals for attending class and studying that are different from what teachers might have. For instance, it is not a disgrace in the Distanced/Personal classroom to enter college simply as a means of training for a good-paying vocation. Teachers see their job as expanding that utilitarian agenda rather than judging it. The Distanced/Personal classroom shares the academic charge to bolster the spirit of inquiry, but Distanced/Personal teachers willingly acknowledge that sometimes the students win the debate and accept their opinions as teachers expect students to accept theirs. Teachers and students are coinvestigators of a problem, much like professors with graduate students. Even novice readers and writers have something to contribute to the investigation, and as teachers, we try to provide them with the investigative tools necessary for making meaning.

The Distanced/Personal course described in this book is designed for a two-quarter, twenty-week teaching period. The Ohio State University at Marion (OSUM), a regional campus of the enormous Ohio State University (OSU) in Columbus, is small compared to many two-year colleges, about 1,000 students compared to the Columbus campus's 60,000 plus. Composed of working-class people from largely rural communities, OSUM's student body must commute to school rather than take up residence on the larger campus. Unlike a community college, however, our regional campus is part of the entire OSU community. Our students, like our faculty, are considered part of the same educational system: the faculty is part of the Columbus campus faculty and the students do not transfer to Columbus in order to complete their degrees; they just continue their education by enrolling for junior- and senior-level courses in Columbus.

It's probably not like that where you are. However, I think that the Distanced/Personal methods will work as well for other types of student bodies at other types of institutions as it has for us. Every academic community—large or small, urban or rural—has mysteries that need to be explored and students who are not quite ready to explore them. I believe that, with some adjustment, our course can be equally effective in a semester schedule. Like any other approach to teaching, our program would be even more effective if students received a full year of reading and writing instruction. Most novice writers need time to develop: time to absorb what they learn and time to practice their skills. No teacher, no theory, no matter how brilliant either may be, can compensate for the abbreviated writing and reading requirements now in effect in most college and universities. I've tried to arrange the material in this book so that teachers can use the ideas within as a starting point for developing their own programs.

Chapter 1 outlines some of the common problems of teaching novice writers in an academic setting. The dissonance between what the composition teachers want, what the rest of their colleagues want, and what the students themselves want, acts to set up learning barriers in the classroom. And since I outline the problems, I naturally can't avoid offering some solutions. Drawing on the work of such theorists as Shirley Brice Heath, Sondra Perl, and Deborah Brandt, I discuss the possibility that ethnographic research, the type of research that can explore nonacademic ways of thinking and acting within an academic framework, might be an answer for uniting expressionist and formalist theories of teaching composition. Furthering the conversation begun in Chapter 1 by offering a discussion of the relationship between learning, knowing, and teaching, Chapter 2 considers the effects of teaching goals on student learning and explores the basic premises of Distanced/Personal pedagogy. In brief, I argue that the narrow grammar and paragraph studies traditionally prescribed by English departments for novice writers defeat these students' attempts to enter the academy rather than help them succeed.

Chapter 3 looks at common reading and writing problems not as problems of illiteracy but as problems of competing and different literacies. I suggest that many reading and writing problems result from not understanding how to enter an academic text or what to do once inside. Moreover, I argue that learning to read and write in the academy means learning to read and write about complex texts that deliberate about complicated issues that extend beyond academic interests and affect real lives. Chapter 4 builds upon the information in Chapter 3 by offering specific suggestions for teaching extended reading and writing. In order to combine theory with practice, I illustrate my pedagogical ideas by describing some of the ethnographic research projects employed in novice writing courses at OSUM. Because I find it easiest to discuss a pedagogical approach by creating concrete examples, this chapter and the following chapters use what I have come to call the education project as an example of Distanced/Personal research. This project has proved one of the most successful in the program. Students read educational theory and interview their former teachers. And since the interview is one of the primary tools used in Distanced/Personal classrooms, and helping students conduct and interpret successful interviews is imperative, Chapter 5 offers some insights on avoiding the pitfalls of collecting this type of ethnographic data, and some explanations for how these pitfalls have been generated.

Chapter 6 is devoted to those academic horrors, grading and assessment. Assessment presents problems that are present everywhere in the university but have dire consequences in the retention of novice writers. How do we grade students who are obviously only beginners as they go about learning to construct informative, analytical, and structurally correct essays? Too harsh a policy results in an increased student dropout rate; too liberal a policy continues the harmful practice of "social passing," which has created the need for college courses that must "remediate" students with twelve years of public school education. I do not wish to imply by that last remark that the public schools are entirely responsible for the writing and reading woes of the nation. Nor are they solely answerable for the growing number of what colleges call developmental, basic, or remedial writing courses. The colleges themselves must share that blame. Who trained the teachers? Who avoids offering comprehensive in-service programs for retraining? Who devises theories that work perfectly well when teachers have fifty or seventy-five students daily and ignores the fact that high school teachers instruct 150 to 200? And finally, who has reduced the number of writing and reading courses in college for the sake of economy, making it disgraceful for a student to need more than one quarter to learn what amounts to a difficult and ever-changing skill?

It only makes sense that to improve pedagogy, teachers and students must work with one another. My decision to work collaboratively with my colleagues and students has affected everything from the activities conducted in class to the text of this book. The *we* that appears in this book reflects the collaborative nature of the project that follows, not an awe-inspiring royal *we*. The pronoun *I* no longer seems appropriate because while *I* taught that first class that incorporated ethnographic techniques, the ideas that began in individual desperation became part of the daily conversations in the office, in the faculty lounge, and in the car on the way to meetings and/or the movies. These conversations between teachers, determined not only to experiment with team teaching but also to find a means of initiating novice writers into the academy a little less painfully, led to the development of the course as it is today.

At the beginning, there were two of us, Lynda Barry, who now runs the OSUM Writing Center, and myself. Without Lynda's enthusiasm and intelligence during the first two years, there might not have been a Distanced/Personal. Called by the students "the two most aggravating women in the world," we taught as a team to develop the first Distanced/Personal sequence, the education project. In the following two years we added two more associates, Sue Cody and Carole Kirkton. The four of us have found this sharing of novice writing pedagogy both mentally and professionally supportive. Working as a team to experiment with the theories that we had learned in graduate school made it easier to develop new projects for the classroom. I would like to thank them for their continued support. And since I seem to have quite inadvertently wandered into that "Thank You" stage of an introduction, I'd also like to express my gratitude to OSUM for financial support through its Small Teaching and Research Grants program and the—unfortunately now defunct—Ohio State University Center for Teaching Excellence, a program that supported educational experimentation. It bit the dust in times of economic hardship.

No other set of colleagues and definitely no funding agency, however, has been more important to me as a writer and a scholar than the group known as The Five Crazed Researchers; Lynda Barry, Anne Bower, Scott DeWitt, and Beverly Moss form the rest of the gang. With their invaluable assistance, I have struggled through the perplexing task of applying theory to practice and the even more daunting task of putting both that theory and practice into words on paper. This book would not have made it to press without their encouragement, good advice, and laughter.

Chapter One

Novice Writers and Academic Discourse

Experts don't know what they are talking about. They just like to hear themselves talk. What people who are experts say is always general, never specific. And each situation is different.

—A College Student
Women's Ways of Knowing

Early in the second year of my position at OSUM, my colleague, Vladimir, stopped me in the hall during a break between classes to discuss one of the new candidates for a position in the English department. "Now my concern is this," he began his preamble, his index finger uplifted in the best cautionary position, chin set, eyes keen. "Does this candidate understand that our mission is to prepare students for real work in the academy . . . not this kind of personal, psycho-babble, expressive nonsense?"

Vladimir's a historian. His use of "our" to modify "mission" refers to the fact that we both teach at OSUM, a two-year regional campus devoted to the preparation of freshmen and sophomores for upper-division courses at OSU in Columbus. Our mission consists of serving students who often have lower GPAs, greater family obligations, and less money than the students who attend the Columbus campus. Fifty percent of our incoming students are

1

over the age of twenty-five and eighty-five percent work forty hours a week to support themselves and their families. Even the more traditional students live at home and work not only to pay for their college education but also to relieve their parents of the financial obligations that naturally arise from feeding and clothing a young adult. Because we are a commuter college of fewer than 1,000 students, the interdisciplinary faculty's connection with the local community is greater than that of the faculty on the gargantuan Columbus campus. On a regional campus, relationships among those of us in different disciplines develops easily— thirty-one faculty members share the same building and classrooms—and the freedom we feel to discuss the goals of other people's instruction grows out of the proximity of both students and teachers. Because we debate curriculum and instructional matters frequently, I was not really offended by Vladimir's charge that the personal essay was not real work. However, I was concerned that he so readily labeled the personal essay as "psycho-babble." I was concerned that Vladimir, and others like him, might too quickly dismiss the personal essay as a means of making knowledge not only in composition but also in other disciplines. But then, I think of composition as a writing process that explores and deepens intellectual experience and promotes thinking skills. Vladimir thinks of composition as a product: firm, crisp copy with argumentative frills and flourishes, free of fallacies and precise in doctrine.

These differences in worldview aren't necessarily a result of competing disciplines. Even in composition studies, debate flourishes as to whether the personal essay can or should be used to teach academic discourse. While I've stood toe-to-toe with full professors from the old school who insisted that "personal essays don't force the students to think rigorously; students need to be introduced to good-old classical rhetoric," I've also hotly debated with other members of my profession who emphasize the kind of process writing that one finds in technical manuals and informative writing tasks that prepare the students to write memos. At this end of the spectrum of writing tasks, the teacher thinks of writing courses as utilitarian preparation for real life: "Students need to know how to write a good letter, how to create a grant proposal, and how to punctuate each of those documents correctly." The concern expressed by my historian colleague about using personal essays grows from his desire to engage the students in a disciplinary conversation about history. In Vladimir's mind, our mission is to prepare the students for the kind of academic conversation that they will find on the main campus. But would throwing out the personal essay, a main-stay of English discourse, in favor of the hard-hitting, focused and—yes, classical—argument, serve students in all disciplines?

Personal Essays

In this book, the term "personal" when used as an adjective for "essay" refers to any essay that places the writer's autobiographical experience at the center of the discourse and that suggests that the writer and the writer alone can know and judge the truth of the topic she or he presents to the audience. Such essays have a long and respected history in English composition and, when used as teaching tools, seem to develop students' descriptive and narrative skills in ways no other type of nonfiction writing can. This sort of personal essay has become standard in the writing curriculum and, in some cases, has gradually taken the place of the impersonal classical argument as the primary expository form in English classes. Robert Conners, in "Personal Writing Assignments," describes the manner in which the elements of the personal gradually worked into the teaching of writing. According to Conners, the focus for college themes has shifted from the rather vague topic "Mountains" to "A Tramp to the Mountains." Instead of "Disease," students began to write about "The Anthrax Plague in our Village." Today, students might write about their family's experience with AIDS. Whether placed in the center of natural wonder or disaster, the individual view has become more important than the impersonal description of grand scale phenomena. Conners notes that in today's high schools and freshman composition courses, essays concentrate on narrations of personal incidents, criticisms of motion pictures, reactions to school subjects, and other topics that ask the student to act as an authority who has experienced or seen events or outcomes (176–77). Every issue becomes relative to personal interpretation, and every argument a matter of personal opinion.[1] Needless to say, this emphasis on the personal puzzles worries many people who see English composition as a service course for other disciplines. Vladimir doesn't want to read essays that discuss the students' personal reactions to history; he wants an ordered analysis of the events leading up to or following historical events.

I admit, reluctantly, that I once stood proudly, and perhaps slightly wrongheadedly, against the use of autobiography and memoir in composition courses for reasons similar to the ones that Vladimir expresses. I saw my composition course strictly as a service course, a place for preparing students to write for other disciplines, not for English, and certainly not for themselves. Now I see such a refusal to incorporate the personal with the scholarly as a strange and somehow disturbing period in my own development as an academic and as a writer. Furthermore, speaking *only* for myself, I realize that my obsession with academic rigor grew more out of my own insecurity with my place in the academy than out of rational thought or firm commitment to formal discourse. The humanist in me believed that autobiography, the memoir, the personal essay, all of these forms fashioned out of individual memory, could be (or perhaps should be) representative of the larger context of times and places that encompass solitary lives. However, the utilitarian, who shared and continues to share residence with the humanitarian, worried about whether autobiographical reading and writing would prepare my students for the world of academic discourse outside the English department.

At that time the personal essays I was familiar with described the students' rooms, or the most interesting characters they ever met—period. Such limited discussions bore an uncomfortable resemblance to the classic "What I Did on My Summer Vacation." They represented to me solitary exercises, almost workbooklike in their performance, rather than attempts to explore a larger community. While I thought students were capable of writing the type of autobiographical narratives and analyses that bring into question the experience and actions of their past, these attempts to invent the truth (to slightly revise the title of William Zinsser's collection of essays about the craft of memoir, *Inventing the Truth*) seemed much closer to creative writing than to composition class. Such essays could, as Zinsser suggests, effectively place the private life in context (29) and, as Anne Dillard asserts, provide the reader with a picture of the self-awakening to the world (Zinsser 22), but they required a proficiency with writing that seems almost literary in nature.

My concerns with the personal essay reflect the larger debate in composition circles. On one side, theorists like Elbow, Hairston, Macrorie, Murray, and countless others, argue that assigning personal experience essays overcomes the students' resistance to writing because such assignments place students in a position of authority that negates their lack of general knowledge about academic subjects. Writing about what the students know provides plenty of grist for the analytical mill. Compositionists on the other side of the argument argue just as persuasively for less expressive writing. That argument is outlined by Mike Rose in "Remedial Writing Courses":

Even when teachers assign such topics in order to provide novice writers with simple tasks involving material that they are familiar with, they do students no service. Limiting discourse to autobiographical experience may help writers develop insight into their own lives, but writing about their own experience tells them little about the world around them and prepares them little for writing in disciplines other than English. (107)

Too often universities instructors unconsciously teach to what Bizzell and others have termed a hidden curriculum, one considered by academics to be universal, one that professors declare objective and based on logic. The context for the English professor varies from that of the scientist or the social scientist because it is a literary one, which in some respects is more cognizant of the interrelationship of thought and emotions. We can extrapolate macrocosms from the microcosm of one life, real or fictional. However, even literary scholars tend to treat that life in a most analytical manner; we deconstruct it, psychoanalyze it, interpret it from the perspective of the new historicism. We continually prod it, poke it, and push it about in an effort to make it give forth meaning that will expand our knowledge about the collective human condition.

Novice writing students, however, take the words "personal experience" seriously and literally, and because they are not ready, willing, or able to be objective about their experiences, the "personal essay" can become problematic for both student and teacher. Take for instance, a student who writes of the heartfelt decision to leave a spouse, defy parents, or (in the case of a placement exam I had to evaluate) turn off the life support system for a dying child. Grading essays such as these for logic and clear argument becomes tantamount to grading the writer's actions in the situation she reports. How can one tell the writer that she has not included enough detail to justify her decision? Can a teacher remark that the essay is not organized effectively if, indeed, the student has organized the essay according to what happened—where it began and how it ended—rather than by some larger more philosophical thesis? What a curious double bind: Students write about personal, private experiences in an honest and sincere manner, but when teachers evaluate these personal experiences, the students' honesty, sincerity, and even motivation become open to question in a most impersonal and dispassionate manner. In effect, we reduce both the essay and the student's experience to a specimen for study and dare to judge whether or not the essay is "honest" or "thoughtful."[2]

The Problem with Significance

Life and death choices aside, developing an essay that is both honest and sincere *and* logical and objective does not present the only problem that the personal essay can pose for writer and reader. What about the student who cannot find anything significant—personal or otherwise—to write about? As teachers, we have all encountered students whose lives have been so enclosed, so restricted, or so limited in scope that nothing, no event, no thought, has touched them deeply. Experienced readers and writers may declare that each life has significance. They could further claim that providing a forum for critical analysis and pushing the student to see how even the most minute event can be significant will help students find meaning where they thought none existed. But those resistant students may be wiser than we think. They may recognize real significance and be reluctant to assign significance to that which is only memorable. For the academic, the quest for the *significant* parallels the quest for *meaning.* Such theory plays an integral role in the pedagogy of David Bartholomae and Anthony Petrosky, who, in *Facts, Artifacts and Counterfacts,* describe a course that uses personal experience essays to introduce students to academic discourse. Students study "Growth and Change in Adolescence," a topic that cannot help but be familiar. Through a variety of reading and writing assignments, teachers introduce some of the basic methods of university inquiry: discussion and debate, research and inquiry, report and commentary (*Facts* 30). In the first part of the course, students read autobiography and fiction about the passage from adolescence to adulthood and write papers that explore their own experiences. Discussion focuses upon significant events that changed, didn't change, or should have changed their lives and the lives of the people they read about. As the course develops, the students locate patterns of behavior in the materials they read and create their own theories of growth and change. Many teachers agree that the students become invested, engaged, and fairly articulate as they perform these tasks—as long as the topics ask for analysis that does not go beyond personal experience. However, when they must expand their knowledge by reading analytical texts—written by more objective writers in sociology, anthropology, or psychology—they falter. Bartholomae and Petrosky's pedagogical theory posits that students who have studied their own lives in detail should be able to engage in a dialogue with more sophisticated authors. However, as Bartholomae reports, believing one can confront the expert in the published manuscript and thereby the academy itself, is not nearly as attractive as believing "can become the source of knowledge, an original, the someone who has the right to make it up as he goes along" (40). I would suggest that novice writers and readers find confronting the academic author less appealing because they still see no way to connect the personal, that which they can make up as they go along, and the academic—the thoughts and experiences of people they do not know, involved in activities they have not witnessed first hand.

This inability to make the leap from personal to academic informs my concerns about converting personal essays into academic analyses. As I see it, even an attempt to make the students gather up all the lives in the class, all the significant events, and all the memories, still creates merely a palette of individual memories, not a portrait of a group in context. The problem is the genre with which the students try to make meaning. Autobiography can be quite deceptive and less than straightforward. It seems easy; it would appear to represent a subject that the novice writers know well, one they can write on with authority. The individual life seems an excellent point of embarkation for a student who wishes to study groups of people. And therein may rest the largest and most fallacious assumption about universal worldviews. Lester Faigley argues that teachers who assign autobiographical essays make a crucial assumption, the assumption that an autobiographical essay can be shaped to reveal an "identifiable 'true' self and that the true self can be expressed in discourse" (405). This traditional approach to content assumes that students can make meaning from events in the past, put that meaning into a perspective the teacher recognizes as true, and tie experience, meaning, and truth into a neatly coherent bundle. Students who can pull off such discourse feats receive As on their papers (or their lives). However, scholars agree that autobiography doesn't necessarily represent the true self; even the examined life can be represented askew. Therefore, compiling a number of autobiographies and treating them as if they were academic case studies is problematic. As Faigley suggests, "the freedom students are given in some classes to choose and adapt autobiographical assignments hides the fact that these same students will be judged by the teacher's unstated cultural definitions of the self" (410).

Novice Writers and Autobiography

Novice writers live in worlds that seldom allow time and space for intensive self-evaluation or for overt scrutiny of actions that seem obvious or natural parts of life. I don't mean to imply that novice writers do not spend a great deal of personal effort in thinking about their lives or examining the issues that control their days and experiences. If they didn't, they probably would not have made it as far as college. Nonetheless, they often see little or no purpose in writing about their lives from what academics call objective stances. Indeed, as Nicholas Coles and Susan Wall suggest in "Conflict and Power in the Reader-Responses of Adult Basic Writers," novice writing students look for education to provide protection against the feelings of powerlessness that they have previously experienced in both school and work arenas (301). For example, since the disasters in our adolescence tend to live longer in memory than our more positive experiences, examining significant events from adolescence often means examining failure of one sort or the other. As one of my students reported, his successes in high school were few. He came to college expecting to start all over, and he found himself going over the same ground once more. For him, it was neither a pleasant nor an enlightening (much less welcome) experience. He wanted a new life, not the old one—examined or otherwise. What most novice writers (and, I would argue, traditional students) want to learn is "how to" improve their chances for employment, make more money, and create a better life. In this improved life, "better" can be defined by learning to control situations rather than by merely pursuing intellectual discoveries.

Grading further complicates the power issues that arise with autobiographical assignments. When the teacher grades an intensely autobiographical assignment, the very act of grading can exacerbate the students' sense of powerlessness. Failing or doing poorly on a personal essay tacitly implies that the students do not even understand the implications of the life they live. What is intended to situate novice writers in the academy can alienate them from the one thing they thought they knew all along: how they came to be the people that they are, people who often have achieved far more than their parents. Autobiography, which Bizzell rightly calls a "supposedly neutral pedagogical technique," can disturb and misfocus students.

Another fallacy in relying on personal writing to introduce novice writers to academic discourse rests in the belief that all analytical tasks are similar in the eyes of the inexperienced writer and reader. The ability to analyze personal experience does not necessarily indicate the presence of an ability to analyze abstract concepts. Perhaps when a particular autobiography offers a life and an experience similar to the student's own, he or she can locate significance. But when *the person* becomes *the people,* and when the single experience becomes the group experience, novice writers lose the ability to objectify and generalize. Their own personal histories tell them that each life contains different versions of truth and experience and that each rule for behavior has an exception; therefore, jumping from the individual life to theories based upon examining collected experience seems, at best, unsound, and at worst, dishonest. The "it depends upon the case" argument informs so much of their philosophical approach to issues and events that they cannot easily accept theories that attempt to explain mass phenomena. And because the easy and fallacious conclusions they jump to as beginners are so quickly knocked down by their academic elders, sticking to the particular is much safer than creating theories about the general. In addition, although college exposes them to texts that explain complex human problems, the writers of such texts are distant; they have no faces or reputations that the novice writers can put together with a name they trust. As far as the novice writer knows, one author's opinion is no more reliable than another's.

The Novice Writer and the Concept of "Knowing"

This state of frustration becomes even more pronounced when the novice students must read and write about cultures other than their own. What might seem to constitute a failure to read and analyze often can be attributed to a failure to find empathy with the population studied. For the novice writer and reader, the gap between books and reality is immense. Books train one for a job or supply relaxation; living and working teach one about human relationships and behavior. Missing is the key concept:

> Learning to read or write is not learning how texts stick together but rather how people stick together by literate means. Learning to read, especially, is learning how what's happening in a text (any text) has everything to do with what you're supposed to be doing on the other end. (Brandt 42)

This lesson is the lesson that academics learned early in their own communities. Through personal experience and schooling, academics become what the authors of *Women's Ways of Knowing* call *separate knowers:* people whose epistemological perspectives allow them to "view all knowledge as contextual, experience themselves as creators of knowledge, and value both subjective and objective strategies for knowing" (115). Separate knowers can make the "intellectual leap" from concrete events to abstract theories that explain phenomena and back again in the opposite direction. As separate knowers, most academics may initially react emotionally to a text, but they usually go on to analyze the written work for the sources of its claims, the proof the writer offers, and the logic of the connections he or she makes. Academics examine the credentials of the writer as well and review other opinions on the subject—in other words, they place the writer's views in context.

Separate knowers, with their ability to think abstractly and their awareness that knowledge is constructed knowledge, form one end of a developmental continuum. In theory, a person begins from an epistemological stance that values connectedness (the need for direct establishment of a relationship between the knower and the teacher) and "progresses" to an epistemological stance that values separateness (the ability to view information and informers objectively). Knowledge itself shifts from *received* knowledge—information taken as true without examination or question—to *constructed* knowledge, a knowledge built by the learner from collected facts and theories. Belenky and her colleagues differ from standard developmental theorists in that they do not suggest that learners "grow out of" one epistemological stance and into a more advanced one, as Piaget, Erikson, and Kohlberg suggest. In *Women's Ways,* they suggest that how one *knows* and what one *learns* grows in direct response to experiences and social community context. Not surprisingly, what passes for knowledge at the Ivy League schools, for example, differs greatly from what passes for knowledge at non-traditional vocational learning centers; however, certain features of connected knowing remain the same regardless of the level of education. At all levels of sophistication, the authors of *Women's Ways of Knowing* argue, most women are connected knowers, needing personal connection of some sort to stimulate learning.

Belenky mentions briefly, and all too quickly, that men also can have this epistemological orientation, and this brief insight seems to me to offer the key to the difficulty that novice students, regardless of gender, have with learning and writing in the academy. I would argue that both female and male novice writers, with their narrow and constrained view of what one can and can't know, tend to be *connected* learners and knowers—people who must have direct connection or relationship with what they learn. While they will often question received knowledge, they do so on a limited basis because they believe truth and knowledge to be personal, private, and subjectively known or intuited (Belenky 15). Some novice writers, like connected learners, go so far as to be convinced that they can know only their own truths that access to another person's knowledge remains impossible (113). This devotion to individual truth causes the familiar complaint, "they can't know that; it's just their

opinion," which confronts the instructor when controversial subjects or writers are presented in class. (I suspect the students repeat
the phrase with reference to the instructor after class.) They look to
professors for facts: the right way to prepare a patient for surgery,
the correct structure of the atom, the time lapse between the bomb-
ing of Pearl Harbor and the declaration of World War II, and the
proper place to insert a comma. They look within themselves for
theories about human behavior: why children defy their parents,
what adolescents value, how a family's socioeconomic background
influences individual behavior. Right answers, as important as they
are limited, come from authority figures; true answers come from
within the individual by route of the still small voice within. I contend this subjectivity explains why novice writers tend to privilege
intuition and attempt to personalize the subjects they study.
Belenky's connected learners

> ultimately come to disregard the knowledge and advice of remote
> experts. They insist upon the value of the personal, firsthand expe-
> rience, and . . . if they listen at all to others, it is to those who are
> most like themselves in terms of life experiences. (Belenky et al. 69)

Novice writers react in the same manner when learning to read
and write. Expanding their experiential base through empathy
rather than through critical analysis, novice students adopt another
person's view of the world if they can find areas of similarity between the person's life and their own; they accept rather than evaluate knowledge based on life experiences (Belenky et al. 115). The
connected learner experiences family life, and later life at school, as
"one-way talk" (Belenky et al. 164). Parents and teachers "talked to"
these children about what they should know, assuming that they
would listen, accept, understand, and most important, obey.
Connected learners could not "talk back"; they could only repeat
what they learned in nonconfrontational, nonthreatening conversation. In school and at home the cycle continues for generations.
Learning becomes the ability to absorb ideas, not the ability to think
things through. In Shirley Brice Heath's *Ways with Words,* we can
see how both sons and daughters are constrained by their parents'
desires to create children who only tell the truth. Children of the
white working-class community may be invited to tell stories, but
they are expected to tell only

> non-fictive stories which "stick to the truth." Adults listen care-
> fully and correct children if their facts are not as the adults re-
> member them. In contrast, fictive stories which are exaggerations
> of real-life books, are not accepted as stories, but as "lies," without
> "a piece of truth." (Heath 158)

Under these circumstances, the truth becomes tight, narrow and restricted to what the child saw or heard, not what the child can extrapolate from several similar experiences. Students who grow up like these children equate passivity with goodness and fact with truth. This fidelity to "the truth" connects the children, and later the adult learners, to a community sense of moral behavior that forbids speculation on nearly all levels and privileges fact passed down from older, reliable sources. A connected learner values verbally imparted, experiential knowledge more than knowledge from books or printed material—books are more often viewed as fictive than as factual. Consequently, when the students approach learning, they look to the teacher as a source of knowledge. Unfortunately, the college professor often insists that the student make meaning from the text. This dilemma might be resolved if the student trusted the teacher enough to accept the way that the academy makes knowledge. But college professors are not always (and my novice writers would argue seldom) perceived as trusted personal models. This simultaneous reliance upon and mistrust of teachers prompts novice writers to remain passive: they hesitate to venture out and offer their own opinions because they are on unfamiliar ground; they are reluctant to accept texts and schools as the ultimate sources of knowledge because they perceive a difference between "book learning" and real life.

Although novice writers generally begin college with a grudging respect for teachers, the connection between school and "real" life remains tenuous enough that they, like the rural populations in *Ways with Words,* isolate what they learn in school from what they learn in their home communities (Heath 166). This separation of school knowledge and home knowledge affects classroom performance at every level. Even following simple directions becomes problematic when novice writers decide to privilege the advice of friends rather than professors. They trust teachers who personalize instruction, whom they can think of as extended members of the family, who know the novice writers' personality traits and home situations as well as their academic ones. Novice writers trust teachers only when they give explicit directions for passing tests or when they create very concrete guides to passing a course. This plethora of factual information and concrete rules lulls the novice students into believing that knowledge is reducible to fact.

In a sense then, novice students become too involved in their writing and reading rather than too little involved: a responsibility to readers and to self requires accuracy and truthfulness; previous training fails to allow for the possibility that knowledge may be amorphous rather than solid; and the moral imperative to stick to what they know brings the realization that they may know very little indeed. The novice writers' world becomes constricted by the personal, and their hold upon what they know becomes so tenuous that they protect it vigorously. For instance, Mike, one of my novice writing students, could not understand why his sociology teacher insisted that women, as a whole, were underpaid. "Your job's your choice," he countered. "If women want more money they should just take a job that pays more." No argument about discrimination could convince him that women have, or ever have had, a problem getting a job that pays as well as a man's. His sociology teacher tried to convince him that some professions, like teaching, pay less because they are traditionally professions that employ a great many women. When the sociology teacher argued that in some cities even garbage men make more money than teachers, Mike retorted "Then let them be garbage men if they want to earn more money! Everyone knows that being a teacher doesn't pay much."

Sherry, another novice writer, insisted that kids fail in school because their parents neglect them. That's it. The sole reason. No other reason could be possible, as far as she saw it. The key, of course, is what she has seen. Kids whose parents don't pay any attention to them drop out of school; it happened to her friend Joan, to Walter who lives down the street, to her nephews and nieces. She had no idea that these personal friends formed a community influenced by economic status, educational background, and/or social standing. Having Sherry or Mike write a traditional personal essay will only confirm their preexisting suspicions and beliefs because their knowledge base is limited by personal influence. Mike will not be convinced that women can't get good paying jobs because the women in his family don't believe it. Sherry will believe that parental behavior alone affects student success since to believe anything else denies her own (and most likely her parents') experience. However, neither Mike nor Sherry nor the countless others like them will be able to progress in the academy until they learn to place what they know from experience into larger, more academic contexts.

Connecting the Personal with the Academic

The answer, as my friend Vladimir would have it, is to eliminate the personal in order to establish what he thinks of as intellectual rigor. For him, and countless others, rigor means a confrontative and sometimes harsh examination of received knowledge. Everything is subject to questioning; no belief is exempt from attack. Critical thinking, or logical thinking, or any kind of analytical skill, we claim, helps the students make sense out of the world around them, puts their thinking, and not incidentally their lives, into a rational context. However, I would argue that directly attacking connected learners' received knowledge without providing alternative strategies for making new knowledge separates them not only from the lives they know at home but also from the lives they would like to develop in the academy. Removing the personal totally from instruction moves the novice writer (and many nonnovice writers) too quickly into the world of the abstract, the impersonal. And many novice writers quit the university rather than give up their personal connections to knowledge. How do we combine the personal with the impersonal so that students can operate from the epistemological perspective that they know while moving into the epistemological approach valued by the academy? How do we demonstrate the process of making knowledge as well as the process of writing?

It's not that theorists and teachers haven't tried to address the problem. But to my way of thinking, so far we have concentrated on developing opposite ends of the epistemological range. For example, the differences between the writing prompt offered by Ponsot and Deen in *Beat Not the Poor Desk,* which uses fable and story writing to teach novice writers, and the more academic prompt that David Bartholomae advocates in "Inventing the University" are rather monumental. Bartholomae's (1985) rubric,

> While most readers of ____ have said ____, a close and careful reading shows that ____ (153)

shares an epistemological grounding with Ponsot and Deen's

> They say ____, but my experience tells me ____ (101).

Both prompts ask students to take traditional oppositional stances, both pit an individual against a rather powerful THEY. In a sense, each prompt asks the student writer to address a received idea and explore it. But the first prompt grounds authority within experience—"my experience tells me"—while the other requires the students to posit their experiences within the world of textual authority—"a careful reading." Both assignments attempt to broaden student perspective, but one argues from the objective world of the academy and the other from the subjective world of the nonacademic community. While both prompts have their merits—as witnessed by the numbers of people who have used one or the other successfully—but neither prompt weds the two worlds of personal and academic. Neither allows the student to work from both worlds at once. Such prompts place novice writers in a two-way bind.

Asking them to do close readings of texts fails because they don't trust the written word as much as they do the oral tradition and, more important, they do not know how to enter texts and construct knowledge about them. Asking students to write solely from personal experience limits their ability to deal with texts and by default with the experts of the academy.

Perhaps we need to start at a midway point between the personal experience and academic discourse. By combining the prompts of Bartholomae/Petrosky and Ponsot/Deen, we can create a mode of personal exploration that is as comfortably personal and familiar as it is academic and rigorous. Perhaps the prompt should consist of several parts:

My book says _____.

followed closely by

Local experts say _____.

ending in

My investigation leads me to think _____.

The key difference in this new prompt is the mixture of scholarly and field research—a mixture of the personal and the academic I call the *Distanced/Personal.* Such a prompt, and such a course of study, allows novice writers to bring the authority of home into the academy rather than tackle the academy by themselves. This approach shares some connection with Ken Macrorie's I-SEARCH paper, which allows students to thoroughly explore a topic that they find useful or interesting regardless of whether or not it meets the criteria of being academic in nature. Macrorie's work, however, dismisses the objective for "the true" and places such a high value on personal voice that instructors outside of English (and some inside the discipline) consider the resulting "research" to be more idiosyncratic than informative or original. The Distanced/Personal bears more similarity to pedagogies that experiment with making students ethnographers. JoAnne Liebman, in "Contrastive Rhetoric: Students as Ethnographers," reports that when her ESL novice writers study their own language patterns and how they fit into the standard English speaking academic world, they learn not only research skills but also language and interpretive skills.

In an ethnographic pedagogical approach, the teacher positions the student in the center of research as a maker of knowledge rather than as a reporter of information, situating the academic within the personal rather than separating the two. Rather than moving from personal narrative—where the student controls knowledge—into the academic—where the student faces overwhelming and foreign authority—this type of field research places academic and nonacademic communities side by side, valuing both. In *Ways with Words,* Heath describes the manner in which this sort of ethnographic research can overcome differences in the worldviews of teachers and students, linking nonacademic communities with the academic community. In one of the schools she studied, she found two eighth-grade boys who struggled with their biology text and the authority represented by their biology teacher. The information in the biology text book meant nothing to them, partly because they could not read it well enough to understand the information's relationship to the world in which they lived, and partly because they did not see why they should learn from a book what they could learn from the neighborhood elders. To overcome their resistance, the teacher created a comparative study. The boys interviewed community elders and matched community lore and practice with the biology teacher's scientific methods. In conducting this research, the boys learned where the worlds of school and community could touch upon and serve one another (315–17). Ethnographic studies such as these combine both personal and academic interests.

The Distanced/Personal Pedagogy and Ethnographic Research

In many ways, our pedagogical goals match those of critical ethnographic narrative. Our students privilege the voices and stories of their own communities; we interrupt the narrative, point out disparities, and call attention to voice and context. In other words, we attempt to create a learning situation that brings about students' awareness of the situated positions that they occupy in society. In addition, we try to move them from writing about the "what" to writing about the "how" and the "why" that characterizes college-level investigations. To tackle this rather monumental task, we base our Distanced/Personal research activities on critical ethnographic methodologies. We want our students to know two things: that "events are worth recording and reporting because they exemplify hegemonic practice" (Brodkey, *WCEN* 70–71) and that "critical ethnographic work . . . leads people to an understanding of the grounds of their own actions in the historically and socially situated context of their lives" (Simon & Dippo 199). Ethnography serves as a particularly good model for critical reading and writing because of the enormity of the experience: from bits and pieces of experience and text, the students must create an understanding of the cultural factors that influence their behaviors and attitudes.

A Brief Discussion of Ethnography

If the overall goals of the Distanced/Personal pedagogy are similar to the goals of ethnographers, perhaps a short, albeit incomplete, discussion of ethnographic research is in order. At its simplest, ethnographic research can be defined (as it is by Janice Lauer and William Asher in *Composition Research: Empirical Studies*) as a form of qualitative, descriptive research that examines "entire environments, looking at subjects in context" (39). Researchers decide upon a population to study, and avoiding (in theory) a set of preconceived notions that could be *proved* by the research, create a *thick description* of the cultural context from which multiple hypotheses can be generated and meaning can be made. The thick description contains a variety of material: interviews with knowledgeable community informants, direct observations of activities, surveys, and collections of cultural artifacts (written and otherwise). These elements provide what can be thought of as the pieces of a sort of cultural puzzle that the ethnographer must piece together to understand various aspects of the community and its members. The empirical nature of ethnographic research places the researchers in the middle of the communities they study. There they participate in cultural activities and attempt to come to conclusions about the nature of the culture informed by and supported by these activities. The goal of ethnographic research, like the goal of most research, is knowledge production. In this case, that knowledge, according to Roger Simon and Donald Dippo, "centers on and makes 'topical' both the actual practices and points of view of people within an organized set of social relations" (196). An interest in people and lived experience is a primary concern of ethnographic research— which causes Linda Brodkey to describe it as "the systematic though admittedly human study of human life as it is lived within the boundaries of human societies" (Brodkey, *WEN* 26).

The original anthropological model for good ethnography posited objective researchers who lived with but remained apart from their subjects—keeping their own cultures and professional judgments to themselves so as to avoid polluting the culture they studied. Presumably objective observers would enter a community and live with its inhabitants—eat the foods they ate, engage in the activities that the community called work, ritual, and play—then generate studies that explained how some aspect of the society worked.

Arguably, the most popular ethnographic study to reach the public was Margaret Mead's *Coming of Age in Samoa*. Mead lived in the Samoan islands, shared habitats and diets, talked with women and men of all ages, observed children, and then came to what she felt were valid conclusions about what it meant to pass through the rites of adolescence and become an adult in Samoa. This sort of researcher and research, as I tell my students, is the model for the *prime directive* that gets bandied about so regularly on "Star Trek" (in all its syndicated manifestations): scientists are supposed to observe, not interfere with, the populations they study. However, in real life, as in the television program, prime directives appear to be incredibly hard to abide by. Teachers and educators who conduct research find it problematic and, frankly, undesirable to remain entirely objective about and distanced from the communities they work with and study. In fact, as ethnographic research becomes more prevalent in education and English, ethnographic researchers tend to take on the roles of social critics and reformers. The rhetoric of modern ethnographic researchers often seems proactive discourse, referring to and questioning cultural hegemony and confronting the validity of perpetuating cultural systems. The following statement by Linda Brodkey is typical. She asserts that

> ethnography creates the preconditions for research and *social responsibility* [italics mine], if only by arguing that the worlds of words separating 'us' from 'them' are not natural boundaries but social borders that we help maintain when we refuse to travel in uncharted territory. (42)

To interject *social responsibility* into ethnographic research, or indeed any sort of research, is to change the nature of both observer and observed as well as the nature of the knowledge derived from the research project. But perhaps this is not a cause for alarm; it's certainly not new. It's not at all unusual for an ethnographic investigator to offer a so-called *negative critique:*

> any systematic verbal protest against cultural hegemony . . . a protest . . . spoken or written, addressed to any number of audiences, and delivered in any of a variety of forms, not the least important of which is our own curriculum and pedagogy. (Brodkey, *WCEN* 67)

Traditionally, this *negative critique* does little more than respond to an already existing academic narrative. The educator/ethnographer—essentially a storyteller—must tell his or her story while keeping in mind a body of established literature that already defines *the story* of a particular group: for instance, in composition, the researcher would have to tell his or her story of a group of writers by fitting it into the context of literature about *basic writers, freshman composition students,* or any other presumably cohesive group of writers whose qualities have been well defined in the literature of the composition community. Juxtaposing the ethnographer's account of activities in his or her current population of writers against accounts of the larger socially constructed and hegemonic populations changes the nature of the narrative: he or she must move from *story* to *discourse analysis,* from what Brodkey calls "the what" of story to "the how" of discourse (*WCEN* 70).

Such moves can be hazardous. The researcher engaged in telling an ethnographic story to other ethnographers finds himself or herself cross-examined, questioned, and generally made to defend the content of his or her story, and even his or her descriptions of what goes on in the group he or she has studied; the very character of the population he or she examines falls under scrutiny. There are other dangers. In the move from storytelling to analysis, the ethnographer may inadvertently create a rather impersonal account, called the *ethnographic present,* which takes on the properties of a monolithic truth "so deterministic that the historically present set of events appears . . . to be unchangeable" (Brodkey, *WCEN* 72). Brodkey argues that the answer to problems with the ethnographic present cannot be solved by simply limiting all ethnographers to personal experience storytelling. She claims that negative critique and critical challenges to the hegemony are more likely to be effective when presented in discourse narrative rather than in mere stories. A critical ethnographic narrative, she proposes, would be a narrative that points out the disparities between the story and the experience, a narrative that constantly interrupts itself to call attention to the voice in which the story is being told and the context that generated the story (*WCEN* 71–73).

The Distanced/Personal Research

Our Distanced/Personal research, given the nature of our students' writing and reading skills and the limits of the quarter system, cannot be called true ethnographic research. The writing tasks of the Distanced/Personal field research can be situated theoretically somewhere between formal ethnographic research methods and Macrorie's I-Search practices. Our research projects are characterized by the activities that Kenneth Kantor, Dan Kirby, and Judith Goetz identify as the relevant features of ethnographic research in "Research in Context: Ethnographic Studies in English Education":

- **Hypothesis generation.** Research assignments promote a sense of discovery, of addressing a variety of questions regarding what is being studied, and a chance to propose possible answers, even alternative explanations for phenomena as the study proceeds.
- **Context.** Research allows students to see that interplay among elements in the physical, natural, and sociocultural environments affect and explain what people do.
- **Thick description.** Students gather and create ethnographic field notes, recorded or transcribed interviews, and explicit descriptions of physical traits of the environment in order to create an authentic written account of the group or culture being studied, knowing that such an account might have to be used by another researcher.
- **Participant-observation.** Assignments encourage rather than discourage personal and even subjective judgments; students begin with their own background knowledge, experiences, and predispositions—even notions of what they expect to see—and continually revise these ideas as their research develops.
- **Meaning-making.** Working with the ethnographic process allows the students to look at ways in which individuals construct their own realities and shared meanings. This sort of meaning-making becomes both something they study and something they do; it provides a significant means for challenging, refining, or confirming the way that they see the world.

In other words, like the ethnographer, the students try to make sense out of the world they investigate. Like the classroom project in Macrorie's I-SEARCH, the world slated for investigation is their own. Unlike the students engaged in an I-search project, our students' don't have the freedom to write on topics they choose. In both cases, the meaning or knowledge that they arrive at must be the result of analysis of lived experience rather than merely textual experience. Just as Macrorie does, we work both *with* and *against* what the students already know, but our goal is to analyze and put that knowledge into an academic context, whereas Macrorie, as always, moves away from the formal aspects of research, concentrating on what it is *to know* only in the sense of the individual student's needs.

Initially our students' sense of what they already know about a topic gets in the way of understanding how individual experience fits into a contextual framework. Kantor contends that although ethnographers may enter a setting with biases and assumptions about their subjects, they "maintain their options until the weight of evidence determines particular directions" (295). Our novice writers are part of the community they study and, therefore come, to the investigation with extreme biases and preconceived notions. From the beginning, we as teachers must persuade the students to rethink or reconceive their biases in terms of the context that creates and supports these ideas and actions.

The expert ethnographer has little or no trouble examining the "dynamic interplay among elements in the physical, natural, and socio-cultural environments" (Kantor et al. 296). All such elements must be brought into play in order to determine what happens to people within a given context. The novice researcher has such a limited view of context that it becomes impossible to see the root experience as embedded in even larger contexts. This limited vision can partially be expanded by developing thick descriptions of the community that is studied. These thick descriptions are a means of "discovering and elaborating upon specific features of context" (Kantor et al. 296), but their effectiveness is inevitably hampered by novice writers' inability to generate careful and close analysis and description of people, places, and conversations. Their inexperience with writing and written material also contributes to their failure to generate texts that might explain these contexts and activities. The students find it difficult enough to actively seek information from members of the community; the task becomes even more difficult when they discover that this sort of critical research sometimes forces them not only to confront their preconceived notions about their culture but also to change their thinking and behaviors.

Confrontation and possibilities for change come about as the students create the thick description necessary to write about their culture. The thick description comes together in the process of triangulation—a corroborative procedure whereby, in our case, student researchers check their interpretations of field notes against statements made by teachers and students. As they gather the material for the thick description and then analyze it in order to make sense of what they have found, the students involved in a Distanced/Personal project[1] are compelled to question *what is* and *what is my role in what is*. Our writing projects, then, must lead the students into making connections between academic and nonacademic communities by employing the following strategies:

- Research starts out with a topic but without a firm direction and allows writing to be hypothesis generating rather than hypothesis driven.

- Reading, writing, and discussion submerge the students in the context of the research activities.

- Activities stress practice: gathering, interpreting, and analyzing information to form a thick description.
- Active-learning projects create participant-observers rather than passive learners.
- Final writing tasks employ meaning making rather than mere information collecting.

This, of course, is theory. What about the practice? How do I describe the recursive, sometimes chaotic, process of teaching writing over a period of two quarters, especially when that process is so intimately tied up with the process of teaching reading? In our two-quarter sequence we follow a pattern that interweaves personal and academic ways of knowing. Each quarter we ask the students to perform the following tasks:

- Read at least two books on a topic.
- Write about both the books and personal experiences.
- Create a hypothesis about topic.
- Interview authorities from the community.
- Create a database from interviews.
- Analyze data.
- Write a thick description.
- Create a theory.
- Write about topic in light of theory and data.

During the first quarter we place a great deal of emphasis on learning to write and research; in the second quarter, we devise activities that provide practice for refining what was learned the previous quarter.

The Distanced/Personal and Knowledge-Making Activities

Distanced/Personal approaches to reading and writing instruction give teachers and students access to the knowledge-making process in an interactive social as well as textual atmosphere. Teachers become privy to all the contexts within which students must operate. Such a pedagogy relocates the site of learning—placing it not just in the classroom, nor solely in the community, but in several arenas simultaneously. Sites of information can be found outside the academy, through experiences and interactions with friends, family, public officials, and former teachers, people who are literally and figuratively brought into the classroom by the students themselves. These added resources of fact, theory, and practice often have as much authority as any the composition teacher assumes and count as much as formal texts when creating meaning. Often a point that the author of a text makes will be lost until an outside authority confirms the theory with experiential data or until the students see the author's theory played out in the lives of those they work and play with. Often the practices of the community find validation or explanation in the texts that the students read.

The teachers' role in the Distanced/Personal classroom is similar to, but not strictly analogous to, that of the participant-observer in ethnographic research. Like the anthropological participant-observer studying a culture, the teacher learns not only what students think about a particular topic or event but also about the ways in which students collect information, process it, and construct new knowledge from what they have observed and analyzed. Unlike the social scientist, however, the participant-observer in the writing and reading classroom purposefully intervenes in the learning activity—providing alternative ways of conducting the process of learning and meaning making, and, perhaps more importantly, listening when the students and their informants devise equally valid but nonacademic ways of constructing knowledge.

The participant-observer experience constructs knowledge in several ways. Needless to say, both students and teachers learn about the research topic. Because teachers are English majors rather than sociologists or anthropologists or psychologists, their knowledge tends to be located in texts rather than in field research involving actual people and social systems. Ethnographic projects allow teachers to construct a more thorough context for what they read. Researching a topic of interest and importance to the local communities provides a chance to learn whether or not art reflects and/or influences life. As the teachers try to make sense of the data the students collect, they need guides as much as the students themselves. In some cases, the students can provide that guidance—acting as the informants, or reliable sources of information in the community. At other times, both teachers and students can find local authorities and experts from the community to add density or to clarify research material.

In addition to collaborating on field research projects with their students, teachers can offer academic lenses for examining the information the students gather and can furnish academic texts that examine the issues from an enriched perspective. The students can get a firsthand glance at all the same sorts of issues in the teachers' world, discovering how we interact with all manners of texts, how we apply our own learning strategies and schemata to our own reading and writing, and (not incidentally) how we proofread and pre-pare written material for outside audiences. They also get a sense of how difficult it is, even for teachers, to risk putting ideas in written form, how scary it will always be to presume to offer the results of research to peers and academic elders. In other words, while mak-ing sense of this mixture of academic and nonacademic points of view, students learn how the academics make knowledge, and teachers learn how the students' nonacademic (and former acade-mic) communities make knowledge.

This collaborative-based research provides still another type of learning, one especially useful for the teacher. By studying the man-ner in which students approach and solve problems of research, writing, and reading, the teacher can build a more complete picture of individual student's learning styles, reading and writing schema, logical strategies, and—yes—grammar and usage patterns. Because students respond to a variety of texts—oral and written, nonliterary as well as literary—the data the teacher has on the students' read-ing, writing, and learning patterns is enriched. With these enriched pictures, teachers can offer better solutions to the problems that plague an individual student.

A Distanced/Personal pedagogy mixes old and new theories about teaching reading and writing—or perhaps more accurately, it attempts to keep in play a variety of the theories that shape the boundaries of our discipline—Burke's conversation theory, Friere's liberatory peda-gogy, and even earlier philosophers and educators. But whatever the-ory informs the practice, a central dynamic remains: teachers must help their students to improve their reading and writing skills because a lack of those skills will interfere with their abilities to understand how the academy affects their lives. What varies are the definitions of *teacher, student,* and *knowledge.* Once the research begins in a Distanced/Personal classroom, the students have as much control over the outcome as the teacher; the data that the students collect is processed and analyzed in the same way as the texts supplied by the teachers. These controlled studies, small and incomplete as they must be, can help the students bridge the gap between home and commu-nity. A chance exists that students like Sherry and Mike, who question both their texts and teachers, will not change their minds, but a chance also exists that they can provide their teachers with new information about the communities they study. To paraphrase the authors of *Women's Ways of Knowing,* research that connects novice students and their teachers with real communities will help each group realize that what they thought was final truth is often merely a starting point for understanding (122–123).

Chapter Two

The Distanced/Personal
Learning, Knowing, and Teaching in the Novice Classroom

To see that all knowledge is a construction and that truth is a matter of the context in which it is embedded is to greatly expand the possibilities of how to think about anything, even those things we consider to be the most elementary and obvious. Theories become not truth but models for approximating experience. . . .
—Belenky, Clinchy, Goldberger, and Tarule
Women's Ways of Knowing

Learning

While not exactly mysterious, the ways in which teaching promotes learning in the reading and writing classroom are at least complex enough to cause confusion. This confusion, in part, results from disagreements about *what* to teach novice students as well as *how* to teach them. In our novice classes, we take as a given the necessity to teach reading as well as writing. This fact alone changes everything, from the manner in which we approach texts to the focus of formal and informal writing assignments. And well it should. As Connie Swartz Zitlow argues in "To Think About What I Think: Inquiry and Involvement," learning goals influence priorities in

teaching practices. When an English teacher has a narrow perception of learning, the goals focus upon a set of behaviors, and the
teacher becomes preoccupied with grade-level facts and skills: literature becomes acquiring information; composition means following set formulae when writing; language is usage and identification
of grammar rules; reading is decoding. A novice English teacher
who works with a narrow range of educational goals tends to value
workbook exercises and simple readers. Some teachers conceive of
learning as a state in which students demonstrate initiative and independence in discovering right answers, so they set up "problems"
that provide opportunities for demonstrating effort and competency. But the emphasis in such classrooms is still on facts and behaviors (54). The workbooks may be gone, but both reading and
writing assignments reflect the teacher's desire to focus the
student's attention toward a formulaic set of skills and answers: the
right mode for a writing task, the correct interpretation of a reading
passage. At the other end of the instructional continuum, a teacher
whose practice is informed with comprehensive learning priorities
promotes a wider range of goals:

> Ideas of awareness, purpose, understanding, reflections, sensitiv-
> ity, and reciprocity appear in *teachers' thinking* [italics mine].
> [Such teachers] tend to stress the essential integrity of mental
> life—cognition is not separated from emotion, nor intellectual
> growth from personal growth. . . . When learning priorities are
> comprehensive, acquiring facts and skills is not seen as an end in
> itself but important in the service of a learner's developing sense
> of purpose. (54)

Distanced/Personal learning, as we define and practice it in our
classrooms, links teacher learning with student learning, integrates
the personal with the academic, associates the subjective with the
objective, and combines the intellectual with the emotional.
Striving to meet these comprehensive goals means that students and
teachers alike begin to see *knowing* in the writing and reading class
as a state that encompasses much more than punctuating a sentence
correctly or reporting on the contents of a chapter.

The goals of our Distanced/Personal classroom reflect the learning objectives set by such organizations as the National Council of
Teachers of English and the Modern Language Association (MLA).
In 1987, the Modern Language Association English Coalition, sixty
teachers of English drawn from all levels of English instruction, met
for three weeks at the Aspen Institute's Wye Plantation in Maryland
in an attempt to define the discipline of English and to suggest
methods of instruction that would improve the teaching of English.

The resulting report, *The English Coalition Conference: Democracy through Language,* written by Richard Lloyd-Jones and Andrea Lunsford, addresses changes in students, curriculum, the school environment, and the larger community over the past ten to fifteen years. Keeping in mind the diversity of America's school populations, the Coalition suggested that the following general principles should inform active and meaningful studies in English (xxi–xxiii):

1. English studies should include a broad range of activities—reading, writing, interpreting, speaking, and listening.

2. Formal, study of English in school is only one of the ways people learn to use and understand their language—classrooms should integrate what the students study formally with what they bring to the classroom from their homes and neighborhoods, especially in areas where uses of language at home and in the community differ significantly from language encountered in the schools.

3. Learning should be active learning—students should engage in self-critical, analytical examinations of their own and others uses of language.

4. At all levels, students should be led to understand how language works, where the words they hear and their own words come from, and what effects these words tend to have—this theoretical understanding will help students to recognize when others use language to influence or manipulate them.

5. English curriculum should focus upon works that challenge students' abilities as readers and thinkers, since meaningful education requires content—however, a list of "core" or "important" works would be reductive and would defeat the goals of engaging students and fostering judgment as well as the acquisition of facts.

Knowing

These principles, which the Coalition hoped would inform practice, reflect a curriculum that posits "knowledge as process" (xxiii). In *What Is English?* Peter Elbow reports that the conference members reached "a remarkable consensus" (15) that learning, especially in English and language studies, involves the *making of meaning* and the *reflecting on this process of making meaning* (18). The Coalition envisions the teaching and learning of English as a meaning-making activity, going so far as to theorize that students come to know what they know by placing their personal, subjective view of a topic on a template of academic discourse. Through understanding each other's experiences and the academy's view of a similar experience, students come to a broader understanding of the larger world and their place in it.

Given the ambitious hope that English teachers will uphold the goals that the Coalition preaches, what is it that students can expect to leave a novice reading and writing course knowing? Perhaps it would be useful to apply the objectives stated by Robert E. Probst, in "Literature and Literacy." He outlines five types of knowledge inherent in the well-planned English literature curriculum:

> *Knowledge of Self:* The curriculum should acknowledge and encourage "the personal significance of literary experience" so that students can "forge some understanding of their own place in the culture" (106).

> *Knowledge of Others:* The curriculum should provide experiences in which students can come to "see and understand one another more fully" (106).

> *Knowledge of Texts:* Students need not only to know how texts are constructed, they need to know how texts "push us subtly or obviously, to accept the writer's assumptions and ideas" (107).

> *Knowledge of Contexts:* The student needs classroom "discussions of and . . . writing about literature [that] moves beyond the text itself and into the responses and associations of the students." Such exploration of context reveals how the circumstances under which a text is created, and under which the student reads, will shape the reading (108).

> *Knowledge of Processes:* The curriculum should offer students a chance to understand all the processes by which a person can come to understand texts: by describing an expressive and introspective reaction to a text, by providing a critical analysis of a text, or by combining these two sorts of responses to make meaning (108–9).

All of these comprehensive goals can be and, I would argue, should be as active in the novice composition classroom as in the literature classroom. Knowledge of the texts created by others and of texts the students write themselves establishes the classroom as the sort of place where, as the Coalition suggests, "people learn to use and understand their language." The goals we set for the Distanced/Personal classroom extend beyond literature and student texts into the many places where novice students might profit from analyzing experience by using scholarship. Context and content become closely associated because the local community becomes a text that must be read in the context of the academy, and the academic text has to be read in the context of the local community. Knowledge in the Distanced/Personal classroom becomes a matter of understanding a process for deciphering and solving problems within a variety of contexts. This knowledge is manifest in the writing that the students produce, which should demonstrate that the students have been able to identify a problem, a phenomenon, or an idea, and put it into a context so that an audience (sometimes, but not always, academic) can understand and make judgments on the issues.

Teaching

Having a definition of what it is to *know* something or to *learn* something does not necessarily help us understand why certain students end up in novice classes while others do not. Standardized tests might indicate a difference between novice students and those who enter the academy with more acceptable scores and GPAs, but the tests cannot explain why some students have progressed while others have lagged behind in academic learning situations, or why some people eagerly seek out knowledge while others seemingly act swiftly to limit their field of experience. The differences between traditional freshmen and the novice freshmen is more likely to be a difference in experience, training, or local community influence than in native intelligence. Those who teach novice courses learn quickly not to dismiss their students as boneheads. In fact, many of us are more likely to characterize traditional freshmen, who sport a facade of bored indifference, as more "dull of eye" than the frightened, belligerent, or anxious novice student. The novice students' very anxiety often marks their potential to become good students because anxiety masks the desire to learn that can characterize the potentially good student.

I find it interesting how often teaching metaphors of the teaching/learning process connect the intellectual with the physical. Theodore Sizer refers to a desire to learn as a hunger; students who want to learn are "hungry," devouring knowledge, asking hard questions despite the fear that they will be marked as stupid, trying the hard problems rather than sticking with those that they can solve easily (53). Not a few educators—led by such notable scholars as E. D. Hirsch and Alan Bloom—seem to associate learning with physical strength and mental fortitude, suggesting that in the public schools the desire to learn dies early from lack of rigorous workout.

The following accusations and stereotypes concerning students and schools are typical:

- **Students are lazy.** We picture them sprawled out before the TV instead of sitting upright on the edge of their chairs, attacking a book.
- **High school teachers don't train students properly.** In our mind's eye, we see teachers content with assigning sloppy little feather-weight paragraphs rather than hefty analytical tomes.
- **Neither teachers nor students can compete with foreign countries or with the golden past.** Our imagination conjures up a sort of contest where students receive points for being able to name authors faster than anyone else, where they break records for reciting key passages from classic texts.

These metaphors of competency seem predicated upon assumptions of the nature of learning that have little to do with the learning goals set by the MLA's English Coalition.

In the first place, such sports and competition metaphors represent the mind as a muscle that can atrophy unless properly exercised. In such a paradigm all the lazy students need is a basic workout, a precision training regime. This mind-as-muscle metaphor is seductive; in fact, I succumbed to it when I first started writing this chapter. In order to get at our philosophy of teaching, I first thought that I'd describe our program in terms of training for intellectual fitness—sort of a mental workout program designed to build inquiry endurance and cranial muscle strength. It seemed apt at the time; after all, physical strength comes from pushing beyond one's limits, and we certainly were asking just that of our students. But the representation, which is tenuous at its best, can lead to teaching practices at their worst. Weight training or any other sort of exercise training works on the premise that the teacher/trainer analyzes the process by which the student/athlete currently performs, breaks him or her of bad habits, then starts carefully and gradually to work toward maximum performance. To use the sports/training metaphor is to insinuate that students just need to work harder, get a better trainer, or try a new approach. It implies that they are somehow "unfit" and need to be retrained to approach writing and thinking "correctly." This sort of metaphor, while not as devastating as the "novice-student-as-cognitively-deficient-patient" metaphor, fits the older, more established goals for teaching reading and writing: start with sentences and simple, short reading exercises, then build up to "real work"; read for pieces of information first, then work up to reading for meaning within context. Unfortunately (or fortunately, depending upon your approach to teaching) learning is not to the mind what body building is to muscle mass.

The sports metaphor continues when teachers are held responsible, like coaches, for turning out a winning team. It's hardly fair to place blame on the public schools for a lack of student enthusiasm or imply that public school teachers, all by themselves, destroy students' curiosity and desire to learn. I would rather argue that curriculums do more harm than individual teachers. Teachers are bound by curriculum. As Sizer has suggested, although school systems across the country may claim to develop a student's "mind, body, morals, values, career" (77), they are more likely to be concerned with custodial care, seeing that "adolescents are supervised, safely and constructively most of the time, during the morning and afternoon hours, and that they are off the labor market" (83). The public demands regimented instruction, emphasis on skills acquisition, and a sort of "equal opportunity" approach to subjects that prevents the classroom from becoming a place for individual intellectual development. For example, sometimes entire classes study each chapter of the grammar book when only a few students lack understanding of punctuation rules. Such intense stress on skills and drills, which many administrators insist teachers must include in lesson plans, leaves little time to introduce material and activities that develop critical thinking or understanding of cultural diversity. Local communities, especially small ones, often strongly resist any tendency on the part of representatives of school districts to explore social and moral issues or to question belief systems. It's much safer to stick to grammar rules or to practice fitting limited content into formulaic essay structures than to discuss Holden Caulfield's musings, to explore the uplifting verses of Longfellow than to reveal the way kids in big city ghettos talk and act, or to adopt a conservative stance in the classroom than to take chances on upsetting the adult members of the community.

Finally, the metaphors that represent students as intellectually flabby creatures—trained elsewhere and delivered to us undisciplined and unready to compete on the playing fields of academe— allows university and college teachers to ignore their own responsibility of fostering and keeping alive the desire to learn. Why attempt to make scholars out of inferior students?

Student Resistance to Learning

In defense of the profession, however, it sometimes seems that the desire to learn is often the last reason that students attend our

classes. Discovering that a class is permeated with that attitude
daunts even the most enthusiastic of teachers. This resistance to en-
gagement in their own learning process often reflects local community resistance to the learning of the academy. James Moffett refers
to this sort of conservative resistance to knowledge as agnosis, "not-
wanting-to-know" (187). Agnosis, he posits, is a quality fostered by
the fear that questioning traditional values will bring about a weak-
ening of those values. And agnosis, he suggests, is rampant in the
public schools, despite attempts of some administrators and teachers to fight it. Students, as might be expected, do not always find
agnosis's conservative stance particularly appealing, and they turn
from school and home to other sorts of activities that will engage
their energies and intellect. Other students adopt the conservative
stance out of a need for a simply explained world and out of defer-
ence to their parents' values. In the first case, students turn away
from formal education altogether; in the second, students pay lip
service to the goals of the educational system, tolerating rather than
engaging in their own education.

Regardless of the reasons students turn from learning and knowing, the legacy of agnosis influences their attitudes and behaviors
when they come to college. They sit passively waiting for "the lesson" to be over with, for the teacher to "cover" the "material," and
for the test to prove them "competent." If they disagree with something the teacher presents in class, they dutifully give the teacher
what she wants on the examination or in the paper and then dismiss
what they "learned" and go about the business of living as usual. To
approach knowledge in this manner rather than to interact with
texts on a personal level allows students to avoid dealing with the
issues presented in class and escape clarifying their own position
on those issues. Participating in learning as inquiry means not only
hard work, but also mental turmoil, for accepted beliefs, moral judgments, and ways of viewing the world might no longer hold true.
Sometimes, especially in matters of religion and related values, students don't want to dissect a matter of faith as if it were a matter of
logic.[1] For some students, religion has proved useful and related to
daily endeavor; education has not. After twelve years of schooling
in which the curriculum emphasizes narrow and middle-range instructional goals, only students with the most rebellious of spirits
will welcome the academy members' penchant for probing every element of thought and action with the questions "What?" "How?"
"Why?" and "So What?"

The clash between worldviews affects teachers also. No matter
how frequently they encounter agnosis, it's always a shock to realize that not every student seeks new knowledge. Instructors sud-

denly discover that they must prove that the books they assign and the types of writing they endorse can be practical and useful. For the academic, *inquiring,* if not completely synonymous with *learning,* represents the first step in constructing knowledge. The students who choose to enter the academy cannot escape the necessity of engaging in inquiry. And here the struggle begins. Novice writers and readers resist inquiry; their teachers resist received knowledge. Because the goals of the instructor and the goals of the novice student seem too removed from one another for learning to take place, students and teachers seem at an impasse. Eventually, however, students who refuse to accept the need to question and inquire about all phases of experience will lose—the teachers set the rules in the context of the academy.

Rather than participate in what comes down to an antagonistic stand-off, novice composition instructors can act as mentors for those who are unfamiliar with the academic system (note that I did not say instructors could coach students—enough with the physical metaphors!). While the responsibility for luring students into the world of academic inquiry does not rest with composition teachers alone, we enjoy an opportunity many of our colleagues don't. Because of the size of our classes, the content of our readings, and the reflection that writing requires, we have an excellent means of introducing students to the possibilities of academic dialogue and dialogue with texts.

But first we must create a desire to inquire and to replace agnosis with gnosis, a reverence for knowledge. This reverence for knowledge, held by educators from Rousseau to Montessori, rests upon the premise that all children possess some sort of intrinsic motive to inquire. Jerome Bruner, in *Towards a Theory of Instruction,* suggests that learning is more effective when it is prompted by intrinsic motive and "does not depend upon reward that lies outside the activity it impels" (114). Learning, he continues, should depend upon motivation in which "reward inheres in the successful termination of that activity or even in the activity itself" (114). Not all learners respond to the same intrinsic motives, and so successful instruction cannot rest upon the effectiveness of any one set of stimuli. Bruner suggests several intrinsic motives that, when put into play with each other, will open the mind to critical thought and inspire spontaneous learning: curiosity, a desire for competence, aspiration to emulate a model, and a deeply sensed commitment to the web of social reciprocity (127).

Bruner suggests that being curious about something implies that the learner sees some concept or event as unclear, unfinished, uncertain, and in need of closure. The *search* for clarity, he proposes, rather than actually finding answers to our questions, satisfies curiosity (114). Narrow instructional goals cut off curiosity before it has a chance to develop. Students come to closure too soon and fail to see the complexity of issues. All too frequently a lack of curiosity exists only in regard to learning in school. Although students talk eagerly about how to get better jobs, the implications of choosing careers, religious and moral issues, and the consequence of politics outside of the classroom, they appear in our classrooms almost devoid of curiosity about the academic implications of these topics. Narrow learning goals have reduced matters of history, literature, science, and, in sociology and psychology, sometimes even human relationships to simple, easily digested formulas that have no relationship to "real life."

Narrow learning goals tend to play more on the desire to achieve competency than the desire to satisfy curiosity. Students expend a great deal of effort on "writing the right way." Grammar instruction takes on monumental importance because students (and many teachers) equate mastery of standard English with intelligence. But such definitions of competence privilege the desire to be "right" about form and formula and cast aside the desire to explore new ideas and concepts in a competent and effective manner. The students tend to define competence in its lowest possible term—correctness. This definition of competence has been reinforced by school systems that evaluate product to the exclusion of process and refuse to acknowledge that competence can mean knowing how to solve problems and interpret data as well as how to perform simple tasks.

Perhaps the most controversial of the elements in Bruner's intrinsic motives for learning is what he labels the aspiration to emulate a model. Bruner relates this aspiration to the strong human tendency to identify not only with specific people but also with specific groups; a student could lack a specific model and still desire to become "a certain kind of person" (122). Inherent in this desire to "be like" someone else is an acceptance of values as well as mannerisms and positions. All too often, academics assume that our students want to be like us, that the model they emulate should be an academic model both in literacy and in values. Indeed, as Carol Severino points out in "Where the Cultures of Basic Writers and Academia Intersect: Cultivating the Common Ground," many of the recent articles on literacy assume that the students will leave their home and community literacies and adopt wholeheartedly the literacy values of the academy. Writers from Heath to Rose use what Severino refers to as transportation metaphors: *bridging the gap,* being *on the way to* or *on the road to* literacy, *crossing over boundaries* (I used the first in Chapter 1). Such movement appears to be unidirectional—toward academic literacy—and undertaken only by the student—the teacher or tutor does not cross over to the students' literacy nor accept their values (7–8). The college or university teacher stands as a model for the student to emulate, and the goal of the student (at least in the view of the authors of such articles) is to join the "club" or "inner circle" of the highly educated in-group (8–9).

The thought of a world composed of model academics leading academics-in-training toward some sort of academic utopian community is somewhat frightening, largely because it smacks of the same agnosis that I previously associated with those outside the academy. Severino points out that, in reality, the ways of addressing problems in nonacademic communities are not vastly different from the ways of inquiry in the academy:

> Consider, for example, the way persuasion is done in writing at the university—with factual evidence, documentation, and appeals to scholarly authority, along with the way persuasion might be accomplished at home—through personal testimony, cajolery, and appeals to parental authority. . . . We should not fail to notice the obvious common features: the common aim of persuasion for getting work done, the common use of evidence, common appeals to authority and audience. (7)

To see the teacher's job as an endeavor that creates more academics rather than more active thinkers is to confuse imitation with emulation. Even as Bruner suggests that learners need models to emulate, he argues that teachers should endeavor to be models to *interact* with rather than models to *imitate.* The teacher needs to become a part of the student's internal dialogue mechanism rather than a prototype to parrot (124). To imitate does not allow students to contribute to an ongoing community of learners. And this need to contribute seems synonymous with the desire for reciprocity, which Bruner defines as "a deep human need to respond to others and to operate jointly with them toward an objective" (125). Learning becomes part of a larger activity: the making of knowledge and the application of that knowledge for the good of the community. This activity not only can be, but must be, shared by groups. Without this reciprocity there can be only limited discovery, only limited progress.

Teachers as Collaborators

Teachers cannot, by definition, create intrinsic motivation in their students; however, the manner in which they conduct their classrooms and the way they construct the goals that inform their practice can provide an atmosphere that brings intrinsic motivation to the forefront and values what the students see as learning goals as well as what the academy recognizes as knowledge. One of the ways teachers can promote learning is to become collaborative learners in the general community of learners that form undergraduate studies. Instead of being specialists, experts, or authority figures, who have transcended general studies, they can pick subjects to investigate that are important for all scholars—not just "subjects the kids might find interesting." Maxine Greene suggests that some teachers think of themselves as a static product, finished educators who are now qualified to impart information. For finished educators, preparing for class consists of reviewing notes and pulling tricks out of the assignment file. Students, however, when asked to identify their best teachers, pass over these finished educators and point to those teachers who continue to be what Greene would call *resilient* inquirers: teachers who constantly explore and redefine not only their own landscapes but the landscapes of those around them (Zitlow 50). Resilient learners find subjects always open, always new. Many of these teachers think of collaboration with each other and with their students as productive not only in what they can "get" from their students, but also in what they can learn for their own enlightenment and pleasure.

These teachers, in every sense of the word, are collaborators, and successful classroom collaboration can not only increase student involvement in the learning process but can also serve as a natural breeding place for Bruner's four types of intrinsic motives. When students collaborate with teachers and other classmates, the classroom becomes not only a community but also a place where teachers become models to emulate. Opportunities to dialogue with instructors as coresearchers allows students to cultivate general knowledge and become competent in basic skills in a far less threatening manner than is possible in the usual "me expert, you novice" traditional classroom. Collaboration with teachers encourages students to develop and/or apply knowledge so that change occurs not only in their own reading and writing but in their relationships to others. Eventually, they can teach and tutor others as well as receive help. In other words, they can reciprocate for past service and kindness.

Theory into Practice: A Personal Journey

My own journey toward a cognizant pedagogical theory might serve to illustrate the means by which composition practice can evolve from and inform theory. For four years before I came to Ohio State

University at Marion, I'd struggled with all sorts of traditional approaches to basic writing instruction. Originally, my instruction included grammar days and grammar projects. I thought that teaching
novice students to survive in the academy entailed teaching them to
be familiar with close reading of texts and formal modes of writing,
so my students explicated essays as my graduate professors taught
me to explicate poems. Ignoring their baffled faces, I led them point
by point and block by block through comparison/contrast essays,
adjective by adjective through literary description. When this approach showed precious few results, I changed direction and
coached skeptical students through Ponsot and Deen's fable exercises. Again they indulged me, but they didn't understand how
learning to create fables would help them prepare a sociology paper.
At last I turned to personal experience essays, relishing what I felt
to be the honesty and sincerity of good essays (actually believing I
could tell an honest and sincere paper when I saw it) or wondering
if the vapid emptiness in an autobiographical piece really reflected
the life of the student who turned it in.

I confess: I could find no way to be at ease with any of these
systems of teaching composition. All through my teaching explorations and experiments, I, too, worried about those sociology papers. None of the methods I used (nor my particular combination
of them) effectively combined the style of writing that I taught in
English composition classes and the style of writing that my students had to produce for other disciplines. Of the many worlds of
discourse that they struggled with—the one found in English
classes, the ones used in the rest of the university's disciplines, and
the ones employed in their communities—the students conversed
comfortably only in the discourse found in their home and personal communities.

I now believe that I unwittingly participated in perpetuating a
"hidden" curriculum, one that I was only vaguely aware of. In
"Cognition, Convention, and Certainty: What We Need to Know
about Writing," Patricia Bizzell emphasizes the importance of considering discourse communities when teaching students how to
write. She notes that even though we might think of teaching writing
as teaching thinking, students do not share our discourse communities, much less our ways of making or analyzing knowledge. When
we teach style and modes and formal ways of approaching problems
(the dreaded syllogism, for example), we think of the writing process
as a set of principles that can be taught easily. We assume that if we
can teach students how to think "logically" and how to consider the
expectations of the academic audience, the students should be able
to manage quite well once they leave our classes.

This pedagogical premise, which is based on the work of "the inner-directed theorists," those interested in the structure of language learning and thinking process in their earliest state, prior to social influence (Bizzell 215), leads to problems and misunderstanding between students and teachers. For example, Bizzell examines the heuristics of composition theorists who believe that writing processes are fundamental and universal (215). Such theorists look at poor writers as undeveloped or somehow deficient in their capacities to engage in the writing process. If students cannot produce coherent sentences or identify and write for a specific audience, the teacher must go back and provide them with the cognitive patterns that they have somehow missed in their development. Certainly this theory motivated my first attempts to teach basic writing. I was in the first stages of learning to teach, the stage Mina Shaughnessy, in "Diving In: An Introduction to Basic Writing," refers to as *Guarding the Tower.* A teacher who is guarding the tower assumes that there is a formal, true (and, yes, superior) way of approaching content and discourse (63). I certainly assumed that my students had some sort of developmental problem with interpreting texts and then producing their own, readable versions of academic discourse. It never occurred to me in my early days of teaching that I should take into consideration the strength and nature of my students' personal discourse community.

Without doubt, I knew at some level that problems with grammar and sentence structure could grow out of differences in cultural communities—like everyone else, I learned in graduate school about the debate over Black English. But I failed to realize, in this period before the university became concerned over issues of cultural literacy, that what I thought of as both grammar and critical thinking problems could stem from the dissonance created when the student's discourse community did not overlap with mine. Like other teachers, I concluded that the student's thinking skills were deficient. The students probably felt the same way about my skills. Obviously, I was not considering, as Bizzell suggests that we should, that "what is most significant about members of a discourse community is not their personal preferences, prejudices, and so on, but rather the expectations they share by virtue of belonging to that particular community" (218). These expectations usually included a system of logic and discourse that bore little resemblance to that taught in universities.

I remember my own frustration in undergraduate and graduate school with attempting to use the syllogism as a means of producing sound arguments. Perhaps I was a bit dense, but I couldn't understand what the fuss was about. Yes, I could break down my argument into three parts, get from the *All men die* to *Therefore* . . . , but I didn't really see the point of worrying about something that was valid but not true. I felt rather like the Old Gentleman coached by the Logician in Ionesco's *Rhinoceros* (18–19):

Logician: Here is an example of a syllogism. The cat has four paws. Isidore and Fricot both have four paws. Therefore Isidore and Fricot are cats.

Old Gentleman: My dog has got four paws.

Logician: Then it's a cat. . . .

Old Gentleman: So then logically speaking my dog must be a cat?

Logician: Logically, yes. But the contrary is also true. . . . Another syllogism. All cats die. Socrates is dead. Therefore Socrates is a cat.

Old Gentleman: And he's got four paws. That's true. I've got a cat named Socrates.

True, valid, false, faulty—it was all very confusing to someone like me, who was trained at home to consider the real person, or real cat, in a very narrow context before making decisions that affected real people. Perhaps my own confusion helped me to understand why my students resisted what I taught; whatever the reason, I continued to move more and more toward a pedagogy that depended on speaking to the students in terms they accepted before I tried to speak to them about the formal principles of rhetoric.

The real breakthough in my attitude toward pedagogy and discourse began when I arrived at OSU, where Bartholomae and Petrosky's *Facts, Counterfacts and Artifacts* provided the theoretical foundation for the novice writing courses. An innovative substitute for the previous skills and drills instruction, the rigorous reading and writing component suggested by *Facts* seemed to combine the academic and the personal in a manner that might lead to good sociology papers as well as good English papers. The level of writing that this approach drew forth from students amazed and excited me.

However, I was troubled by certain aspects of the *Facts* theory and practice: the implication that a short essay necessarily implied a lack of serious thought; the assumption that all writers had the same ways of knowing and same manner of expressing that knowledge. I must confess that in many ways, I felt that teaching by the *Facts* model represented still another step along Shaughnessy's ladder of teaching involvement: *Converting the Natives,* the perception that students are "empty vessels, ready to be filled with new knowledge" (64). In this case, the instructor not only had to fill the students with knowledge, she had to carefully demonstrate the right way to approach the well and the proper ceremony for sharing the water.

In addition to my concern with what I perceived to be academic rigidity of the *Facts* model (and my feminist perception that Bartholomae and Petrosky's book endorsed a male model of discourse), I had another concern. The *Facts* model advocated the personal essay as a basis of writing; the student was encouraged to view significant personal experience as the objective subject of academic investigation. My discomfort with the Bartholomae and Petrosky approach was further complicated by my own hesitancy to invade students' privacy; the *Facts* pedagogical emphasis on developing academic discourse through autobiographic narrative became problematic almost immediately. Too often my students' discussions of what was significant or not significant involved revelation of information that I, as a teacher, wasn't qualified to deal with or that the students were hesitant to reveal to their peers. At our school, students live and work in a tight community where families had known each other for generations—a situation that was not necessarily true on the campuses of large schools, like the University of Pittsburgh or the Columbus campus of OSU where students are removed from their families and friends.

For example, in my first class of novice writers, two students wrote about being abused by parents and spouses, three described the difficulty of dealing with the death of a loved one, and five or six raged against their parents' divorces. Needless to say, everyone was hesitant to become involved in peer editing, and many wanted assurance that I would be the only person to read their papers. Even more disturbing to me was the students' assumptions that I was there to help them work out these nonwriting, nonacademic problems. Making me the audience of the essay privileged me to information that ordinarily would have only been shared with close friends and members of the family. In that first semester alone, I referred four students to the advisers here at school, and I suspected that other students were equally disturbed by the investigations they conducted, but chose to keep silent. They didn't want to know some of the things they found out, and I found this type of personal responsibility for student problems overwhelming. Despite my belief in connecting the personal with the academic—I never felt particularly outraged if a student wrote "I feel" instead of "I think"—this emphasis on analyzing personal feelings seemed a dubious goal for an academic writing course. True, at the end of the quarter, my student evaluations were quite favorable. However, over and over again students would report: "I learned to understand my feelings" before they reported, in an almost offhand manner, that they had learned to write for college. Furthermore, when the students came in for help on other writing projects at the writing center, we discovered that they did not automatically apply the analytical skills we taught them in English to the writing they did for classes in other disciplines. They operated by a familiar assumption: English was about feelings; history, sociology, biology were about facts. Those who did well in our course experienced confusion later because their other professors didn't want to know how the students felt about observing a butterfly, just what the butterfly looked like and how it acted. A chasm still remained between the students and the academic discourse of other disciplines.

My working-class students also found it difficult to identify with the readings in the *Facts* syllabus. Novels about young boys in eastern prep schools—*Catcher in the Rye* and *A Separate Peace*—meant little to my students. *Ordinary People* seemed to them to be a story of Spoiled Rich People; Maya Angelou's autobiography proved equally alien to their experience.[2] Discussion of the novels went slowly, and the students' alienation from the characters kept them from equating the characters' experiences with data for the topic at hand—growth and change in adolescence. More than once I was faced by a group of sulky students, arms crossed and eyes defiant, determined not to find "the universal" in the texts.

In my search for ways to engage these recalcitrant students, a study by Elizabeth Flynn, published in *Gender and Reading: Essays on Readers, Text, and Contexts,* was particularly helpful in understanding their reactions. Flynn's study described male and female students' reactions to three frequently anthologized short stories: James Joyce's "Araby," Ernest Hemingway's "Hills Like White Elephants," and Virginia Woolf's "Kew Gardens." Flynn contends that

> reading involves a confrontation between self and "other." The self, the reader, encounters the "other," the text, and the nature of that confrontation depends on the background of the reader as well as on the text (267).

If the world depicted in the text is similar to the students' backgrounds or at least accessible in some manner,

> the self and other, reader and text, interact in such a way that the reader learns from the experience without losing critical distance. . . . Self and other remain distinct and so create a kind of dialogue (268).

But if readers cannot make a connection between the self and the events in the story, they fall back on one of two reactions: they will attempt to "dominate" the text, rejecting it as useless and irrelevant to learning; or they will let the text dominate them, assuming that they do not have the ability to understand the important points of the text (268).

In her study, Flynn found rather distinct gender differences in student responses to alien texts, texts that did not relate to either the students' past experience or to texts they had encountered in the past. Males tended to try to dominate stories they did not understand by rejecting the stories as "stupid" or "boring" and the characters in the stories as "crazy" or "insane." The women in the study, on the other hand, tried to put the characters into personal contexts and avoid outright rejection. The women assumed that the text had meaning, but that the meaning was beyond their understanding unless they understood the situations in which the characters found themselves.

These reactions certainly echoed my students' responses to fiction. In both cases, readers dismissed the texts or became mystified by them. However, my class exhibited one notable difference: among the Marion campus novice reading and writing students, the tendency to dominate and/or be dominated by texts knew no real gender distinction. Across the board, readers faced with unfamiliar situations in texts repeated the same message: "I really can't identify with the character. His [or her, depending upon the reading] life has nothing in common with mine." Frequently, the dialogue would stop there, despite my attempts to link my students' experiences with those of the characters.

But if the novels were difficult, the students could at least follow a plot; reading Gail Sheehy's *Passages* resulted in an interpretive disaster. The students not only read the narrative sections badly, treating them as analysis of situations rather than as example, they also ignored or completely misunderstood the sociological explanations Sheehy offers of her subjects' experiences. After several days of fruitless class discussion, the students rebelled and simply pronounced *Passages* a dumb book. "Who are these people?" they asked. "Why would anyone care what their lives are like? What's this got to do with learning to write?" Then they leveled the supreme denouncement: "It's boring."

Faced with a room of recalcitrant students and a book they found impossible to read, much less analyze, I would have tap-danced on the desk if that would have engaged my class in their studies. But fortunately, for myself and the desk, I didn't have to resort to such outlandish methods. By happenstance, I had been reading *Sometimes a Shining Moment,* Eliot Wigginton's account of the early years of the *Foxfire* project. This was two years before Wigginton's conviction for child molestation, an act that has cast doubt on his pedagogy as well as his character. Admittedly, even as I write this, I struggle with separating Wigginton-the-man from

Wigginton-the-teacher; however, I still find his teaching experiences to be compelling and intrinsically important to my own development as a teacher of students the world refers to as *unprepared.* In *Sometimes a Shining Moment,* Wigginton describes the bleak day that, frustrated and discouraged, he walked into his classroom, which he had begun to think of as a battlefield, ready to try anything to reach the students. He climbed on his desk, but instead of tap dancing, he crossed his legs, and said quietly, "Look, this isn't working. You know it isn't and I know it isn't. Now what are we going to do together to make it through the rest of the year?" (32).

His question turned the problem over to his students. Furthermore, it required them to define the problems that kept them from learning and to suggest a way of presenting the stuff of English courses in a manner that would make English seem worthwhile and at least a little interesting. Amazingly enough, his belief that the students were responsible and intelligent beings *did* engage his class and led to a solution for the immediate situation that has become one of the mainstays of English education in the past twenty years.

Wigginton's Rabun Gap students, although younger, shared certain characteristics with my students. Like the Rabun Gap population, our students are place bound. The Marion campus serves a rural/blue-collar area whose population historically has had little use for either secondary or higher education. Many of our students, being honest about their ambitions, reveal that they attend college because they have no choice in today's economy. Factory jobs are no longer abundant; family farms are rarely self-sufficient. Our students' parents decided to finish high school in order to compete in the job market, and many of our students have decided to try for a college degree for the same reason. To Marion campus novice writers, as to other novice writers, a college education provides a license that will entitle them to a better paycheck. Exploring the world of intellect is seldom even an attractive side benefit.

Wigginton lamented the fact that in Rabun Gap "all the disciplines and beauties of English are as foreign to [students] as an opera, and that's the way they want it" (26). Our students, too, make little pretext of enjoying or even seeing a need for English literature or any of the humanities core curriculum. Composition may be one of the few English courses that they accept as practical; some of the students pay lip service to the idea that everyone should learn to write, and others begrudgingly confess that writing might serve some purpose in their future careers. Our students don't generally hate English, but they don't suffer it gladly, either. Because of similar student attitudes toward English, Wigginton discovered that merely asking his students for methods that would make English a relevant and interesting subject didn't immediately result in new earth-shaking strategies for teaching English. Initially the students could not conceive of writing as other than a negative experience. "To read out loud is like ordering a big fat F," one student reported (18). And there was little doubt that the same went for writing. His students had experienced few positive experiences with English or English teachers. The conventional pedagogy he had learned in college didn't have a place in Rabun Gap. Assuming that there could be connections between teachers and students, he reflected on his own education and started a list of educational projects that had, over the years, engaged and inspired him when he was a student. The list led to a series of teaching guidelines. Learning, the final list revealed, became more attractive when

- visitors from the outside world attended class
- students left the classroom on assignments or field trips
- activities and products of the classroom had an audience beyond the teacher
- students were given responsibility of an adult nature and were trusted to fulfill it
- students took on major independent research projects that went far beyond simply copying something out of an encyclopedia and involved them in periods of intense personal creativity and action

From these principles of learning and with the help of his students, the *Foxfire* project was born, a project that has had great influence on high school programs throughout the United States, but which has only peripherally touched college and university writing courses.[3]

College English objectives, of course, need to be far more comprehensive than high school objectives. Wigginton struggled to teach basic skills; we have to push past simple learning tasks and introduce critical reading and writing. *Foxfire,* as impressive as it was, required the students to collect material and report findings of research. Wigginton himself reported that the curriculum only tangentially touched upon the sort of examination of culture and community that a college-level course might be expected to develop:

> Basically, it's a composition course. The students, in twelve weeks, make demonstrable gains in terms of skills—organizational, grammatical, and mechanical—and I can document that fact not only to my own satisfaction but also to the satisfaction of a department head or an administrator. (382)

These goals, however, were not, and still are not, adequate for the novice writing classes on our campus. Not only must the students demonstrate competence with their skills, they must be prepared to demonstrate an ability to engage in formal oral and written conversations about the texts, ideas, and philosophies of various disciplines. I could not merely adopt Wigginton's curriculum any more than I could wholeheartedly adopt Bartholomae's and Petrosky's. But I could use his strategies and I could use the students' ideas to supplement my own. I, too, was ready to try anything. Although I do not remember climbing on the desk in this particular incident, I did appeal to my students for help. We were in the middle of the course; I wanted to finish what we'd begun. Straightforwardly, to their infinite amazement, I put the task in their hands. How could we make sense out of the tasks before us and, not incidentally, have some fun with learning to write?

As might be expected, their first suggestions echoed their years of previous English instruction:

> "You could write notes on the board about what we're supposed to get out of each chapter."

> "You could give us a list of questions to answer after each chapter."

> "You could explain it to us, so we could know what you want."

These suggestions reflected narrow learning objectives and a knowledge base that depended upon extrinsic rather than intrinsic motivation. Learning by these methods would involve little curiosity, no modeling of inquiry, and no sense of reciprocity. I refused to play.

"Those methods won't develop the skills you need to master," I explained. "Textual interpretation, critical/evaluative writing, and correct grammar and mechanics can't be reduced to formulas that can be memorized and spit out. What you suggest puts the responsibility for learning on me; that responsibility is yours, not mine."

While a few students looked at me as if I'd lost my mind, most of them just nodded and grinned in agreement. So we began again, this time drawing upon ways they learned best at home as well as at school, drawing upon theories of learning from Wigginton and Bruner, and struggling to translate their ideas into classroom theories and learning strategies. Our final negotiated plan bore only a surface resemblance to the program Wigginton proposed for Foxfire. Instruction grew out of the students' attempts to understand their own world as well as the worlds depicted in the books they read. The project emphasized interpreting and verifying the ideas in written texts rather than in creating, as Wigginton's students did, entire texts from whole cloth. The major complaint about all of the books, but especially about Sheehy's *Passages,* consisted of the students' claim, "It's not like that here." None of the adolescents Sheehy uses to represent typical adolescents fit my class's conception of "normal people." The class had serious reservations about the inevitability of the crises experienced by Sheehy's respondents, and they flatly re-fused to believe that the problems and conflicts she considers central to "the average person's" life cycle were in any way connected to the life experiences of people in central Ohio. Her portraits produced neither curiosity nor a sense of social connection.

"It's not like that here," the students kept insisting. "People can't worry about being fulfilled, or having jobs they *like* if their families are hungry. They do what they have to do." It was, as my colleague Lynda would say, a teachable moment.

"Is Sheehy only talking about self-fulfillment?" I asked. "Why are these people so interested in their careers? What makes the fam-ilies Sheehy studies different from yours?"

For those of you not familiar with *Passages,* Sheehy collected the life stories of 115 people who belonged to what she identified as "America's 'pacesetter group'—healthy, motivated people who either began in or have entered the middle class" (23–24). She chose these people for three reasons: (1) she *had* to limit the study to a special group in order to trace inconsistencies in attitudes and actions; (2) she views the members of the middle class as carriers of American so-cial values; (3) she thinks the members of the educated middle class have more options and fewer obstacles to shaping their lives as they desire (24). Her male subjects included lawyers, doctors, chief execu-tives, middle managers, ministers, professors, politicians, students. The women were "top-achieving women [as well as] those who fol-lowed the steps of many traditional nurturing women" (24). Most of her subjects lived in metropolitan areas, and their interests and atti-tudes reflected the diversity found in large urban areas.

"So," I asked my students, "what do these people have in com-mon? Do you see your family represented?"

We took a quick survey of occupations, educational back-ground, and family history in order to produce some demographics of our class. While a number of students had family members who taught elementary or high school, no one's family could claim any of the other college-trained professionals that Sheehy listed. Women either worked at jobs they despised or stayed home; choice was rarely a factor in their decisions. Most of the parents had only high school educations, and many of the grandparents quit school in the sixth or seventh grade. The difference between Marion, a town of approximately 30,000, and the cities that were home for

Sheehy's subjects was plainly and almost laughably clear. Fairly quickly the students concluded that while what Sheehy had to say might be applicable to the people she studied, it was not relevant to working-class rural people—people like their parents and like themselves. Curiosity, which had peaked when they discovered that they might be right when they declared there was a difference between Sheehy's population and the population of their own communities, began to die quickly. In fact, at that moment, they would have liked to consider the matter closed. I, however, chose to model a more extended inquiry.

"How do you know your families are representative of all the families in this area?"

This question led to a series of "Everybody feels . . ." "Everybody knows . . ." "Everybody thinks . . ." statements from some of the stronger personalities in the class, and surprisingly, an equal number of "Not in my family . . ." statements from people who usually didn't speak at all. Suddenly the clear-cut nature of what it was like "here" fell apart, giving an opportunity to discuss generalizations, interpretations, assumptions, and various influences on personal opinions. It became obvious that no one knew exactly how it was here. But they became intensely curious about whether their families represented average families or stood on the fringes of normal as far as attitudes and beliefs were concerned.

"How do we find out?" I asked.

"Do what Sheehy did?" someone replied. Everyone else moaned.

I already held the chalk in my hand. "Suggestions?"

The activities they devised fit the criteria that Wigginton set for Foxfire: hands-on activities instead of traditional composition class activities. But the activities also required developing strategies for mastering texts, because before we could replicate Sheehy's study, the students had to find out how she went about gathering information and how she interpreted what she found. Our distinct purpose for close reading the text became learning how to do something rather than learning about something. As luck would have it, some of the students were taking sociology and speech, and both courses offered at least some preliminary information about doing surveys and questionnaires; these students shared their notes and insights into gathering data. I dug though material from my own days as a student researcher and prepared some lessons on interviewing. Discovering how to uncover information, interpret it, and write up the results taught the class more about collaborative research and academic reading and writing than all the other methods that I'd tried before.

To make the search more manageable, we divided the class into four groups—"the Trying Twenties," "The Thirties," "The Forties," and "An Overview of the Life Styles of People Over Fifty." Each age group corresponded to one or more chapters in *Passages.* After much discussion and debate about balancing the study, each student in a group interviewed three people in the community, making sure that each group obtained information from both men and women in the age group they studied. We did not consider matters of race in our first research for one reason only: we had decided to make the study reflect the experiences of the students in our class, and there were no members of minority groups enrolled. In subsequent projects, we have made an effort to create ethnic as well as gender balance, regardless of the character of the class population.

After completing their interviews, each group of students typed up a summary of the information gleaned from the individual interviews. They made enough copies of the summaries so that every member of the class could have one. This sharing of information opened up chances for discussion between the students about various subjects. It also revealed problems in the interview data: what was left out of the summary became as much an issue as what was recorded. Since the groups needed accurate information to complete their studies, interviewers suddenly found themselves responsible for accuracy in a manner they had never before encountered. Demands for more information abounded:

> "What do you mean, you don't know how old she is? That's your job; the data isn't valid if you're ten years off."

> "Does this woman have children? What age are they?"

> "How long did old Jimmy here work? You say he's taken early retirement—how early?"

> "Can you call this guy back and get some more information? I just don't see why you think he belongs in this study."

The first set of interviews proved so inconclusive and incomplete that the students decided to go out for a second set. This time they insisted that the interviewers produce a transcript of new materials or at least a copy of a tape so that they could have a record to work from that might contain some actual passages from which they could quote. They wanted to judge for themselves what was important and what was insignificant in the respondents' statements.

After the second round of interviewing, the students discovered that reading the interviews was not sufficient preparation to come to conclusions about the groups of people they studied.

Experiences were different, attitudes varied, no clear results popped out and presented themselves. It was time for me to step in and demonstrate how to analyze data. I asked each group to put what they considered to be major findings from their study on the blackboard, so the whole class could approach the task of making sense from the diversity of information. "What do we make of this data?" I asked. Everyone sat very still. "Can we say that this group has a set of common experiences? Do you see any sort of attitude that prevails? What are we to do with these people who stand out as really different? No, we can't drop them from the data. They live, breathe, and exist in central Ohio. They're part of that HERE you keep talking about."

After the discussion, I left the groups to develop their own theories about the passages experienced by members of the Marion community and insisted that they compare their findings and theories to the work developed by Sheehy. Each group wrote a paper explaining the conclusions they reached, and some groups included minority reports from those students who were not convinced of the conclusions supported by the rest of their group.

The student researchers discovered many differences between the passages that Sheehy describes and the passages that their families and friends experienced, but they also found unexpected similarities. The collaborative and individual writing they did gave them a much better sense of how to process and interpret information and the problems that resulted from having incomplete data on a subject. They couldn't have discovered this by merely reading and studying *Passages* because their conception of how knowledge is created from research was limited. They realized that interviewing their friends and families skewed the data about the nature of Marion's occupants, but despite the fact that they knew their work was limited in scope and execution, they found reasons to be proud. One student even argued that our study was probably more valid than Sheehy's because our sample was larger and we applied it to a more contained group. While the final report would be judged incomplete by an anthropologist, it provided a means of experimenting in another form of formal discourse—one that was not English and one that was not in the comfortable language of the community.

IMPRINTS, the newsletter sponsored by the Columbus campus Writing Workshop, published the report. Not only thrilled to see their work in print, my students had a new sense of their ability to handle "real" research. Our study had allowed the students to work from a position of authority: they knew and trusted the people they interviewed and reported upon. For the first time, they understood

how authors and, by extension, academics, construct knowledge
and transform it into the stuff of books.

At the end of that long autumn quarter, thoroughly exhausted by
feeling on the edge of either an abyss or a pedagogical breakthrough,
my colleague Lynda and I sat by the fire and reflected upon the outcome of my quarter. I had combined the personal with the academic
by making the population of our area the subject of our study and
source for information. Valuing what the students had to say about
the nature of their own lives and experience engendered that ever
elusive quality of student investment in learning that Bruner discussed. But what was it I thought I was doing? Could my success be
duplicated? Was there a theory in this practice? At this point I could
have stopped the inquiry and rested upon the success of the program. Like other composition practitioners, I had created a program
that would probably serve me well for years to come. But like my
students, I was affected by intrinsic motivations: curious about what
might happen with the next group of students; spurred on by the desire to be a better teacher; inspired by models such as Murray, Emig,
Elbow and Belanoff; and desirous of contributing something to my
colleagues as well as to the students I teach.

Lynda and I decided to team teach the ENG 052/053 courses the
next year, and thus began our process of reflection and experimentation. Because naming creates legitimacy, we temporarily labeled
what we were doing as ethnographic research, partly because we
did not know what else to call it and partly because what we were
doing resembled the types of ethnographic writing that both Shirley
Brice Heath and Sondra Perl advocated as teaching tools. Heath,
whose work I discussed in Chapter 1, advocated ethnography as a
means of connecting cultural and educational differences. In
"Reflections on Ethnography and Writing," Perl outlines the similarities between the process of ethnography and the process of writing. Although she uses teachers rather than students as researchers,
her points are equally applicable to student-based ethnographies.
Indeed, they connect quite remarkably with the principles that
Wigginton outlines for encouraging active learning in students and
with instructional goals advocated by the MLA Coalition. Perl discusses the seven common features that the writing process and the
ethnographic process share:

1. Writing and ethnography require that we analyze the process as
   well as the final product in order to understand the way people
   function. In the writing process, breaking down the activities so
   that we can see how the student constructs the paper helps us
   understand the final product. In the ethnographic process, out-

lining various activities and histories allows us to understand a cultural phenomenon.

2. In both writing and ethnography we learn by doing. We must, as Perl says, learn by "rolling up our sleeves and getting our hands dirty—in other words, we have to do it in order to learn it and to get better at it" (11).

3. In ethnography, as in writing, we discover what we want to say as we go along, allowing the meaning to grow from observation and reflection rather than imposing meaning before the research is complete.

4. Both ethnography and writing are recursive processes. Students of each must go back to the original texts (or contexts) constantly—reviewing, reinterpreting, deepening our sense of what our observations mean.

5. Both forms of process involve mastering or learning diverse points of view and a variety of ways to share and interpret information. Writing requires mastery of various but equally effective forms; ethnography recognizes various but equally valid versions of truth.

6. Ethnography, which grows from anthropology, allows the individual researcher to "immerse [himself or] herself in and come to understand a foreign culture" (11). His or her findings cannot be reduced to sage generalizations about people and things. In a like manner, the writer responds upon a human level rather than an abstractly objective one; both viewing the world from a personal context and acknowledging that context.

7. Above all, both ethnography and writing can be instrumental in developing trust between teachers and students. Allowing the students control over what they study and an authoritative voice in the conclusions they reach, makes them more comfortable about taking risks in writing and in thinking (11).

But as we read and explored the goals of ethnographic research, we discovered, as Michael Kleine has noted in "Beyond Triangulation: Ethnography, Writing, and Rhetoric," that what we tried to think of as student ethnography differed from the ethnography of anthropologists and educators. Professional ethnographers, especially the early ones, "enjoyed the illusion that their work was scientific and non-rhetorical" (118). In other words, they believed it represented the truth. We did not hold any illusions that what our students knew about their communities, even after research, was at all representative of complete, objective truth. The studies were incomplete, limited, and often convoluted by individual assumptions about the nature of living in central Ohio. While we wished to examine and critique what the students claimed to know about the population in this area, we also wished to introduce them to the idea that researching and writing about a subject or a population could raise questions more frequently than answer them. Ethnography in our class was less a means of studying a population than a means of connecting the students with the research process that goes into academic study and writing.

So we abandoned the idea that we were ethnographers and began to think of what we did as a new sort of rhetorical stance: the "Distanced/Personal." The *personal* element allows students to speak as authorities about what they have experienced—educational practices in their home town, the importance of cultural literacy, the supposed difference between popular and "real" art. It does not require them to reveal traumatic or sensitive moments in their own lives. The way of life in their communities becomes the data they analyze rather than the events of their own lives. The *distanced* element allows them to look at themselves and their communities as subjects for academic research, to take a somewhat objective look at what they believe they *know*.

As we worked out the first of our planned, Distanced/Personal projects, we tried to keep in mind several principles and objectives that embodied the comprehensive learning/knowing goals we felt the curriculum should stress. The curriculum we devised was designed to draw on student interest and stimulate intrinsic motivations for learning:

- The topics for study would be ones that none of our students could deny pertained to them and to future and past members of their communities.

- The topic would be broad so that students could retain a great deal of control over shaping it, following those elements that peaked their curiosity.

- Investigating the topic would involve students in field work—hands-on, active learning that takes place outside of the classroom as well as in it.

- The desire to exhibit competence could be stimulated by publishing student findings.

- Integrating reading, writing, and research assignments would insure that the students could not find, nor attempt to appease us with easy, unconsidered answers to questions.

Because students had to leave our courses and go into other disciplines, we felt that we needed to prepare them for changes in disciplinary discourse. This meant introducing such writing tasks as summarization, reporting, paraphrasing, and formal essay development. But at another level, we realized that our students will always know more about the nature of their communities' discourse than we, as academic outsiders, can possibly understand. Therefore, we decided, it was imperative to treat the students' worlds and their conceptions of what constituted knowledge as respectfully as we would have them treat ours.

Thus began our search for topics to investiagate. Topics fit within the realm of the Distanced/Personal, we concluded, if they meet the following standards:

- The topic can be construed as personal—located within the students' range of experience.
- The topic is connected with the experiences of new and old acquaintances that the students can interview, observe, and survey.
- The topic is researchable, preferably as the topic of (multi)disciplinary research, and a reasonably accessible, book-length example of research is available.
- The topic, as an overall guiding principle, concerns some common, immediate problem of human interaction and connection rather than an abstract or a future problem in some specialized area.

After close to two months' worth of discussion and research—developing a topic, looking for books to use as texts, and devising research projects, we settled upon the topic of High School Education, a topic with which students are and have been actively involved. Well within their range of experience and problematic during most novice students' lives, education touched each of them. They all attended high school—some years ago, some recently. Even adult learners could remember their high school education fairly vividly, and those with children in the system now would be especially aware of classroom practice. While they could declare, "I wasn't really interested in school" or "School never meant that much to me" or "I hated high school; it's wasted time," they couldn't say, "I never experienced it." Although some of our students had been out of high school for more than ten years, each student had attended high school at some point, even those who had dropped out and finished with a GED. We decided not to ask them to concentrate solely upon their personal experiences in the classroom; individual woes or successes had to be put in context with other students' experiences. The course would begin with an investigation into learning experiences: Why are some teachers effective in the classroom and others not? How does the course of instruction affect particular segments of the student body? What makes a student want to learn? Personal experiences and the experiences of their friends in the classroom could constitute legitimate proof for making a point, but their essays had to go beyond the autobiographical. By analyzing reactions, both positive and negative, we hoped that our novice writers' would eventually see their own experiences as important pieces of data in a larger inquiry.

As we worked, the requirements for completing the course grew as demanding as they were complex. Some of our colleagues questioned whether novice students could complete such a difficult set of assignments. However, insisting on more instead of less formed a central part of our pedagogy. We agree with Vygotsky's premise that the highest order of thinking develops when the learning environment provides challenges that make new demands upon the students and introduces them to a sequence of new goals (58–59). As we continued to develop new topics and new ways of teaching reading and writing, we continued to look for complexity rather than ease. Mike Rose said it best: "Students will float to the mark you set" (26). We raised the water line enough that they had to swim.

Chapter Three

Starting with the Basics
An Overview of Reading
and Writing Problems

Learning to read and write depends critically on imme-
diate social involvement with people who read and write
and who can show you how the work goes . . . ordinary
social ties with others [act] as the very means that en-
able reading and writing and the very essence of literate
reflection.

—Deborah Brandt
Literacy as Involvement

Novice Readers, Problem Readings[1]

Few people deny that the novices who populate what we call developmental, basic, or remedial writing classes have reading problems as well; yet we tend to take their explanations for the nature of
that problem as gospel. When students pronounce a topic to be
"boring," "stupid," or "a waste of time," they imply that the right
reading material would erase their objections.

Isn't that a seductive thought?

I certainly would like to believe that the mere selection of a
topic will overcome all reading problems. We've all read the leg-
ends of individual students, labeled slow or deficient, who became

inspired by an interesting topic and began to read marvelously well. My favorite example concerns a young girl with a deep-seated interest in sailing, who suddenly started reading *Moby Dick*. Equally impressive is the legend about a whole tribe of motorcycle jocks who rushed to read Kerouac. I'm sure that these students did undergo a sea change of sorts—but did they ever read anything else? Could they decipher an anthropological text on Eskimo whalers or a psychological study of the Beat Generation?

The *reading* problem, it seems to me, is probably situated not in the students' *interest* in the subjects but in their inability to understand the nature of complex expository prose. In my experience, students who don't enjoy reading on some level don't change their minds permanently as a result of a few changes in reading material. Unlike those of us who enjoy reading and decoding texts, students who hate to read do not consider books to be conversations between authors and readers about ideas. They think of books as pages that must be read, pages containing information that must be absorbed. Struggling through the reading, alternating between feeling lost, bored, and frustrated, they often come to class hostile, not so much from what they've read but from having to read. Frequently, the range of behaviors that greet a teacher when she enters the classroom merely reflect her students' inability to respond rather than their unwillingness to participate. They won't discuss the text, but not for the reasons we usually attribute to them. They simply haven't understood what they read. Please note that I said "haven't understood what they've read" rather than "haven't read" or "can't read." While our midwestern, rural college may occasionally admit a student who reads at the elementary school level and a few who hope to beat the system by faking their way through both class and books, most of our students can read and attempt to keep up with the reading. They just read expository prose poorly.

Every year, teachers face students who don't realize that reading should open thinking, not close it. Nor do they understand that these carefully wrought texts are, in a sense, unfinished, permitting the reader to agree, resist, or puzzle over a topic until she or he completes the meaning. It doesn't help to tell them that authors and texts can be ambiguous. The novice readers I've encountered don't like ambiguity: most of them want straightforward prose that says what it means; many want simple and obvious meanings. But just because they want simple and obvious meanings doesn't mean we have to supply or accept that level of work. As Dennis Baron has said about beginning writers, "If novices do not grapple with hard forms, they will never master them" (28).

I advocate serious study of one or more pieces of extended text, books that cannot be raced through in a day but must be read over a period of weeks. Such reading allows practice of the difficult tasks involved in piecing together an elaborate and thoughtful conversation about a topic. Yes, I know, novice readers have trouble with even the shortest of essays; the length of most nonfiction books—scholarly or otherwise—becomes daunting. But they need practice and guidance in nonliterary textual analysis, and, like learning to write, the only way to learn to read texts is to grapple with them.

Recognizing Reading Problems

The first step in teaching students how to read is, quite naturally, recognizing their particular reading problems. That initial identification needs to be made in the classroom rather than in the psychometric testing lab. Just as Mina Shaughnessy suggested that teachers watch *how* students write, I suggest teachers arrange opportunities to watch *how* students read to themselves. Reading silently in class can reveal a great deal about students' reading habits and problems.[2] I'm looking for more than moving lips when I watch students read. I'm looking for attitudes and facial expressions. Like the dentist who checks the effects of Novocain by watching his patient's eyes for flinching eyelids, I watch the students for outward manifestations of inward turmoil.

Most novice readers attack a book rather like they attack a meal that they dislike but know to be good for them. Rather than savor the content, they attempt to devour it whole, and not in the Baconian sense. Skipping front matter and epigraphs, starting at the first word of chapter one, they read about half a page before they stop. At this point, the observant teacher can witness an almost clear break from the material. Some students start a conversation with their classmates in order to avoid going back to the page. Some stare into space. Others begin to doodle in the notebook beside them. Still others shift in their seats and drum their fingers trying to keep their eyes on the page. Whatever the behavior, little reading takes place. Sometimes these breaks with the text can indicate a problem with attention span. If that is the problem, the student will also have difficulty with paying attention while others speak, keeping "on task" (as elementary school teachers say) when working alone or in groups, and concentrating on any but the shortest of activities. But, of course, it could also indicate the student is having outside interference—problems at home or school, or simply the seduction of spring or fall air. Just watching students isn't enough to identify their reading problems.

We are compelled to look closer. Observe the open books, for instance. Novice readers' texts usually fall into one of two categories: unmarked and marked. In the first category, pages lack any handwritten annotations. Often the reason for the pristine cleanliness has nothing to do with not recognizing important points. For many of the students, writing in or otherwise marking a text constitutes a sacrilege. Furthermore, either from the grapevine of student knowledge or from the *buy back* instructions in the bookstore, they have learned that writing in a book affects how much they can sell it for at the end of the quarter. Few novice readers see books as items to be kept and used again after a course is over; books represent money spent and money to be regained.

In the second category, texts are marked, not with annotations, but with brightly colored lines. Making a visible effort to "get something" from the books, students underline and highlight everything that seems to be important. They look for the substance or the core of the information—that which will be on the test, that which the teacher will discuss in class. These students wield highlighters with a heavy hand because the *How to Succeed in College* study guides emphasize underlining important passages. But it's important to look at *what* they highlight: seemingly irrelevant individual words, dates, and names; the first sentence of every paragraph regardless of what it says; contiguous paragraphs; entire pages. Regardless of whether they mark or don't mark in their books, the problem has the same root: novice readers don't know what they're looking for.

The students' problem with deciding what's important in the passages signals their lack of familiarity with formal written discourse. Never having worked with complex expository texts, novice readers have limited schemata with which to decipher what they read. In theory, the students' schemata, or methods of making associations between what they read and what they already know, should have broadened and become more enriched as they encountered new texts in high school. In many cases, however, reading tasks remain at the same level of difficulty year after year—witness the fact that sophomores in remedial tracks in high school read simplified "young adult" novels, high on action and low on word count, rather than lengthier, more difficult, and—we would hope—more meaningful texts. These simplified reading tasks have not broadened their interpretive schemata any more than they have broadened their knowledge of genre, form, literary allusion, or vocabulary. Students often fail to understand a text not because they cannot decode individual words but because they do not know that they should try to decode the text *as a whole.* Applying old methods of understanding high school texts to new texts proves unsuccessful. The college-level texts demand quite different schemata to facilitate understanding. High school texts tend to be informative rather than speculative. They present facts, dates, formulas, explanations. Their authors do not tend to pose questions for examination or pit theorists against each other in order to prove a point or create a context for their own theories.

Even more problematic are the students' tendencies to read spatially rather than globally. Deborah Brandt points out that while expert readers "create and maintain a network of immediate and long-range plans by which they manage and monitor their progress and level of understanding . . . poor readers tend to focus on what the text is saying next" (37). Poor readers attempt to move through a text without an overall plan or an understanding of how the pieces of the text work together to construct a whole meaning. They begin by moving word by word through the text. When they find themselves in a muddle of strange and incomprehensible phrases, they abandon their original strategy and develop a new, equally ineffective process: they concentrate on the words they understand and ignore those with which they are unfamiliar. In a similar manner, they read the sentences that they can easily understand and skim the complex ones. The text develops holes where the readers didn't understand a word or a passage, or where they left out something that seemed unimportant. Such readings not only destroy the nuances and tone of a text, they also obliterate important details in the writer's argument. The students end up merely reading words. And individual words cannot make sense or create interest in a topic. It's rather like reading a series of unrelated paragraphs—unless readers are devoted to making meaning from the elements that confront them, the enterprise seems endless and pointless. The inability to see the text as a whole contributes to the boredom students experience when reading and fuels the feeling that reading wastes time.

For expert readers, the conversation between writer and reader and the aftermath of that conversation forms the basis of knowledge. As Brandt argues, writers and readers must do more than merely make sense of a text: readers must understand what to do as one reads and after one finishes reading (38). A text calls for action: "knowing what [the text] is saying about what you need to be doing, right here, right now" (38). Because novice readers don't understand what they need to do with a text either during or after reading, their ideas about content often seem ridiculously off-base. They misread in ways the teacher often finds amazing. Take, for instance, the misreading made by most of my students when reading

Passages. They came to the erroneous conclusion that Gail Sheehy was male merely because she described being caught in the cross-fire during Ireland's Bloody Sunday. They further concluded that *he* was writing about some of *his* weird friends rather than exploring the crises that occur in Americans at various ages. In a later class, when the students misread a case study of censorship, they attributed the motives of the censors to people who were actually advocates of the First Amendment.

Before those of us who know the conventions of reading become judgmental or write off the problems as learning disabilities, we need to think about our own misreadings. Even the best of readers, caught up in some highly intricate argument, will occasionally miss the quotation marks, insert a "not" where only a "does" exists, or misread a statement so that it fits one interpretation rather than another. In these days of intensive critical jargon, it's rather commonplace to guess at word meanings; academics do it far more than it's comfortable to admit. For novice readers, the problem is just exacerbated.

The ways to misread are as numerous as the students who misread, but the primary reasons students misread aren't especially mysterious. Students skip block quotations, reasoning that they are just examples covered elsewhere. They privilege the first line of each paragraph, seeing no real reason to read further "to get the point." Unattuned to written language, they even miss direct textual clues. If, for instance, an author writes, "There are four reasons to believe *this-y-which*," the practiced reader starts counting. Novice readers just keep reading, missing clues like "First," and not noticing that "the second reason" follows close behind. Even when the section they read starts with the assertion, "Some people believe *such-and-such* while others believe *so-on-and-so-forth,* but I believe *this-y-which,*" the students miss the fact that such a rhetorical strategy is a means of placing ideas in a general framework. Even quotation marks confuse the novice reader. Sometimes they read over them, attributing the remarks in the quotations to the author. This has disastrous results when trying to decipher an argument and can be even more disastrous when trying to piece together the arguments that are spread out over a book. These faulty reading practices, and others like them, indicate that novice readers do not have Brandt's network of reading strategies, and without such strategies, the words just flow together, the continuous print creating a sort of textual overload.

Think again of those faulty or incomplete schemata. The students' previous reading has been carefully constructed to provide information, but college readings often supply information only as part of a larger search for understanding about motivation, purpose, or being. References to other books and scholars, quotations from other sources are used as supporting evidence, not as discrete parcels of fact to be memorized. Given the shift from factual to speculative discourse, it's not surprising that the students' formulaic strategies for deciphering the written word frequently fail. To illustrate my point, I offer the following selections of first paragraphs from the four texts we read in the first Distanced/Personal reading and writing sequence. Yes, *Sometimes a Shining Moment* is among our selections; Wigginton's personal life was not a problem at the time. Even after his arrest and conviction, we were able to use the book. Students were quick to see the difference between his pedagogy and his personal life. In fact, for many of our students, it opened up conversations about their own need to understand how someone they respect as a teacher of a subject can fail to meet their expectations of ethical behavior:

Eliot Wigginton

Sometimes A Shining Moment

I am a public high school English teacher.

Occasionally, on gloomy nights, my mood shifts in subtle ways, and familiar questions rise in my throat; in social situations, confronted by those whose lives seem somehow more dramatic, an implication in the air is that I will have little of interest to contribute to the conversation; many people with fewer years of formal education make more money. Then the mood passes, for I know that surface appearance is deceitful and salary is a bogus yardstick of worth. (x)

Ann Tracy

Higher Ground

Historia, quoquo modo scripta, bona est.

In the seventeenth century, when inquiring minds still swung between magic and science, one popular experiment professed to "revivify" a plant from its own ashes. Even Sir Thomas Browne, that famous exploder of popular error, avers in Religio Medici that the thing can be done, that the "art of man" can "from its cinders recall [a plant] into its stalk and leaves again." (Indeed, the manuscript version seems to imply that he has done it himself.) I, for one, hope that it's all true, that those Renaissance dabblers revivified not only stalk and leaves, but bud and blossom and the very scent of the rose. My intentions in this book, you see, are analogous. I propose, from faded photographs and dead jokes, from memories and memorabilia, from letters and ledgers, to conjure up the late Higgins Classical Institute, alive and educating before your very eyes. (1)

Theodore Sizer

Horace's Compromise:
The Dilemma of the American High School

Of all the stages of life, adolescence is the most volatile—full of promise, energy, and because of newly achieved freedom and potency, substantial peril. In its freshness, adolescence is attractive. In its enthusiasms, it can be, to older folk at least, exhausting. For most people, it is pivotal: it is the time of life when we find out who we are becoming, what we are good at, what and whom we like. What happens in these years profoundly affects what follows. (1)

Mike Rose

Lives on the Boundary
The Struggles and Achievements of America's Underprepared

Her name is Laura, and she was born in the poor section of Tijuana, the Mexican border city directly south of San Diego. Her father was a food vendor, and her memories of him and his chipped white cart come back to her in easy recollection: the odor of frying meat, the feel of tortillas damp with grease, and the serpentine path across the city; rolling the cart through dust, watching her father smile and haggle and curse—hawking burritos and sugar water to old women with armloads of blouses and figurines, to blond American teenagers, wild with freedom, drunk and loud and brawny. She came to the United States when she was six, and by dint of remarkable effort—on her parents' part and hers—she now sits in classes at UCLA among those blond apparitions. (1)

The differences in these texts and students' expectations about texts range far beyond the obvious differences in vocabulary and sentence length. Experienced readers will not immediately try to locate a series of important facts to be underlined, highlighted, or memorized in these introductory remarks. They hold what they have read in reserve, knowing that the writer's purpose or argument will emerge gradually. The idea of spotting a "thesis statement" at once, much less in the first paragraph, seems ludicrous. Only Wigginton starts out with a necessary fact: "I am a public high school English teacher." Situated in that stark opening paragraph it seems at the same time monumentally important and rather small. It is hardly a thesis statement. Only Tracy's opening paragraph describes the task at hand, and her announcement of intention is preceded by an elaborate analogy that only experienced readers can easily decipher. Seasoned readers know that they must continue reading to discover the full extent of her purpose. They also know that the other authors are setting up premises and introducing images that will not be explained until much later in the chapter. To find these intentions, the students must read much further and delay the satisfaction of knowing the point until the writer, determined to construct a more elaborate explanation of the problem, can work up to it.

These opening paragraphs may be difficult, but such readings are not out of line with the reading in other freshman courses. To illustrate, I've sought out examples of reading from courses on our campus, which I'll wager aren't that different from courses on most college and university campuses. For instance, many freshman composition teachers assign Plato's "The Allegory of the Cave":

> And now, I said, let me show in a figure how far our nature is enlightened or unenlightened: Behold! human beings living in an underground den, which has a mouth open toward the light and reaching all along the den; here they have been from their childhood, and have their legs and necks chained so that they cannot move, and can only see before them, being prevented by the chains from turning round their heads. Above and behind them a fire is blazing at a distance, and between the fire and the prisoners there is a raised way; and you will see, if you look, a low wall built along the way, like the screen which marionette players have in front of them, over which they show the puppets.
>
> I see.
>
> And do you see, I said, men passing along the wall carrying all sorts of vessels, and statues and figures of animals made of wood and stone and various material, which appear over the wall? Some of them are talking, others silent?
>
> You have shown me a strange image, and they are strange prisoners. (1116–17)

Novice readers do not, in the words of theorists, know how to enter this text. They cannot identify the "I" or the "you" of this selection, even after reading the explanation that usually precedes the text itself. What this first statement means, why the writer isn't using standard punctuation, where the conversation takes place, and who's being held prisoner, eludes the novice reader, as it often does students in higher-level writing courses. However, while students in *regular* freshmen courses will have similar questions, they consider it almost a game to decipher the messages, to answer the questions. The novice readers reject the text as boring, or sit quietly, assuming they aren't bright enough to understand rather than attempting to decipher the allegory. Since not knowing what to make of the text makes readers feel stupid, the safe course is to declare the work itself stupid, or old-fashioned, or nonsensical. After all, the literal-minded student may argue, no one has been or will ever be a prisoner in a cave from infancy.

The reading tasks in other disciplines are no less difficult. Supplementary history texts in college consist of more than dates and events arranged in chronological order. History has the same sort of mysterious, cross-disciplinary, narrowly focused reading tasks as English. The autobiographies of Frederick Douglas, collections of letters such as *Down and Out in the Great Depression, The Great War and Modern Memory* (surely an interdisciplinary text), and other books attempt to re-create a period rather than merely list dates. The following paragraph begins a passage from a collection of readings for a freshman world history course compiled by a colleague of mine (in fact, Vladimir of the first chapter):

> A Bodhisattva resolves: I take upon myself the burden of all suffering, I am resolved to do so, I will endure it. I do not turn or run away, do not tremble, am not terrified, nor afraid, do not turn back or despond. (Riley 87)

The immediate reaction to this piece from fact seekers with highlighters in hand can only be panic. What should be underlined? What does a Buddhist resolution have to do with world history? What does the writer mean by *all* suffering? Is this Bodhisattva character a priest like the hero of *Kung Fu?*

Geology texts are not straightforward reading either:

> The spectacular eruption of a volcano, the terror brought by an earthquake, the magnificent scenery of a mountain valley, and the destruction created by a landslide are all subjects for the geologist. . . . The study of geology deals with many fascinating and practical questions about our physical environment. What forces produce mountains? Will there soon be another great earthquake in San Francisco? What was the Ice Age like? Will there be another? What created this cave and the stone icicles hanging from its ceiling? Should we look for water here? Is strip mining practical in this area? Will oil be found if a well is drilled at that location? What if the landfill is located in the old quarry? (Tarbuck 2)

The questions in this opening paragraph are the questions of a discipline, not the idle speculation of the authors. Our students seldom understand this; they look for the *important* facts.

If the first paragraphs of texts are difficult, texts in their entirety are daunting, and, especially to the novice student, practically unreadable. Imagine the students' surprise and frustration when assigned Lewis Thomas's *Lives of a Cell* in Introduction to Biology, or Paul Fussell's *Class* in Introduction to Sociology, or works as diverse as *The Education of Henry Adams, The Myth of Sisyphus,* and *Lonely in America* in other classes.

Novice readers miss the sense of connection between the subjects being studied, themselves as students doing the studying, and the actions suggested by the writer. Furthermore, they would be astonished by Brandt's contention that our ordinary social world is "constituted and sustained" by the collaborative involvement of readers and writers such as these (31). Mike Rose, echoing Kenneth Burke, refers to this sense of connection as "entering the conversation," but finally, whether teachers think about books as conversations or as connections, the problem becomes establishing links that will stimulate curiosity and create analytical dialogues about and with subjects that students think of as set, unchangeable, and unrelated to everyday life.

Recognizing Writing Problems

As urgent as it may seem to identify exactly what's wrong with a paper and as necessary as it may seem to respond immediately to problems ranging from organization to surface error, it might prove more useful to decipher why students make the writing choices that they do. Let's face it, it's hard not to concentrate on the paper as is—in the form that the teacher receives it. The novice writer's paper often rocks a teacher's senses. Take these first paragraphs of a first draft of a paper that is supposed to be describing an incident that typifies a student's high school learning experiences. She has chosen to write about her experiences in a band. [In time-honored tradition, the names have been changed to protect the innocent, or not so innocent.] This draft is rather typical of the novice papers our students turn in. They could be worse; unlike other teachers, we do not have to deal with students who have the additional problems caused by ESL interference:

Conficts in Band

Band is partially a learning process till conflicts interfr with this process to create a disastor. The problems which most frequently cause conflict are lack of communication, too much discipline, under qualified teachers, and canges of Elwood's tradition.

A definition of communication is to pass along; transmit by Webster's New World Dictionary. If you don't have communication, you will have a lot ofmisunderstandings and a lot of confusstion. The students at Elwood High feel Mr. Lemer talks and talks and doesn't let them express there opinion. When I went to Elwood, I didn't fell this way. I felt that if you had a opinion, raise your hand and express it. You just had to be patient and talk at the right times. The times I remember to state this as a fact is when we waited till we ran the drill , and the leader of our section raised her hand and said," Mr. Lemer, I feel we should be anotger yard line over; would you please check our laocation on the drill sheet?" It turns out we were correct. Like I said there is a right time to state our opinion about a subject. You have to displine yourself and have the patience of a saint.

—Laura

Where should a teacher start? She, too, needs the patience of a saint. To attack the surface-level errors in this paper—starting perhaps with changing Conficts to Conflicts—much less to comment on the organizational or rhetorical issues in the work, would be like attempting to bring order to chaos using only a broom.

Cherryl Armstrong-Smith, in "Reexamining Basic Writing: Lessons from Harvard's Basic Writers," suggests that teachers would better serve students by addressing the underlying difficulties the students encounter when writing rather than concentrating on the obvious flaws in their texts. Pedagogy, she argues, should be "less guided by the question, 'What is wrong with this prose?' than by 'How did it get to look this way?'" (74) As she points out, "The basic writers' problems are problems basic to writing" (71). To demonstrate this fact, she lists nine writing problems that were shared not only by her students at Harvard but also by the students she taught at Queens College, an open-admissions, inner-city institution:

1. Lacking confidence in one's ability to write

2. Having trouble getting started on writing tasks

3. Becoming easily discouraged during writing tasks

4. Composing by what Peter Elbow calls "the dangerous method," (*Writing With Power* 39–46) trying to get it right, paragraph by paragraph or line by line, the first time

5. Attempting to write a one-draft version of a paper

6. Thinking of writing assignments as tests one will either pass or fail

7. Trying to write down only what seems already clear or known rather than using writing as an aid to learning or to discovering ideas

8. Believing that one's writing problems are primarily the fault of poor vocabulary, inadequate style, difficulty with "grammar," or the inability to write quickly

9. Having greater concern for form and appearance than for meaning in one's writing (75–76)

These problems also affect the novice students in our classes, and I suspect that they affect developing writers at all institutions and in all areas of the country. Therefore, finding out how this paper got this way guides much of the pedagogy in the Distanced/Personal classroom. Just as we attempt to understand why novice students misread, we try to understand why they miswrite.

Not surprisingly, our first discovery concerns the students' understanding of the writing process. It's clear that our novice writers know little or nothing of what we call process (in any of its manifestations). In fact, of all the new experiences novice writers encounter in this first college writing class, the concept of process writing seems to be one of the most amazing and distressing. Like Armstrong Smith's Harvard students, our novice writers tend to view writing as a product rather than a process: the shorter the paper the better; the quicker the paper is written, the more likely it is to be inspired. Even surface-level revisions or corrections annoy them. Although they worry constantly about grammar, vocabulary, and form, they—ironically and a bit unbelievably—resent the idea of working to improve those problems after the paper is *finished*. While they will begrudgingly accept the idea of *reading it over* for correctness, they often think that even minimal proofreading is a waste of time. It's right or it's hopeless. Besides, the teacher should know what they meant. Furthermore, if she does understand, she should let the errors pass.

Like the problems with reading, the problems with writing grow from the inability to understand what an academic text should be doing. Once again we can see that the students work from a network of strategies or what could be called a writing schema; however, just as in reading, the methods of composing that are adequate for writing in high school prove inadequate for college. Take, for example, the writing formula prescribed in this passage from *The Lively Art of Writing*, a typical high school composition text:

The Introduction

One paragraph is usually sufficient to introduce an essay. The structure of this paragraph is different from the structure of any other paragraph in the essay because its function is different. *The function of the introductory paragraph is simply to introduce the subject and come to the point.*

This neat formula gives the impression that introductions always consist of straightforward paragraphs characterized by a simple triangle. Following the formula, the author claims, will keep the student's introduction from "stagger[ing] in mid-flight like a faulty rocket" (56–57). Not surprisingly, more than introductions can be highly structured. Even the *Big Middle Section,* as the author refers

Figure 1—The Short Essay

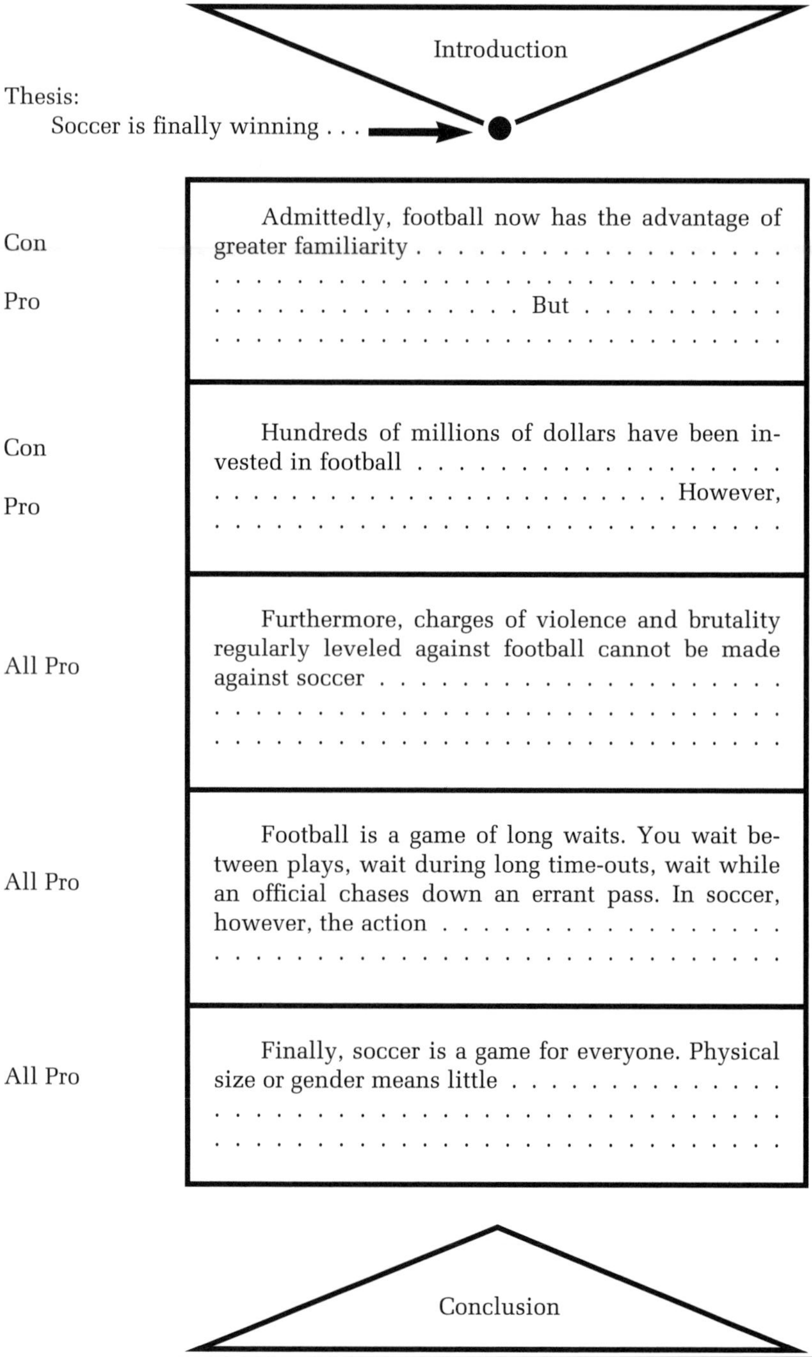

Introduction

Thesis:
   Soccer is finally winning . . .

Con
Pro

Admittedly, football now has the advantage of greater familiarity . . . . But . . . .

Con
Pro

Hundreds of millions of dollars have been invested in football . . . . However, ...

All Pro

Furthermore, charges of violence and brutality regularly leveled against football cannot be made against soccer . . . .

All Pro

Football is a game of long waits. You wait between plays, wait during long time-outs, wait while an official chases down an errant pass. In soccer, however, the action . . . .

All Pro

Finally, soccer is a game for everyone. Physical size or gender means little . . . .

Conclusion

Figure 2—The Longer Essay

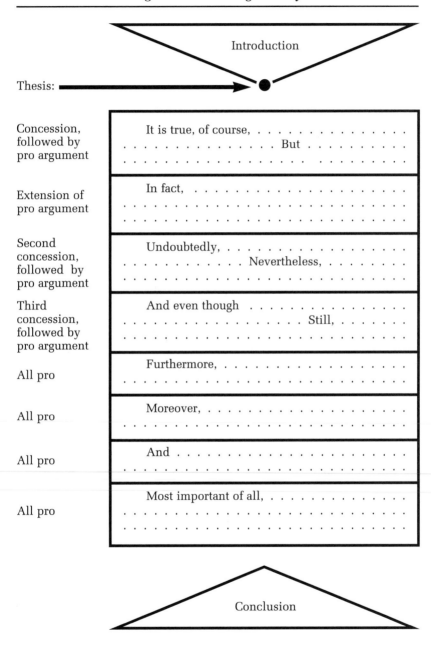

Thesis:

Concession, followed by pro argument
> It is true, of course, ...
> . . . . But . . . .
> . . . .

Extension of pro argument
> In fact, ...
> . . . .
> . . . .

Second concession, followed by pro argument
> Undoubtedly, ...
> . . . . Nevertheless, ...
> . . . .

Third concession, followed by pro argument
> And even though . . . .
> . . . . Still, ...
> . . . .

All pro
> Furthermore, ...
> . . . .

All pro
> Moreover, ...
> . . . .

All pro
> And . . . .
> . . . .

All pro
> Most important of all, ...
> . . . .
> . . . .

Introduction

Conclusion

Bear in mind that the arrangement of early paragraphs here is suggested only. You may want to devote an entire paragraph to a concession or add extra "extensions" of pro arguments. But later paragraphs should concentrate on pro arguments only, as shown.

to the body of the essay, is blocked out into sections that represent formulaic *logical development.* The logical development is illustrated by an even more elaborate series of geometric figures—depicting both the short and long essay forms—filled in with transitional statements (see Figures 1 and 2).

The student merely has to fill in the blanks with information.[3] This example of textual construction, more representative than we would like to believe, not only encourages the student to fill in the blanks in a *correct* form—introduction, body, and conclusion—it implies that all good writing will fit this pattern. Writing is a simple matter of formula over matter.

But there are other reasons students produce undeveloped or meaningless texts. When we discuss the essays with the students, "how the paper got to look this way" becomes more obvious; they usually can explain their abbreviated texts. These explanations fall into categories that more than one teacher will find familiar. The student usually starts with the statement, "I know my essay's too short, but . . . ," followed by one of the following excuses:

"Every reasonable person knows what I'm talking about . . ."
This statement attempts to squash any request for more information by making a time-honored reference to common knowledge—the rhetoric of all right-thinking persons. It assumes a shared knowledge between writer and reader. Probably the gutsiest of attempts to silence the teacher and avoid revision, this excuse may at first seem tantamount to the parental reply, "Because I said so." It is often used in tandem with the next excuse.

"It's my opinion; I don't have to justify it . . ."
In making this statement (usually rather forcefully), the novice writer endeavors to dismiss the ambiguities of the essay by using the logic, "It depends on the case—here's the answer in my case—that's sufficient." However, it also indicates the student's misunderstanding of the concept of opinion, which I will discuss later in this chapter.

"I wasn't sure what you wanted . . ."
The students who make statements like this hope that wandering about free-associating on the topic will produce at least one idea that will be right. If they plead uncertainty, the teacher may take responsibility for the stunted nature of the piece. This sort of behavior results from years of having teachers spell out strict formulas for writing—formulas like those in The Lively Art of Writing. This excuse, used mostly by students who had college prep courses in high school, can be accompanied with or followed by the following excuse, which is more likely to come from those who have had no formal essay writing experience at all.

"These are my ideas, I just didn't know
how to arrange them . . ."

Loosely translated, this means the student has stacked up three or four sentences, hoping that they will pass as an essay. Often such strategies indicate that the student has no idea what an essay is or how it's put together. The sentences usually have something to do with the topic, but a pattern of logic or development is not apparent. If the student would just "talk out" the ideas in his or her head, then the essay would probably have the beginnings of a shape and form, but the urgent need to produce an essay undermines genuine expression.

"This is the way it happened . . ."

As this statement implies, the essay is probably a narrative without obvious analysis. Sometimes a point may be tacked on the end, but, for the most part, the student assumes that the story will carry the point. There has been no culling of events, no shaping of story to prove a point, and no sense that some details of stories are more important than others. The essay stands as a monument to truth. However, without analysis of the situation, what the truth might be is not as obvious to the reader as it is to the writer.

"It's over a page long now; I thought you would be bored . . ."

Some students who use this explanation for a brief essay have been told to limit their writing in high school classes, required to keep answers short on essay tests, and taught to value brevity above all else. Make your point and get on with life. Other students really know what they produce is too short, but because they have no real investment in or knowledge of what they are writing about, they have lost interest and assume that the teacher will be grateful that they cut it short.

"I worked so hard on spelling [grammar] that I didn't have
time to write a longer piece . . ."

This is the defense of very novice writers. Writing proves so formidable a task that they'll concentrate exclusively on correcting spelling or sentence structure or any of a variety of grammar errors, which are at least identifiable problems. When this problem surfaces, the teacher would be wise to spend some time determining whether or not the student has a learning disability. While this inordinate fear of being wrong can result from being the victim of a beast of an early English teacher, most of the time this struggle with elementary concepts to the exclusion of all else indicates the student's attempt to compensate for some other problem.

No matter what explanation, excuse, defense, or justification the students come up with, the results are almost always the same:

short, fragmented, undeveloped essays rarely over four-hundred words in length.[4]

Connecting the Reading/Writing Problems

The problem most often comes down to this: students lack the mastery of both form and content required to shape complete explanations or to justify their thinking. Dennis Baron, in *Declining Grammar,* declares that successful, or expert, writing depends upon mastery both of subject matter and of the conventional context of writing. Novice writers are hampered as much by their unfamiliarity with the subjects they write about as with the process of writing. The reasons that they fail to develop essays often can be traced to the fact that they don't understand the topic. This lack of knowledge causes them to narrow the scope of their discussion. Novice writers, for example, tend to "proceed directly to simplistic solutions, failing to consider related problems, alternative strategies, or complications that might arise [when considering a subject]" (Baron 55). In other words, they cut analysis in favor of simple and factual answers to problems whose nature they don't understand.

Interpretive answers are the province of expert writers, whose analyses tend to "go beyond the words to the underlying conceptual relations, weigh a variety of answers, and examine the implications of solutions, preferring general approaches that will solve a number of subproblems" (Baron 55). Expert writers use writing to come to an understanding of the topic they are studying. Beginning writers stick to what they know or facts that they have recently learned—little wonder that their texts appear stunted and disorganized. Most developing writers feel little compulsion to explain or explore *why* they think as they do. On the one hand, their thoughts about a subject fall under the sanctity of the personal opinion: "I believe it; I'm entitled to my personal opinion!" On the other, their teachers, especially those outside of English, have repeatedly emphasized that knowledge comes from without rather than within: "Tell me what experts think; rely upon outside sources." The students, caught between competing epistemological and discourse perspectives, struggle with the idea that personal opinion, although relatively safe from criticism in most social interactions, is often inadmissible as evidence in formal essays.

Much of the teacher resistance to personal experiences as explanations or evidence for academic arguments results from the fear that personal opinion, which is strictly forbidden in high school essays, will corrupt what can only be described as institutionally correct ways of viewing subjects. Personal opinion will create subjective rather than objective texts because personal experience cannot be statistically valid. The experiences of *the one* will not adequately reflect the experiences of *the many* because the freshman *one* is still unfamiliar (read—uneducated) in the subject. A pedagogy that completely forbids personal opinion except in the mode labeled *personal narrative* values the experience of the academy, or the experts, over the experiences of those who merely live the lives that are under examination. Personal opinion, goes the thinking, forms too narrow a base for academic research. And this, to a certain extent, is true. However, it is not necessarily true that *opinion* must be considered either unacceptable (because it is subjective) or inviolate (because it represents lived experience). Certainly a middle ground exists. And, as you might expect, dear reader, I'm about to offer you one.

Just as we believe that novice readers must grapple with difficult texts, we believe that novice writers cannot become expert writers by limiting the number of words they write or the amount of information they must learn to juggle. The details, the *how-does-it-work-in-practice,* of our pedagogy will be outlined in the following chapters, but the theory behind the practice can be reduced to two rather simple (and not necessarily new) factors: novice writers must write a lot; novice writers must write about subjects that are as important to their nonacademic communities as they are to the academic community.

First, the length issue. Expressing complex thoughts takes more than two pages and five-hundred words (or less), so we have our students write at length and often *on the same topic over the entire two-quarter sequence.* While most of our students can speak thoughtfully and at length about a problem or orally *render a description* (as Elbow suggests they must learn to do in "Reflections on Academic Discourse: How it Relates to Freshmen and Colleagues"), they hardly ever produce more than a few stunted paragraphs of prose even when asked to thoroughly examine or think through a problem in writing. The actual number of words or pages a student can generate is not the point. We recognize the fact that our students may seldom write again at such length in other courses—multiple-choice exams abound; we hope to bring them to understand how writing can be an integral part not only of expert research and study of any topic but also of problem solving and personal satisfaction in non-academic communities. Like Elbow, we argue that students generally have little use for what we call academic discourse once they leave the academy. They do, however, need more complex writing skills than they have when they enter college. More important, they need to be able to apply at least some of the things they learn in college to situations that arise long after they have left the halls of academe. Writing about how academic knowledge intersects with nonacademic experience can be useful in determining whether or not the theories of the academy have been integrated into the students' ways of knowing. After all, "the best test of whether a student understands something is if she can translate it out of the discourse of the textbook and the discipline into everyday, experiential, anecdotal terms" (Elbow 137). As many a teacher has discovered, the fear associated with academic texts isn't sufficient to inspire learning. Students know instinctively what Elbow means when he says that "life is long and college is short" (136). They won't employ the strategies of academic inquiry unless they see a nonacademic purpose worthy of the labor that goes into such actions.

I maintain, as always, that the secret of successful inquiry is curiosity, the first of Bruner's internal motivators. When students are curious, even the most commonplace of topics can open into an almost continuous set of problems that they can investigate. And—I guess that brings us to the second premise—novice writers must write about subjects that are as important to their nonacademic communities as they are to the academic community. This problematic requirement harks back to the discussion that opens Part II of this book: the need to construct research projects that will create a climate of pseudocuriosity if not actual curiosity. Therefore, we construct extended reading and writing units that simulate the research done in the academy and the investigation that has to be done to solve problems in real-life situations. In these research projects, each new assignment connects—sometimes in obvious ways, sometimes not—with the reading material, the students' own experiences, the data from interviews, and earlier assignments. By the time the students write their final essays, they have—usually as much in practice as in theory—a wealth of material to draw upon. During the process, they also come to know that reading and writing need to be thought of as connected rather than separate means of inquiry. Extended writing/reading assignments also help students understand that knowledge is not the isolated privilege of members of the academy, unconnected to the ways in which people live their everyday lives, nor constructed by stacking blocks of information together loosely, one fact on top of another. The information, or right answers, they collect can be interpreted in many different ways and applied to many different situations.

Chapter Four

Putting It Together
Reading, Writing, and Research

Bit by bit,
Putting it together . . .
Piece by piece—
Only way to make a work of art.
Every little detail plays a part.
Having just the vision's no solution,
Everything depends on execution:
Putting it together—
That's what counts.
      —Stephen Sondheim
    Sunday in the Park with Georgey

At the beginning of the first quarter, I type up this verse from "Putting It Together," from Stephen Sondheim's *Sunday in the Park with George,* pass around copies to my students, and post it on the board in the classroom. Although, in context, the song is largely about relationships between artists and art foundations, I indulge in time-honored tradition and appropriate the sentiment for my own use, discussing what I see as its relationship to writers and their texts. Through my own writing, I know the difficulty of bringing together vision and execution; I know they're two different things. But somewhere between elementary school and high school, in the mire of grammar workbooks and topic sentences, my students have completely lost the connection between having an idea and laboring to express that idea for others. The song seems an appropriate introduction to the type of writing that we're about to attempt.

No students drop dead from insight. One or two of the older ones will acknowledge that they understand my point. The rest will very quietly and respectfully read the song, listen to my comments, and file both under "weird stuff your teacher asks you to read." They listen carefully as I explain that writing, like painting, like any worthwhile project, requires conscientious selection of detail, diligent attention to word use, and meticulous attention to audience demands. After all, I elucidate, the song is as much about attracting patrons as it is about creating a work of art.

"Oh," they say.

But their lack of spontaneous enthusiasm doesn't bother me much, for the song also serves as a reminder for me that basic writers don't develop into nonbasic writers after some great burst of rhetorical vision. They become competent writers by putting limited skills together bit by bit and developing those skills into a system of composing. They need help not only sorting out the pieces but also discovering the way in which the fragments of ideas go together. As experienced writers know, sometimes this involves taking the entire vision, breaking it down, and reassembling it. I try to replicate this process by breaking down their previous conceptions of research and writing, then replacing it with a multifaceted research assignment. Bit by bit, we explore a topic and write about it. Every time they think they're finished with the project, I up the ante, requiring them to integrate yet another "bit" into an investigation that they consider to be complete. As they work, they come to understand not only the writing and research process that takes place in colleges and universities, but also the knowledge-making process that is the goal of scholarship.

Research writing, as our group of writing instructors construct it in the classroom, only remotely resembles the high school research paper our students know and hate. Like the schism between high school rules about introductory paragraphs and the actual introductory paragraphs of college-level texts, a gap of immense dimensions exists between our students' idea of research papers and the academy's goal of creating and incorporating new meaning into old knowledge. To our students, *research* consists of spending several weeks putting together a paper on a topic like "Cheese in America." In order to begin this paper, the student forms a thesis statement, "Cheese can be a healthy substitute for meat," or a thesis question, "Can cheese be a healthy substitute for meat?" During the next four to six weeks, the students follow detailed instructions from the teacher about how to find and copy material from library sources. This intensive "research" will yield two magazine articles (usually from *Good Housekeeping* and *Ladies Home Journal*), two books on diet and nutrition, three quotations from the encyclopedia, and a definition from Webster's dictionary that goes into the paper like this:

> Webster's defines cheese as "curd that has been separated by whey, consolidated by molding for soft cheese or subjected to pressure for hard cheese, and ripened for use as food."

Then, usually overnight, the high school researcher arranges the material so it looks like an essay, creates 25 note cards, makes a sentence outline, and plugs in a set of footnotes. Voila! The research paper extraordinaire! A research paper fit for an English teacher! The fact that neither student nor teacher likes the final result (much less finds it useful) doesn't seem to matter. How to use the library and how to arrange information seem more important than any intellectual investigation.

Our agenda differs. We introduce not just topics, but problems, problems that cannot be solved by these high school research techniques. The thesis statements for student papers grow from the study rather than shape the exploration, and the data that supports student assertions comes from the books assigned for the course and interviews of people in the community.[1] Students can, and do, resort to library research when their personal interests demand more information, but this research is not the principal means of gathering information or developing an understanding of the research problem. They build a new set of skills to complement the old ones, learning to interpret primary sources as well as secondary ones. During the entire process, they turn in no note cards, compose no elaborately numbered sentence outlines, and write no predetermined number of paragraphs. We substitute prewriting techniques that serve to help clarify, explore, or explain an idea, rather than these rigid information-gathering and organizing techniques that often only demonstrate that the students know the mechanical processes of gathering information.

And what do we study? What problem do we investigate?

While the research problems posed in our basic writing sections have varied over the years—censorship, divorce, work, the American Dream—one stands out as an excellent means of connecting students' lives to academic research: what constitutes an adequate and meaningful high school education for American adolescents. When we explore this problem, our research assignments move the students from a contrastive study, which juxtaposes accounts of other high schools with their own, to the study of American high school systems in general, and back again to a study of their personal experiences with learning and the educational system. Our goal is always to keep the students' own experience in view while examining academic viewpoints about education. Juxtaposing individual experience with authoritative texts creates a dissonance between experiential and textual knowledge that the students must reconcile.

This search for a way to reconcile multiple versions of experience is something the students have not encountered before. Bartholomae and Petrosky have pointed out that most remedial reading courses ask the students to find "a single, identifiable main idea that all readers can agree upon" (12). This approach to knowledge, which in many ways resembles the approach to high school research, consists of finding the *true meaning* of a text—information that is verifiable and correct. The search for the main or right idea in a text undercuts the students' own sense that their experience counts, and it limits their ability to build upon already existing ideas. We want our students to learn to view reading as "a transaction [with a text] rather than an attempt to guess at meaning that belongs to someone else" (Bartholomae and Petrosky 12), and to come to terms with the fact that academic knowledge generally results from negotiation with texts and experience rather than from blanket acceptance of either experiential or textual truths. The major objective of our study of the educational system consists of introducing the students to the idea that they can contribute to academic knowledge, that they can construct their own version of knowledge rather than merely identify and accept someone else's theories, and that their lives are affected by the theories that inform educational practice.

As I revise these words, I realize what a demanding task we take on. Juggling reading, writing, and research becomes quite complicated, especially since, as any experienced teacher/writer knows, all of these activities take place at the same time. Students must master content so that they may master writing techniques; they must put together a number of reading and writing *bits* in order to create their particular vision of the problem. In this context, exhibiting *mastery* means being able to effectively understand and manipulate data from diverse sources of information in such a way as to create a comprehensive picture of thoughts and ideas. The material varies according to the instructor's approach to the problem, but the tasks remain largely the same. The students read three to four books during the two-quarter sequence, conduct and transcribe interviews, and write essays that report the results of their thinking about the problems involved in providing adequate high school education in their communities, in particular, and in America, in general. The essays they write during the first quarter (a ten-week period) respond to ideas posed in the books we read; at least two of the essays draw upon interview data that the students gather. During the second quarter, they write only two major six- to eight-page essays. However, the first of these essays consolidates three preliminary explorative or *miniessays* into a more comprehensive final essay, and the second brings together two quarters of research in order to allow the students to propose and confirm hypotheses about their own educations. The research material the students and their colleagues have gathered during the two-quarter sequence can be (and is) shared by everyone. We sequence the reading and writing tasks so that we accomplish the following objectives:

- Provide a knowledge base for research.
- Create a personal, cultural, and academic connection to education.
- Introduce the students to unfamiliar reading and writing tasks.
- Supply a theoretical framework against which students can examine their own educational experiences.

Providing a Knowledge Base for Research: The Education Series

The problems involved in providing effective secondary education make a good reseach topic for two reasons. First, the problems cross disciplinary lines in the academy, providing reading that employs different discourses and different ways of providing evidence to support points. Second, high school education is of particular importance, if not interest, to our students because a failure to understand or a refusal to participate in the rather rigid educational systems landed them in remedial courses in the first place. Our students have an urgent "need to know" about education; their lack of knowledge about the system continues to interfere with their learning in college.

The reading in our courses exemplifies the art of inquiry about education at its most personal so that the students can find people in the text to identify with; however, the very fact that the authors combine the autobiographical with the theoretical moves the students from the realm of the strictly personal into the realm of the academic. Placing the students in the position of joining and often reconciling the personal with the academic serves several instructional goals:

- They discover how personal interests can become community and scholarly interests.
- They acquire mastery of a variety of discourse strategies.
- They learn a variety of techniques for melding together fact and theory.
- They come to understand that it is not only possible to connect nonacademic and academic communities, but that it is also advantageous.

What we have come to call the Education Series involves four core books: Eliot Wigginton's *Sometimes a Shining Moment,* Ann Tracy's *Higher Ground,* Theodore Sizer's *Horace's Compromise,* and Mike Rose's *Lives on the Boundary.* These texts provide excellent examples of the Distanced/Personal position we wish the students to master. All of the authors describe and analyze some aspect of American high school education against their own personal experiences, attempting to understand why various high school curricula, both past and present, fail or succeed in nurturing students who are not in the middle-class mainstream. In order to fully understand the dynamics of the educational systems they write about, the authors incorporate comments from the students, faculty, and members of nonacademic communities in the cities and towns that participate in the local school system. Evident in each of these strong narratives is a sense of the importance of the local community as well as a driving curiosity about the educational systems that either stimulate or kill a love of learning. Sometimes the students read all four books, sometimes we cut back to three. A great deal depends upon the individual teacher, who sometimes uses alternative materials. If there is a change in text, it generally occurs in the first quarter, which always seems to be the most difficult for student and teacher.

These four books serve as more than sources of content or paradigms for discourse; they also provide models for academic research. The four writers create studies—part ethnographic, part oral history, and decidedly interpretive—that model the sorts of inquiry we believe forge a connection between our students and the act of knowledge making. The common research strategies used by the four writers—reading, observation, interviews, surveys—demonstrate how writers make sense of their own and their communities' experiences. By emulating these writers, by appropriating their methods, our students can experience themselves as knowledge makers, not merely passive receivers of knowledge. They can use their own experiences yet distance themselves in such a manner that these very personal insights can contribute to our knowledge of the educational process.

As in the project developed for the eighth-grade biology students in Shirley Brice Heath's *Ways with Words,* our students encounter two perceptions of a topic—their own and the experts. Learning becomes a process of comparing nonacademic and academic sources on education. The students must make sense of both and understand how they affect each other. Such a project, needless to say, is initially embraced more enthusiastically by teachers than by students, who would just as soon have their teachers make the knowledge while they take an easier road to passing English.

Creating a Personal and Cultural Connection: Understanding Teachers and Writers

During the first quarter, we attempt to connect the students' personal experiences with those of the students they read about in Eliot Wigginton's *Sometimes a Shining Moment* and Ann Tracy's *Higher Ground.* Although our students don't recognize the similarities at first, Wigginton's Rabun Gap students and Tracy's HCI (Higgins Classical Institute) students greatly resemble the students at OSU Marion. All three student populations come (or in HCI's case, came) from working-class families, do not really expect to go to college, and are interested in high school more because of the diploma it provides than because of an innate love of learning. Despite these similarities, students have a difficult time entering texts. They attribute their difficulties with the texts to differences in cultural values and experiences: Appalachian culture versus rural Ohio culture or, in the case of Tracy's book, boarding school versus public school conditions. They miss or do not recognize the evident similarities. Seldom do they attribute their difficulties to the common problems of reading texts: understanding new and different discourse strategies, deciphering extremely complex sentence structures, and interpreting literary metaphor and allusion.

In theory, students who view learning as connections and conversation between people should be able to follow Wigginton's conversational explanation of how he developed his educational theories—the book begins with several diary entries and continues with a description of his successes and failures as he journeys toward establishing the *Foxfire* magazine. The students, however, have a hard time understanding "what's going on." To say that they are lost in a maze of words and events is to understate the case. Wigginton's journals annoy them; his conversational letters to his friend Howard are anything but interesting. Their inability to understand what motivated Wigginton in his teaching and what shaped him as a teacher limits their ability to understand the pedagogy he devised. Even their preconceived notions of gender roles affect their interpretation of the material. The Wigginton of the text doesn't behave as they feel a man should, so they don't like him very much. Several factors work against him: his pacifist attitudes toward war, his choice of teaching as a career, and the fact that his letters to his friend Howard concentrated more on his problems as a teacher than on his social life (the concept that he had edited the journals and letters for publication never occurs to them). When Wigginton became infamous rather than merely famous, the students had an interesting reaction: they felt justified in their evaluation of him as a human being but saddened and angry to discover such a wise teacher had betrayed the students that he wanted so desperately to help. In many ways this new revelation about Wigginton was merely an extension of their original frustration with the book. Even without the complication of scandal, our students, like most students, didn't understand the educational values or experiences of Wigginton, *the teacher,* or of other teachers. From the beginning, Wigginton's attitude toward teaching baffled them, and what they did not understand made them angry.

The first reading of Wigginton's personal journal and letters, which open *Sometimes a Shining Moment,* always brought the more vocal students out of passivity and directly into personal attack:

> "This guy's a draft dodger, writing to his friend, *Howard,* and whining. It should be called *Sometimes a Whining Moment.*"

> "Why's he wasting our time with his journal? I mean, no offense intended—you must have chosen this book for a reason—but who cares what he did in the sixties?"

> "Is this guy a nerd, or what? Did you see his picture? No wonder he has nothing better to do than teach."

> "What have hillbillies and high school teachers got to do with learning to write?"

I must confess I still find their reaction to the personal voice disconserting. It amazes me that students who respond so well to the personal when talking with friends, teachers, and family have infinite trouble deciphering written material that so strongly mixes the personal with the theoretical. The clue to their problems with such texts seems to be their sense of what a text, especially one used in a course, should do.

Their inability to think of teaching as an art and intellectual activity hampers their overall understanding of the book as a work of pedagogy. As far as they know, teaching takes no special preparation. Teachers go to college, where they major in a subject; school districts provide new teachers with a set of lesson plans. Teaching is simple: teachers conduct classes and then return home to do something more interesting. Our students don't even *suspect* that good teaching involves incorporating pedagogical theory into precise and carefully developed practice. As one student put it the first time we taught *Sometimes a Shining Moment:* "Anyone can teach. All you need is a book and a red pencil."

Distressing thought for Lynda and me.

"You mean I spent ten years of my life in school when all I needed was a book and a red pencil?" I responded (and it's important to remember that I asked with a grin on my face rather than a frown).

I did not take, am not taking, and will never take an objective stance in the classroom—possibly bad form for most academics since it violates the notion of proper professional distance. However, taking a personal rather than an objective stance helps my students understand that, in some ways, my career parallels Wigginton's. My obvious attachment to the idea that teaching can be an art opens conversation about the book and about education as a whole. At this point in the two-course sequence, they don't know me well, but we have been in the classroom together long enough for them to suspect that I am a person of good will whose major eccentricity seems to be a preoccupation with the idea that reading and writing can be both useful *and* fun.

At the time, my obviously defensive posture led to questions:

"What do you see in this guy?"

"Do you think he really cared about his students?"

"Why do we need to read all his diaries and his letters? Normal people don't publish their personal writing."

Invariably, each new class makes some assertion about the ease of teaching, and each quarter my defense of teaching as an intellectual pursuit leads to the humanization of the teaching process and of the teachers whose books we read. As we discuss my education and career, Wigginton and his career, the spirit of the sixties, and what really constitutes teacher training, the students begin to think of teachers as persons capable of approaching teaching as more than just a job. Everything connects, and the rather vague world of

Wigginton and his explorations in education take on relevance and become part of the conversation about teaching and learning. We form a symbiotic relationship wherein they depend on me to understand Wigginton and I use Wigginton to develop issues about the educational process. Together we wrestle with the book in order to link personal and academic issues. The implications of educational theory become extremely personal because I value it and because they come to understand that their individual problems with schools and learning are representative of major problems in American education.

The humanization of Eliot Wigginton, however, does not automatically endow all the teacher/writers we study with human qualities. A different failure to connect occurs when the students start to read *Higher Ground*. Wigginton might not fit the students' stereotype of a macho man, but Tracy fits their stereotype of an "English teacher" to a tee. Her fascination with HCI and its students completely escapes them. Why write about a school, especially one which has already closed—forever? "A Necessary Introduction," designed to provide her readers with the background of her project, confuses rather than enlightens our students. I've included the first paragraph of that introduction in the last chapter, and I'd like to quote from the end of her introduction in order to remind readers of Tracy's prose style:

> All I can say is that a dispassionate picture is not a whole one. This revivified rosebush of mine will have its roots sunk in as much solid fact as I can scrape together, but that's not what makes the perfume. Facts are only the substrata of truth. I've pretended to myself as well as to officialdom that I can stop being an English professor and take up being a social scientist for a year. I've been lying. Lean closer, reader, and I'll confess it in your ear: this isn't just a history—it's a love song. (7)

Even if I didn't know Ann Tracy, and I do, as a reader familiar with the literary community for which she writes, I would recognize certain characteristics about her prose style. The ornate imagery, the Victorian address to the reader, the hint of subterfuge, and the quick dig at sociological *truth,* indicate a woman possessed of a learned and keen mind, not to mention a definite sense of humor. The students don't see her that way, and that failure to see the *person* in the text, a writer who lives and breathes and makes jokes about English, hampers their ability to read or to enjoy *Higher Ground*.

In addition, the purpose of her book eludes the students. *Sometimes a Shining Moment* offers solutions to the educational problems Wigginton encountered in Appalachia. *Higher Ground* does not define or offer solutions to any problem of teaching. In fact, it doesn't recognize problems with classical education. No advice on *how* to implement or reform schools finds its way into her text. Her audience remains a mystery. Who would read this book? Why? The students can't understand why anyone other than the graduates of HCI would want to read *Higher Ground,* and they frankly doubt that even former HCI graduates would rush to purchase it. After all, the narrative and its few accompanying photographs concern people long dead (which loosely translated, to my horror, means anyone who went to high school before the 1960s). This inability to understand why local experience might be valuable in and of itself reveals their inexperience with academic scholarship. They struggle to come to grips with *Higher Ground* as required reading. Certain facts indicate that the book has value in the academy: we use it in class; a publisher invested the time, effort, and money necessary to publish it. As they begin to search for relevance, confusion opens conversations about publishing houses and authors; those conversations lead to discussions about the missions of both groups. Then as we push the students to consider possible audiences for *Higher Ground,* they begin to consider the types of people and the disciplines that might find the book useful: historical societies, educators, tourists. The list remains sketchy, and even if they knew the answers to "Who would read this book?" and "Why?" the problem of the voice in the text remains. Tracy, even more so than Wigginton, seems too removed from student experience.

I could, and did, talk about my friend. We even brought Ann to Marion and videotaped her discussions of her book. However, it became obvious very quickly that such conversations didn't help with the text. If we let them, they would forsake Tracy's text and privilege my discussion of her and of the text itself; they would rather rely upon classroom conversation and discussion to find meaning rather than try to puzzle out the theories embedded in the texts. This *let-me-explain* method of teaching and learning is practically traditional in schools. As Lynda pointed out, some teachers (she meant me—but I'm symptomatic of a type) love to talk as much as their students do; being *the expert* can create an immensely delightful illusion of power. However, being the authority in a course and pontificating about the meaning of a text deprives students of the challenge and opportunity of working out their own reading transactions. In short, it deprives them of the practice they need in order to sharpen their own interpretive and meaning-making skills.

Introducing Unfamiliar Reading and Writing Tasks: Understanding Discourse Strategies

The reading problems students have with paragraphs that don't meet their expectations become magnified when they approach the books in the Education Series. The discourse strategies of the authors can't be deciphered with students' high school reading schemata. *Sometimes A Shining Moment,* for example, begins with a diary entry and ends with an annotated course syllabus. Lacking a sense of how personal history can shape ideas and actions in the academy, the students fail to see how such different types of writing can inform each other, much less how practice can become codified as theory. A basic schema that we try to develop for the students involves three activities: prereading, rereading, and writing to understand. Despite the linear nature implied by lining up these activities one after another, these activities that open up texts become a single, recursive act that has rather broad and vague boundaries. We break them down into separate activities initially so that the students can internalize what they previously missed in their reading/writing educations, but as the students become more proficient in reading, they learn that these interpretive strategies can be used anytime they have a problem with the text.

Prereading activities, which most academics have internalized, need to be introduced to novice readers and constantly reinforced. At the beginning of the course, we initiate reading assignments with detailed discussions of the ways to approach the material. Outlining the chapter, the note-taking strategy used most in high schools, seems self-defeating, so we don't do it. Because we want to put an author in the text and humanize the topic, we carefully discuss the background of the book, the author's reason for writing (as best we know it), and the audience the book was intended to reach. We make an effort to describe the authors as human beings: discussing where they work, where they went to school, what they look like, and revealing any other material about them that we might happen to have at hand. We explicitly state the reasons this topic, these books, and these writers seem particularly appropriate for a basic reading/writing course. The students are not told that they *must* appreciate or like the writer—*like* is not as important as *understand.*

The next step involves putting the book within an academic framework: explaining the goals of the discipline the writer works within, discussing the philosophy that guides certain types of study, and elaborating upon the author's reputation in his or her field. In addition, we pose questions about the connection of such work to what students think of as the *real world.* Why would someone want to write such a book? Who's the audience? Why would someone want to work in such a discipline? What contribution does, or will, this book make to the writer's discipline? To those outside the academy? To this writing class? Obviously the students can't answer our questions yet, but we insist that they keep them in mind as they read. To reinforce these questions, we repeat them regularly, so regularly, in fact, that the students come to ask them before we do—though not always in a kindly manner. During these discussions, the students don't have to sit quietly and absorb our wisdom; these are not strictly lecture activities. We divide the class into groups and have them ferret out as much information as they can—lecturing only about the elements of text and discipline that they don't understand or can't find out on their own.

To most expert readers, leading students through these activities appears rather simplistic. Expert readers preread automatically: going over the introduction to the text, the preface, and the table of contents before venturing forth into the body of the text. But the students, for the most part, have not read academic nonfiction and have no ready-at-hand template for deciphering these texts. When approaching *Sometimes a Shining Moment,* for instance, an experienced reader would not fail to notice that Wigginton divides the text into several distinct parts: an introduction, a prologue, and three books. It's obvious from the table of contents that the first book outlines the intellectual as well as chronological history of the *Foxfire* project, the second offers a discussion of the principles of good teaching, and the third contains what amounts to a "how-to" section for teachers—complete with discussions of instructional goals, practices, and objectives. Expert readers use this information to decide where to start reading, knowing that reading the preface or introduction to a book not only reveals whether its contents hold any interest but also can save time since prefaces and introductions summarize the entire contents. If the contents of the preface don't address the problems they study, they often abandon the book and go on to another. We surprise the students by encouraging them to read the afterword, if there is one, along with the introduction. They seldom realize that reading for the academy is not like reading a novel; sampling the middle and end doesn't ruin the excitement of discovery.

Our students have never had to look at front matter before and see little purpose in looking at it now. They have been trained to believe that readers should study the *whole* book from the first chapter to the last, so prereading activities seem irrelevant. (I don't mean to imply in the least that students follow up on that training, they merely have been subjected to it.) If you've got to go from the beginning to the end anyway, even looking at the table of contents seems like an extra step, an unnecessary effort. As the course continues, we spend a great deal of time comparing the front matter of different books, discussing the perspective that both table of contents and introductory remarks can create, the clues that they put forth about what items the author considers important, and how they allow readers to preview the material and recognize the author's premise long before the end of the book.

Most novice readers want to jump into Chapter 1 immediately. There they meet the greatest obstacle to understanding—not just the author's writing style—the overall discourse strategy of the book itself. When reading *Sometimes a Shining Moment,* for instance, the internal relationship of the three parts that form the whole proves practically undecipherable to our students. If they approach the first section of the text as they would a personal diary, Wigginton's experiences become narrow and unattached to their own. If they read the text as an informational or how-to work, his development of the *Foxfire* course syllabus holds little relevance because they have no sense of what was innovative about Wigginton's pedagogy or how Wigginton's practice differs from their own high school teachers' practice. Their inability to pin down the relationship between the style and the purpose of the text causes them to question what they're supposed to learn from it. *Sometimes a Shining Moment* doesn't teach a skill, so it isn't a handbook or a writing textbook— the *important stuff* isn't highlighted in bold print. High school reading assignments were usually literature-based and meant to *broaden their horizons*—whatever that means—but *Sometimes a Shining Moment* can't be classified as fiction, poetry, or drama. They don't have to memorize what happened; they aren't being asked to outline the plot. The class stresses writing, but this book, despite its claim to be about teaching English, contains practically no advice for constructing sentences or correcting errors.

The students have never encountered this type of personal nonfiction writing. Their reactions illustrate Brandt's theory that nonreaders don't understand that books act as conversation for literate people. Certainly our students do not recognize or participate in the literate tradition of gleaning information and insight from the personal writing of those involved in experimental or research activities, nor do they realize the immense benefit a scholar finds in personal correspondence with a supportive but challenging friend.

Entering the Text

To help the students enter the text itself, we avoid traditional question-and-answer sessions about what they are about to read, are

reading, or have read. Each class period, unless some unusual oc-
currence throws us completely off balance, begins with a short writing exercise related to the previous night's reading. (As you may
have guessed from simply looking at the list of books we expect the
students to read, a night without a reading assignment is a rare night
indeed.) These in-class writing assignments promote in-class rereading of difficult passages.

We learned the hard way that not all writing activities promote
interaction with the text. At the beginning of our project, we simply
asked the students to write about some element of their reading that
they didn't understand. This got us nowhere fast. The responses
tended to look something like this:

> "I didnt realy have trouble understanding it just meant nothing
> since I'm not intersted in his topic."

> "I understood everything, but was boring so i had hard time keep-
> ing mind on the page."

> "Wiginlton wouldn't serve in our country I think we shoun't read
> about draft dodgers."

Displeased with these rather mediocre or off-base remarks, we
asked the students to respond to the books by comparing their own
experiences to what they read. This, too, created problems. In my
notes I made the following entry:

> The older students were better at responding, but tended to place
> too much emphasis on their own experience and not enough on
> the book. The younger students tried to keep to a much abbrevi-
> ated version of their own experience and employed the "it's sim-
> ple, of course" rhetoric that implies that there is nothing to discuss
> really. The material in books seems isolated and irrelevant to their
> own experience.

At last we stumbled upon the following activity that we now
use routinely. We ask them to write out three or four events or statements that seem to be significant clues to understanding the chapter. A sort of puzzle approach, these statements have to be related to
each other but cannot be found on the same page. After locating
what they feel to be key statements, the students must explain the
connections between the statements and why they seem to be representative of the author's ideas. Such an exercise might at first
seem mechanical and pointless, but it proves most useful. Released
from looking for topic sentences (only a bit of explication reveals
that such beasts don't exist in most of the paragraphs), they can look
for meaning in content rather than allow form to guide their search

for meaning. They begin to be aware of the many different ways in which writers elaborate upon and expand important points, recognizing that what the students often think of as repetition is a fine tuning of logic or the creation of a context for making an assertion.

This exercise also provides us, as teachers, with a map of the students' misreadings and miscues: What points do they think are related? What do they privilege as they read? How do they interpret relationships between passages, ideas, sections? When do they mistake a narrative or a quotation for the author's opinion? In short, the exercise reveals whether or not they can follow a significant line of argument and if they can judge between a main point and a minor one. Their schemata become obvious to us rather than hidden. In individual conferences and in class discussions, we can point out how their reading can become confused and where misunderstanding can occur. Gradually, they also grow aware of the schemata they use.

Appointing a student discussion leader and asking her or him to outline the results of this writing exercise on the board leads the entire class into a deeper discussion about the material than a teacher-initiated dialogue will. One student's observations nearly always bring out another's. Since a peer is easier to confront than a teacher, the students feel freer to suggest alternative readings. When the discussion leader presents her outline to the class as a whole, the other students seldom agree completely: they see other relationships or different points, or they fail to understand what the group found significant. At this point, they welcome rather than resent our intervention, which tends to be a (mostly) neutral-focusing action rather than a pontifical clarification of the right way to deal with the chapter. Usually all we have to do is point out ways in which the divergent views represent, in reality, parts of multiple arguments supporting multiple points. The interchanges between teachers, students, and text highlight the various connections readers can make. Our writing/reading/presentation exercise, then, serves as a dialogic activity, rather than as one merely intended to determine if students have read. The students do not have to fear being *wrong* since the connections they make are their own. They're free to discuss these connections since the object is to make sense of the whole rather than to break the text down into discrete bits of information.

Another writing/reading/presentation activity usually follows this discussion. After we establish that the chapter can be read in several different ways, we ask the students to find more support for particular interpretations of the text. They may not merely locate another related phrase and read it to us; they must go back and write down the passages that support their statements and explain *in writ-*

ing how these thoughts connect with or dispute what has already been discussed. We usually do this second activity collaboratively so that locating supporting data does not come off like a test. Defending conflicting interpretations does, however, tap into the students' natural desire to compete, and the activity often comes to resemble a contest.

The extended collaboration and concentration on the text allows us to once again do a close reading of the students' reading strategies while they are in class. We can actually watch them think about what they have read as they work to defend their interpretation of the text. Even with limited skills, the students are quite capable of discovering or making meaning from text *if they are allowed time to work it out for themselves.* The dynamics of the group activities bring out discussion about the nature of texts that would be missed if a teacher tried to cover them in advance. The students can be rather demanding of each other. Instead of letting misreading go unchallenged, they question each other until they come to consensus. The group activity also juxtaposes various opinions from the groups, revealing differences in reading and differences in attitudes. Reconciling or explaining these differences compels members of the group to contend with each other about individual statements, which leads to the realization that some differences in reading and in opinion are impossible to resolve.

Writing to Understand Reading

Toby Fulwiler suggests that most compositionists would not disagree about the purpose and value of journals: "Writing helps our students learn things better and these notebooks provide a place in which to write informally yet systematically in order to seek, discover, speculate, and figure things out" (9). This theory sums up most teachers' use of journal writing as a teaching aid: we assign journal writing to help our students understand what they've read. However, the theory doesn't always suceed in practice, especially with novice readers and writers. I have found that when these students first attempt to write in journals, their entries fall far short of the discovery or speculative inquiry that more expert readers and writers (and students) can produce. This failure to use written language as a means of intellectual exploration should not be surprising. Having never written willingly for school, novice writers are not likely to begin producing pages of introspective prose just because the process is informal. Like the reader who doesn't know what to highlight, even the most willing novice writer doesn't know how to respond to the text. Their entries often reveal no more than whether they liked or disliked some aspect of the narrator's actions. Commonly, students will attempt to pass off quick judgmental pronouncements about pieces of the text or about the narrator. For instance, we wanted the students to get a sense of why Wigginton begins his book with his own journal entries, so we asked what the students see as a rather difficult question as a journal prompt:

> Wigginton wants us to think of his journals as a reflection of the historic events that helped shape his life. Can you see that history? Why is it important to know about his life before he left for Rabun Gap? Why would the Kennedy years have shaped his actions?

The quality of journal entries varied greatly, but the majority of the students wrote entries that fell between the two responses that follow:

> Most of my teachers are different from Wigginton. One of them particularly was Mr. Reitz he was always doing something different. Unlike witlington a the begginning of the book. Mr. Reitlz has more experience than wittington did at the beggining of the book. Wittington seems to be very creative which is much like Mr. Reitz so I really cant compare the two very well.
>
> —Brian

> In class today someone brought up that the book is not interesting and boreing. And alot of babaing. and It may be all of them. But I did understand or tryed to understand where he is coming from. That is Eliot Wigginton. From his interduction I belive he is a very intellagent preson who likes to teach but hopes he don't have to do it for the rest of his life. I also get the feeling that he dont care (I hope thats the appropriate pronoun) what people or socity thins about where he works or what he looks like. I say that because people think being a doctor is more noble than being a teacher. Thats the way socity thinks. And knowing that he drops out of med school to become a teacher. I admire that and the fact that he will take a pay cut to be where he wants to be as he says it in the mountains. One thing I don't like about Mr. Wigginton is that he did not enlist or want to enlist in the military. I see him as a coward from this aspect. I fell every American should help serve to protect when called to do so. I don't feel running or avioding the draft is a true american thing to do. I hate to end the days journal on a bad note. But I'am sitting here watching the news while writing and there is nothing good tonight to tell about. It looks like Hurricain Hugo is going to hit South Caroliana.
>
> —Michael

Neither student addresses the prompt, although Michael comes close to discussing Wigginton's history. In order to encourage speculative writing, we focus our journal prompts so that they address questions that we will bring up in class discussion and bring out problems related to reading and understanding the text. In addition, we ask questions that will connect the students' experiences with both this author's experiences and theories. These exercises address the students' inability to find meaning, purpose, and even factual detail in extended narrative or exposition. At the beginning of the sequence, for example, the journal entries lean heavily toward finding factual information and interpreting it in light of the overall tone of the book. We try to avoid the "questions at the end of the story" syndrome (although it's extremely hard to accomplish) and address issues of meaning and interpretation. The following questions and writing tasks completed the first collection of journal prompts:

1. Entering or leaving school often represents a "crossroad" in a person's life. For example, Wigginton tried several educational paths before he decided what to do with his life. What about you? What brought you here to OSUM? Do you have a plan in which school plays an important role? Do you have the freedom to change it?

2. *Sometimes a Shining Moment* starts with a physical description of the school and then goes on to describe the rules that govern the school and the living conditions for students and teachers. Why does he begin this way? Did it catch your attention? Was his use of old letters effective?

3. What would you describe if you had to describe your high school? What would you want people to know? Start several descriptions using as many types of writing as you wish.

Extra Credit:

1. Write a letter to a friend of yours comparing your first week of school at OSUM with your high school experience.

2. Give a general reaction to any of the reading or any of the activities so far.

The journal activities, largely comparison/contrast writing, enable us to point out differences in what the students choose as important details to describe about their own schools and experiences and the types of detail that Wigginton provides. Wigginton's experience creates a focal point for discussing educational problems; the reader gets a comprehensive picture of how and why Wigginton came to Rabun Gap, the changes his decisions brought about in his lifestyle and his future expectations, and the very practical educational reforms his experiences brought about.

As we move through the text, we shift journal strategies. Since the discourse changes from the strictly personal to the instructional, the students' reading problems become even more evident and the students' resistance to the type of text even more vehement. For example, Book III of *Sometimes a Shining Moment* consists of practical and theoretical advice for teachers—knowledge that most of our students think they will never use. Ironically, the conversation they avoid by dismissing Book III as irrelevant is one that might explain their own faulty preparation for school and study. Not surprisingly, they have never considered their own educations critically, nor have they made the connection between how the educational system has affected them and how it may eventually affect their children and other family members.

To make this personal connection, we return to the first section of *Sometimes a Shining Moment,* review the content, and prepare to write the first essay. In the essay, they must make connections between what Wigginton refers to as Shining Moments and the educational practices that made (and make) our students feel uninvolved in their own educations. We give them the following essay prompt:

> One of the chapters of *Sometimes a Shining Moment* is entitled "So What *Did* I Learn in School, Anyway?" In it Eliot Wigginton presented statements from high school students which detailed what was important in their education at Rabun Gap and discussed what was valuable in his own high school education. From this chapter we began to understand the conflict between what teachers believe they are doing and how students see their efforts. In your essay you will want to answer some of the following questions:
>
> What did you learn in high school? How did you learn it? Which teaching methods were effective and which ones merely created hostility and indifference? Where were the dissonances between what your teachers thought they were doing and what you needed? Where were the shining moments when knowledge and interest came together?
>
> Do not limit yourself to these questions; you may have more important issues you want to address. If you are concerned that what you want to write about will not meet the assignment, discuss it with us; we will decide together how to pursue your interest.

The journal assignments change so that they now provide critical evidence for completing the essay assignment. Using Wigginton's text only as a template, we ask them to delve into their own educational experiences. In addition, we ask for feedback on their own learning and writing processes and experiences in class, once again trying to determine where the problems in reading and writing occur. What don't they know? What do they need to know? We ask a variety of questions:

> Is Wigginton's class at Rabun Gap different from those you've experienced? How? Is your experience unique or common? How do you know? How can you verify your opinions?

> What did you learn in high school anyway? How did you learn it?

> Decide upon three possible *Shining Moments* for your paper. Why were they so good? How do they fit into Wigginton's descriptions of his *Shining Moments?*

> React to the assignment—what will be hard? What will be interesting? What don't you understand?

> How's English going these days? Just let me know how you feel you're doing and what I can do to help.

We repeat these journal strategies throughout the two-quarter sequence, adjusting the questions according to the book we're reading at the time. At the beginning of the quarter, students have no idea what goes in a journal and so they tend to write little. By time we start reading the last book, Rose's *Lives on the Boundary,* the students generally can formulate their own journal prompts. However, we give them a list of suggestions so that they do not feel completely lost or abandoned:

**To design your own prompts, you can approach the text
in several ways:**

- Ask yourself how the information Rose presents matches your previous experiences.

- Ask yourself where you disagree with what Rose is saying. In what ways are his experiences and thoughts so different from yours that you think he's crazy?

- What new concepts seem immediately to make sense? In other words, when you're reading this type of passage, you're saying, "This is exactly what I've observed; he's just putting a label on it."

- What terms are so abstract that you have a hard time following Rose's train of thought? What was your previous understanding of those terms and how can you provide concrete examples to help you through the difficult passage?

- Which passages seem to substantiate something else you have read or heard? What further information can you add to what Rose is espousing?

- What does he say that you absolutely love—quote him if you want. Why is it so significant?

- How do the titles relate to the chapters? Rose had a reason for choosing these titles; what do you think he had in mind? How does the theme in the title recur throughout the chapter?

You might also do the following types of responses:

- Outline any section that confuses you so that you understand the point Rose is making.

- Make personal observations about yourself as a student and how you're changing as you learn more about school.

- Respond to discussions in this class and other classes.

- Discuss your thoughts about teachers and teaching at the university or at your high school.

- Create character descriptions of Rose, Sizer, or anyone else you encounter that will help you understand how their personality and background affects what they think.

- Connect learning experiences that take place out of school with the experiences you have in school; tell us how they differ and why. Which do you prefer?

  Use these ideas as you work or invent your own ideas and ways of dealing with the book. You may be asked to lead discussions on the reading without prior notice. These journal entries will give you something to talk about.

We suggest that this list of journal activities could be useful in other classes, and many of our ex-students tell us that they now use their journals as problem-solving devices to prepare for class presentations in other courses or to make sure that they've sorted out the important points of whatever they're reading. This sort of interplay between text, lived experiences, and academic analysis draws the students into the idea that their own histories—while unique in many respects—duplicate and, therefore, can be seen as representative of the experiences of other students in other places. Even when their experiences don't match those in the text, the students have a concrete example to serve as a sort of touchstone. When the students begin to comprehend this theory of journal writing, they come to understand that journal entries require focused rereading and that rereading enables them to use the text as evidence and resource rather than as grist for the testing mill.

Recognizing a Writer's Choices

We use a variety of books so that students can understand the variety of choices that a writer makes when composing a text. While a simple comparison might do to make that point, I find that the discourse strategies of *Higher Ground,* which on the surface seem more straightforward than those of *Sometimes a Shining Moment,* offer an excellent opportunity for discussing alternative strategies for handling a complex body of data. Tracy's book, while only 270 pages, covers the history of a school that served the rural population of Maine for over one hundred years. The book avoids a strict chronological order: Chapter 1, "A Necessary Introduction," gives a brief history of the founding of the school, which is not explored in more detail until Chapter 12; Chapter 15, "The Last Days," recounts the final demise of HCI but is not the last chapter of the book. In between the covers of the book, readers find chapters entitled "The Student Body," "Courses of Study," and "Love and Other Unscheduled Recreations." Each of these chapters could stand as independent essays because they move back and forth over the hundred-year period of the school's existence. This nonchronological presentation extends the students' reading task—they must make sense of a history without a straightforward chronological approach.

Since *Higher Ground* obviously could have been arranged in a number of different ways, we encourage the students to speculate about alternative ways in which to organize the material. To point out that the arrangement of the text is determined by a purpose other than creating a factual history, we purposefully rearrange the order in that the students must read the chapters: first, they read the chapters that directly address the educational goals and character of HCI, then undertake one or two chapters that elaborate upon social relationships. The assignment puzzles the students:

Reading Instructions:

Read carefully the following chapters IN THIS ORDER:
Chapter I—A Necessary Introduction
Chapter IV—Tone and Philosophy and Chapter VI—Courses
    of Study
Chapter XV—Last Days

Skipping about in the book in this manner does more than just point out the nature of Tracy's organizational strategies; it allows the students to develop and justify alternative organizations. In class, we discuss those alternate organizations, asking the students to speculate about the changes in the text that a different rhetorical strategy would necessitate.

Equally important is the issue of how data can shape the organization of a book. Since the students have no idea about what goes into researching such a book, we examine some of the research material that Tracy drew upon. Anticipating such a discussion, we had requested and received from Tracy the following materials: several surveys completed by former students of HCI; copies of newspaper articles, eulogies, and commemorative speeches about HCI's one-hundred year anniversary; competing biographies of the founder of HCI and his family; excerpts from yearbooks, budget reports, and annual dispatches from the headmaster to the board of trustees. The sheer diversity of the sample material astonished the students—especially when they learned that Tracy had two standard-sized filing cabinets full of additional material.

Looking at the research data occasioned a discussion about the way in which Tracy had gathered this information: how she developed the survey, how she hunted down former students at HCI, how she handled the rather tricky task of interviewing and retelling the stories of those who were involved in HCI's eventual demise. In addition, we discussed the way she pieced together bits of information to solve mysteries in the history: what happened to various people after they left HCI, when and under what circumstances dancing was finally allowed in this unquestioning religious atmosphere, how her father managed to keep students in school when they obviously could not afford the tuition. It became obvious that such a project could not be accomplished quickly or without a great deal of revision and experimentation with form and order.

Such explorations in data collection and organization led to several discoveries on the part of the students and several benefits as far as their own writing was concerned. They became privy not only to some of the agendas that inspire research but also to the processes that scholars use to collect and interpret data. They did not miss the fact that Tracy's desire to re-create HCI "alive and educating before your very eyes" (1) was inspired more by her love for her father and the institution than by her love for scientific or humanistic research, and they came to understand how that love shaped not only the choices she made from the data she gathered but also the collection of the data itself. When they wrote about their own schools, they could not avoid being keenly aware that even researchers who speak from the authority of personal experience *and* outside data could still present subjective, rather than objective, points of view. We have since used this reorganization exercise with other books. Since we usually analyze books that do not depend upon a chronological development, we have a number of chances to discuss the authors' organizational strategies.

Crossing from the Particular to the General

By far the most difficult reading task for the students in the two-quarter sequence was Theodore Sizer's *Horace's Compromise,* a work that would present no problem to a seasoned reader. Divided into a prologue, three sections, and an afterword, the book leads the reader from point to point in an almost predictable manner. A classic example of extended argument, Sizer's text deals with a complex problem—American high schools are offering students an inadequate education—and offers a series of suitably complex solutions. In the prologue, Sizer takes the reader through a typical day in the life of a teacher, Horace Smith. He follows this narrative with three related sections—"The Students," "The Teachers," and "The Program"—which explain the educational, social, and economic conditions that interfere with Horace Smith's ability to teach and his students' ability to learn. These three sections are followed by a conclusion, "The Structure," which pulls together the discussion. The book's afterword, "An Experiment for Horace," suggests changes in both instruction and in overall goals while calling for greater empowerment of teachers.

"Students," "Teachers," and "Program" begin with narratives, similar to the one found in the prologue, that represent people and situations that Sizer encounters as he visits a variety of American schools. The exposition that follows each composite portrait offers a careful explication of the conditions that hamper educational processes and prevent curriculum reforms. Novice readers, not being seasoned in rhetorical forms, initially have a great deal of trouble making sense out of what most of their teachers would consider straightforward reading. Although they may recognize themselves or others in his composite portraits, they do not understand how the theories of education that Sizer presents to his readers have affected and will continue to affect their own educational experiences. Obviously, any author who attempts to answer the question, "What's wrong with American high school education?" expects that readers will pursue such a topic through many layers of complexity and that they will possess a well-developed sense of how texts hold together; readers need such a sense merely to keep abreast of the various lines of argument. Because they lack that sense of texts, we must provide a schema and a template for reading that covers the book's rhetorical strategy.

The first step is pointing out the book's recursive organizational pattern and discussing the function of the composite narratives within this less-than-personal text. Although we once again start with the table of contents, this time we seek to demonstrate how the organizational strategy connects the parts of an argument. By using the table of contents as an outline and reading back and forth in the various sections, we lead the students toward recognizing that each section is a microcosm of the overall discourse strategy. This recognition becomes the first block in building the foundation for the students' new schema.

The conventions of Sizer's organizational strategy is harder for students to identify than one might think. Some are simple to explain as part of our prereading discussions. For example, we have consistently found that the students are unaware that empty space between sections of text within a chapter, or what proofreaders often refer to as page breaks, function as a means of dividing related but slightly different ideas within a chapter. The students often read over these page breaks, trying to make sense of the text despite the lack of obvious transition. Naturally, such ignorance of textual convention causes confusion when trying to follow the author's argument. In a related problem, the students fail to fathom the relationship of chapter titles, epigraphs, and footnotes to the main text. All of these valuable clues to meaning appear to be like so much window dressing to the novice reader. Once novice writers understand that these items are not arbitrary affectations of writers and can be used to clarify the author's intention, they routinely include them as part of the textual puzzle.

Other reading problems, more serious and less easily solved, interfere with the students' ability to analyze this and other texts. For example, without an understanding of how quotations can be employed in academic texts, the students cannot make sense of what they read—the author's voice, the quotations from other sources, even snippets of conversation that often punctuate discussions, meld into one. While novice readers usually recognize the conversational dialogue that quotation marks signal in fictional texts, they do not recognize that, in academic discourse, quoted material represents a conversation between texts.

Intrusions of other people's opinions in the author's text or even slight digressions from the main text force novice readers to reconstruct the text as best they can. But without a real sense of the purpose of the quotations, the results can be chaotic. It's easy to assume that the resulting chaos in papers or in classroom discussions stems from the fact that the students haven't read carefully. However, I would argue that the chaos comes from a faulty processing of the elements that make up the arguments rather than from a failure to read. When novice readers encounter a text that depends heavily on outside sources to back up arguments, they reconstruct it; in the new text, all quotations, paraphrases, and exposition—regardless of their original sources—are attributed to the author of the students' text, creating a confusing conglomerate of conflicting ideas.

Part of the failure to recognize multiple authorities in a text results from the students' tendency to read from word to word rather than from idea to idea. They skim through a text either so rapidly that they confuse the person who is speaking with one or more people being quoted or so slowly that they lose the connections that let them know who's saying what. Even when an author quotes from someone who holds an opposing viewpoint, the students often attribute the statement to the author and quite naturally become bewildered about what seems to be the author's contradictory ideas. They ignore obvious introductions to quotations such as the following:

> Jerome Bruner, among psychologists the most persuasive advocate of intuitive thinking, put it well in his *Process of Education:* (105)

> John Dewey argued similarly: (94)

This inability to pick up textual cues creates an interpretive snarl; therefore, many students solve the problem by skipping block quotations altogether. But even more confusing for them are passages in which authors paraphrase in order to prove points or to further their arguments:

> As part of his Paideia Proposal, Mortimer Adler made a useful distinction between three spheres of learning: the development of in-

> tellectual skills, the acquisition of knowledge, and the enlargement of understand of ideas and values. (99)

> Aversive behavior, B. F. Skinner has amply demonstrated, may have short-range benefits (the class may become quiet), but is likely to leave long-term scars (the seething resentment in the class distracts everyone from learning the subject under study). (169)

The parenthetical phrases and convoluted sentence structures in such paraphrased remarks confuse inexperienced readers, and the confusion stops reading and understanding quickly.

References to outside sources also present the students with a conceptual dilemma. Why should one "expert," such as Sizer, resort to discussing the ideas of another? Who are these people, and why do they appear in this book? Once again, the students' first inclination is to skip the reference.

As part of our reading instruction, we teach students to find textual clues that will help them decide how much weight to give a quotation and the person who is being quoted. This can be achieved by doing some simple explication exercises with the class, concentrating not on whole chapters, but on individual quotations in context and their function in the passage. When the students learn to take apart the text, they come to understand that B. F. Skinner is probably only in the paragraph because he developed a theory about the efficiency of using threats to motivate people. They don't have to know everything there is to know about Skinner; they can concentrate on the more important claim that Sizer makes—angry students don't learn.

Given their inexperience with the multiple voices that appear in academic texts, it is not surprising that the additional mixture of narrative and exposition distorts the students' reading. Sizer's composite portraits, or "word pictures," drawn from his visits to various schools, are designed to make his book more accessible to laypersons. The following statement, found in the introduction, helps us introduce this strategy to our students:

> The characters here portrayed are real people, and the places described are all actual places. With but a few, mostly personal, exceptions, however, I have masked true identities. It has been my experience that educators tend to ignore something not exactly on their own turf. "Oh, that's Lincoln High School," they say; "it can't apply to us." The points I am trying to make do in fact extend beyond any one high school, and I wish no reader to be encouraged to think otherwise.
>
>   More important, brief portraits such as these inevitably distort. One can describe faithfully, but in making choices of what to

represent, one inevitably shapes a point of view. While I have struggled to be fair, I want no persona or school identified with a particular portrait. My purpose is not to tell their special stories, but to use aspects of their experience to make some useful general points. (7–8)

Concentrating on this passage also helps us to address the students' continual objections to much of the general theory they encounter when reading abstract exposition. Sizer's discussion of his own rhetorical strategy paraphrases the students' favorite complaint, "it's not like that here." His explanation of how a limited emphasis on particular experiences can hamper thought about larger issues reinforces and expands upon our attempts to encourage students to see their experience as representative rather than as exclusive. This epitomizes the Distanced/Personal stance we wish to introduce. Perhaps not so surprisingly, Sizer's text proves a model for bringing together our students' experiences with the experiences of students described in all the texts we study.

At first, these word pictures prove to be merely distracting. However, as the quarter progresses, the students begin to see how composite portraits illustrate and strengthen Sizer's major generalization: that very little differs in school curricula regardless of whether the district is affluent or poor. For example, the first composite character Sizer creates, Horace Smith, a sort of EveryTeacher, represents the experiences of teachers across America. The students initially have difficulty differentiating between Sizer and Horace Smith, and even those who do recognize Horace as an imaginary character have trouble understanding why Sizer devotes a twelve-page prologue to the events in Horace's day. The prologue has no real purpose: it doesn't, like Wigginton's prologue, reveal anything about the author's personal thoughts or, like Tracy's introduction, lead into a historic account of high schools in America. The composite picture seems to have no "so what," no purpose or information that couldn't be solved by jumping to the rather brief summary at the end. They are greatly relieved when we confirm that the "so what" in this section is slight, that this prologue simply illustrates Horace Smith's life as a teacher—creating a context for the chapters that will follow. (To their credit, some students are not confused by this prologue; they recognize immediately that Sizer's portrait of Horace Smith in many ways serves the same function that an introduction should serve in an essay.) In order to make Sizer's organizational strategy clearer, we ask the students to jump ahead in the text and read a number of the composite pictures, pointing out the parallel structure of the various sections of the book.

Discussing these composite portraits and their function eases the students' problems with entering the text. Knowing that Sizer's portraits will always be followed by a related discussion gives them a way of dividing the text into readable segments and provides a familiar context. Despite the complexity of the text, *Horace's Compromise* has one quality that the others lack. While the narratives of Wigginton and Tracy provided different cultures to which our students could compare their experiences, Sizer's theories, coupled with his composite pictures, provide a means of connecting the students' own experiences to the abstract world of educational theory. Because they can "see" the common problems that affect the American high school system, they can place themselves among the students and classrooms that Sizer describes.

Deciphering and responding to the exposition that follows the composite portraits is a completely different matter. The students, while better readers than they were at the beginning of the sequence, cannot follow Sizer's more theoretical arguments. This difficulty with argumentative prose is most pronounced when they read "The Program," the section about American high school curricula. Sizer's claims are based on abstract philosophies and are not easily translated into actions. Only the fact that we have already begun the examination of their own high school educations in the previous quarter keeps the students from floundering entirely. The previous quarter of study, in effect, provides a contextual schema as well as a textual schema for reading *Horace's Compromise.* The studies of Wigginton and Tracy, coupled with the interviews they conducted with their former teachers and peers, introduce the students to the idea that each school has a set curriculum and that each curriculum represents more than the hobbyhorses of individual teachers. Moreover, our discussions of pedagogical theory as the backbone of classroom practice and teachers as professionals provide an important cultural background for Sizer's discussions.

The composite picture that heads this chapter on high school programs speaks to the students' experience much more closely than any other. As usual, Sizer begins with a carefully drawn character, Mark, a "genial eleventh-grader" (71), and follows him through a rather confusing and uninspired day at school. Mark drifts from class to class, never connecting the material he studies to present or future experiences. Sizer ends the composite picture with this rather bleak observation:

> Tomorrow, and virtually every other tomorrow, will be the same for Mark, save for the lack of the assembly: each period will be five minutes longer. (76)

Sizer switches from narrative to exposition without transition, immediately presenting his readers with several types of curriculum goals. The first, a set of 1979 objectives from a California school district, represent to him a typical, almost national, model of curriculum. He argues that these objectives can be found, with only slight variations in wording, in almost every school he visited in his travels about the country. Students from a multitude of diverse school systems, economic status, and social backgrounds are expected to graduate from high school with the same qualities:

- Fundamental scholastic achievement . . . [being able] to acquire knowledge and share in the traditionally accepted academic fundamentals . . . to develop the ability to make decisions, to solve problems, to reason independently, and to accept responsibility for self-evaluation and continuing self-improvement
- Career and economic competence
- Citizenship and civil responsibility
- Competence in human and social relations
- Moral and ethical values
- Self-realization and mental and physical health
- Aesthetic awareness
- Cultural diversity (7)

As Sizer notes, this list is distinguished by its completeness: the goals, if met, will affect the students' minds, bodies, morals, values, and future careers (77). Unfortunately, his argument continues, despite grandiose goals and objectives, most high school curricula consist of courses that provide "a systemized, conveyer-belt way" to keep students supervised, make parents happy, and preserve the labor market for adults (83). Sizer maintains that current educational practice stresses the memorization of facts and submission to discipline rather than an introduction to and practice of critical thinking skills. He suggests that students would profit from a much narrower set of curriculum goals if educators would prepare them in literacy, numeracy, and civic understanding, and leave moral and values instruction to parents. Such curriculum goals would, of course, require a much more critical and individualized set of courses (86).

To our students, Sizer's goals initially seem far more limited than the ones set forth by the California school, and they make the goals even narrower by equating curriculum goals with courses: literacy means English, numeracy means math, civic understanding means courses in American and Ohioan history. To familiarize them with the broader curricula Sizer speaks of and to connect them with the issues he discusses, we send them out into their own schools, requiring that they use Sizer's discussion to determine what educational goals have been set by their own high schools.

Through interviews, documents from administrators' offices, and their own experiences, they discover that Sizer's curriculum objectives can't be met merely by introducing a single course. They also find that their teachers have little control over either curriculum goals or course requirements, and less over instructional objectives. Driven by frustration, many of their teachers have abandoned the abstract principles and objectives of the official curriculum guides and have settled for teaching what they feel to be *the basics.* In fact, locating copies of the local high schools' mission statements proves extremely difficult; everyone knows that, by law, each Ohio school district has to have a mission statement, but since it is only pulled out during formal review periods, many of the teachers have never seen the official document. Students and teachers alike confuse the mission statement with the course objectives and the course objectives with state-mandated curriculum objectives.[2] When the students compare their high school educations to the educational practices described in *Horace's Compromise,* it becomes obvious that vague and received notions of educational philosophies affected not only how they were taught and what they learned in high school but also how students and teachers interacted. Kay, an older student enrolled in the course during the second year of the project, reported what most of the students seemed to feel:

> My thoughts of what kind of education I want for my children have really been challeneged these past few weeks. That surprises me for two reasons. First, because I was getting annoyed at the constant thoroughness of dissecting the book Horace's Compromise by Theodore Sizer. And second, because I had a cocky attitude, (in my heart) thinking I knew enough to already be discussed with the school system. The persistence of not just reading this book but writing journals and essays. Along with the constant discussion in class (my favorite part) brought me to a different understanding of the dilemma of the school system.

Without exception, year after year, the students embrace Sizer's concept of "less is more" in education. They, too, reject the idea that schools should teach all students the same subject matter—regardless of individual inclinations and abilities. They agree with Sizer when he proposes that four general principles should govern the choice of subject matter for high schools:

- If students have not mastered the fundamental standards of literacy, their programs should focus exclusively on these.

- Choices of subject matter should reflect the tastes and priorities of particular schools and communities.
- Subject matter should support the students' learning of skills.
- Subject matter should lead somewhere in the eyes and minds of the students. (110–112)

Since most of the students readily recognize that their school systems have not provided them with what Sizer refers to as "ultimately useful or patently interesting high school experiences" (112), they begin to look for scapegoats. At this point, teachers and administrators seem the most reasonable candidates, and some students are willing to hold them responsible for everything that is wrong with the high school education system. However, Sizer's description of several very different teachers and their classes not only forces our students to recognize how the bureaucracy and structure of school systems affect teachers, but also cause them to reconsider their own part in making the educational process successful. Sizer's argument, in part, claims that

> if effective learning is to take place, student and teacher must agree on the objective and on the means to reach it. For the student, this often requires trusting the teacher, as the objective and the ways to it are obscured by the student's inexperience. . . . Any person who sees, at least to some extent, why he or she is asked to do something is ahead of the individual who is merely absorbed into some inexplicable but compulsory activity. And if those reasons are persuasive, the energy and effort that are provoked will help the individual learn. (159)

Students, who up until this point, have maintained that they learn only when they "enjoy" a course, suddenly begin to consider what part trust in the curriculum and in the good intentions of the teacher plays in that enjoyment, the resulting motivation, and the eventual learning. Previously, most of them considered the entertainment level as the primary factor in effective learning. Sizer's discussion of agreement, trust, and mutual purpose put learning in a new perspective. The students begin to admit that they find it difficult to pay attention to the many subjects in high school (and college) that suffer from what Sizer calls "the castor oil problem: Take this and you'll feel better some time in the future" (159). While nearly all students can recount an experience in which they gladly participated in learning with a trusted teacher, equally prevalent are accounts of experiences that recall teacher-student "agreements" that led to what Sizer labels "conspiracies for the least"—classrooms where both teacher and students agree to maintain the peace at the expense of learning.

Most of our students, divided between those who have just finished high school and those who have been out of high school for years, can match their experiences with Sizer's composite descriptions of American high schools; yet those who finished high school recently continue to argue mightily that their high school education has prepared them for college. Even when faced with the fact that they have been placed in remedial English and math courses and are having difficulty understanding what they're supposed to be learning in other disciplines, they hold on to their claim that their local high school education was sound. If they blame anything for their current difficulties, they blame their own early disinterest in education and lackluster efforts to complete homework. The older students, however, most adamantly blame the school systems for student failure. They have been out of the educational system long enough to be objective about it, and they fear that their children will be underprepared and turned off by the same system. However, these older students still feel the authority of that past educational process: they are reluctant to claim the training, the experience, or the right to confront those who teach the classes or those who set the policies. Reading Sizer and writing about high school helps both sets of students approach education from a more academic perspective—as a process to be examined and held up to scrutiny.

Brian, for instance, a traditional student who spent the first half of the ENG 052/053 sequence being laid-back, polite when spoken to, and generally irresponsible, found Sizer's book to be a revelation, especially when it came to the sort of passive agreement that shaped his own high school education and was leading to problems in his college career. I've included the following essay on his high school experience in its entirety in order to demonstrate how he uses Sizer's text to work out his understanding of the damaging effects of his own particular *conspiracy of the least:*

> When I was in high school I was in a classroom of the conspiracy for the least. Which is a classroom in which the students and the teachers have an unspoken agreement in which the students give the teacher no trouble and in return the teacher does not intellectually challenge the students. A good example of this was my algebra I teacher my sophomore year, who's name will remain anonymous. Our class was very quiet during the period. After the bell would ring, all us would be in our seats copying notes from the over head projector while the teacher sat at the desk with his feet propped up with the daily newspaper at hand. During this time our class was restless and bored because it only took five minutes to copy the notes and he always took fifiteen minutes to read the paper out of each period. Since he had the paper in his face

most of the time he wasn't able to see the paper wads flying across the room and the students shooting baskets into the trash can. After finishing the sports page he would stand up and briefly discuss the basketball game from the night before. Since he coaches the team he would always find a reason other than his own fault for losing, and then invite all of us to watch their next game. We could easily predict what kind of mood he was going to be in by how well his team was doing. After twenty minutes are rapped up in all of this talk he would go over the notes and make it fun by relating it to the basketball game or telling a joke in between ideas. While explaining the notes, he would pick on the girls in a flirting manner and they would joke back with him but there were very few times when he picked on the guys. After going over the notes, he collects the homework from the night before and then tells us our assignment for that night and to start it.

We were not intellectually challenged in this class and by the description of the class a student could easily slip by the teacher without learning. After this poor influence of seeing the teacher sit for fifteen minutes a day one hour and fifteen minutes a week and five hours a month that could really have negative affect on the students. After that year in algebra I was never able to understand it very well because I was introduced to the subject by a teacher, who is supposed to be a role model for the students, who was sitting around being very aloof concerning the subject. That type of teaching had a negative affect on me and after talking with several students in my class and some other classes he taught I discovered that they also had similar problems. A friend of mine in the class was having trouble understanding a few chapters in the book. He confronted the teacher for help several times and the teacher would send him to the smartest student in the class. My friend still was having great difficulties understanding the material because the supposedly smartest student in the class didn't know any more than my friend. This supposedly smart student had managed to slip by the teacher unnoticed, by doing the minimum of what is expected of him and was able to pass the tests by memorizing most of the material.

This problem seemed to evolve from the overall attitude my teacher expresses to his students. Perhaps this attitude is caused by the neglect of the administration not applying enough pressure on the teacher to teach in an organized by progressive manner. Its possible that my algebra teacher was severely underpaid and had no incentive to teach the class. There are several reasons that could make a teacher teach in such a way but I agree with Sizer in saying there is no excuses at all for this type of teaching. Sizer gave examples of several teachers and the one I found most similar to my algebra teacher would be Mr. Broday a social studies teacher. The school in which Mr. Brody taught was more concerned in looking like a good school [teacher] rather than being a good school. Therefore Mr. Brody taught the class accordingly he only taught the minimum of what was required and only expected the minimum from the students so they were not intellectually challenged in any way. Sizer explains that it is sometimes necessary for a conspiracy for the least since the teachers and the students cannot deal with the rigorous activities all day. Both my algebra teacher and Mr. Brody were teachers that could keep the students attention for a whole period but just how much of that time had anything to do with school. Which is better a teacher that has some type of control over his students or a class that has no agreement and is in total chaos. Both classes will accomplish very little so neither type of class would be better.

In Sizer's book "Horaces Compromise", he uses several teachers as examples of different types of teaching methods and there is one particular teacher that I feel could fit into my algebra class to solve our problems. That teacher would be Mr. Curtis a computer teacher who has a very unique approach to helping students learn. Sizer explains that Mr. Curtis assigned the class to do a simple program on the computer if they understood the program from the day before if not to work on it and he would walk around and answer any questions. Some of the students worked in the advanced groups and the strugglers in another. But one girl stayed in the back of the room by herself she was fiddling around and messed up the first problem and was on cloud nine so to speak. When she thought he noticed her she would sigh and act confused and he just ignored her. He continued helping the other students and ignored her pleas for help by just telling her to think for herself. After realizing that he was not going to help her unless she really tried it herself she got to work. When he noticed that she was working he watched to see how she was doing and when he seen that she was getting close he walked up to her and said really loud "That's great!" and all the students looked up noticing. By doing this Mr. Curtis instills confidence in this girl who doesn't believe in herself.

If Mr. Curtis was my algebra I teacher, our class would definitely improve. Our class suffered from the lack of concern as well as the lack of confidence which Mr. Curtiss would be able to help regain. I think that Mr. Curtis would teach this class in a very different way. He would probably give the class a list of problems from what they did the day before and break them up into groups, ones that understand and ones that had trouble. Then if any students had trouble they would have the help of the students surrounding them and the help of the teacher if so desired. By teaching this way it can eliminate the chances of students getting by the system without learning.

Seeing my algebra teacher and the way he teachers the class and then seeing Mr. Curtis teach you can see that Mr. Curtis's method of teaching is much more affective. Mr. Curtis uses a method in which the students think for themselves instead of memorizing material like that of my algebra teacher. And that proved to be a more affective form of teaching in my high school.

Sizer's book helped Brian understand his experience in the public schools. It's true that his paper remains far from perfect: he abandons commas rather than figures out where they go; he hasn't fully mastered the art of paragraphing; he still makes mistakes in syntax, subject-verb agreement, and word usage; the conclusion falters slightly. However, I would argue that he exhibits a maturity of style and thought that he was incapable of at the beginning of the year.

This maturity grows from the extensive reading the students do, rather than from writing alone, and from studying one topic at length, rather than moving too quickly through a series of neat, concise arguments on different subjects. Sizer's book, with its careful delineation of a complex problem, contributes to our students' sense of addressing a situation that was common to all of them. His examples gave Brian, for instance, a means of illuminating the problem; his vocabulary and terminology provided a means of discussing what went wrong in Brian's algebra class. Sizer's book also helps our students come to terms with the manner in which we conduct the ENG 052/053 classroom. They recognize in Sizer's descriptions of Mr. Curtis, Sister Michael, and other teachers who demand students work out problems, echoes of our own demands that they figure out what to do—how to decipher mysterious passages, what to write, and how to write—using the skills they already possess. I've explained how we use Sizer's book rather extensively so that readers can develop a sense of how the Distanced/Personal combines lived experience and academic theory. Will other books work as well as Sizer's does? The answer is obviously "Yes." Over the course of six years and four different topic developments, teachers and students have found such diverse books as Katherine S. Newman's *Declining Fortune: The Withering of the American Dream,* Judith S. Wallerstein and Sandra Blakesless's *Second Chances: Men, Women and Children a Decade After Divorce,* and C. Wright Mills' *White Collar* equally effective for studying the meaning-making process.

Applying Theory To Personal Experience

By the time the class begins to read Mike Rose's *Lives on the Boundary,* the nature of the students' questions and responses have changed radically. While the rest of the books generally bring on some form of groan or protest on the first day we discuss the reading, this book brings about an entirely different response.

Over the years, we've repeatedly heard affirmative comments. For example, "This book is about my life," claimed Morgan, who wasn't exactly like Rose—he defied his parents by taking vocational education *instead* of college prep courses in high school. Returning to school after working for two years as a professional welder, he had recognized welding wasn't, in his words, "a life that was ever going to change."

As we delved further into the book, and Rose describes Lucia, a returning student who was also a single mother, Anita, one of our older students reported, "When I read about that woman carrying her baby around to classes, I think of myself." Although Anita was happily married and the mother of older children, she could readily understand the problems of mixing motherhood and school. Indeed, our students' baby-sitting problems are such that we have visiting children in class occasionally. But what particularly drew Anita to Lucia's story was the account of Lucia's struggle to understand the reasoning of the academy. Rose describes one of Lucia's problems with scholarly texts, this time Thomas Szasz's *The Myth of Mental Illness,* as resulting from a clash of intellectual and religious belief systems: "Working-class Catholicism made it difficult for her to go along with, to intellectually toy with, the comparison of Freud to God" (184). Nor did she, he continues, have the background to appreciate Szasz's discussion of Freud as creator of a movement that took on an almost religious character.

Anita, too, felt these conflicts. As a born-again Christian, she had carefully structured her world, and her children's world, around her belief in absolute values and in the personal guidance of a supreme being. Needless to say, this belief system came under attack in nearly every class that she took, every intellectual (and sometimes, I regret to report, personal) discussion she engaged in with professors. She, like Lucia (and like many students with similar belief systems), was determined not to give up. Her days and evenings were filled with tension between her own expectations of herself and her struggle to come to terms with the difference between what she wanted to believe and what she felt she had to accept to be a good student.

Whether the stories match exactly or merely touch similar chords in our students, the stories of Rose's students affect the way our students think about themselves. But it is, as could be expected, Rose's own growth from underprepared student to educator that gives the students permission to speak about their own educational needs. In a sense, his experiences and words help them when they have to argue with family, friends, and various members of the faculty about whether or not they are college material.

Anita, for instance, found herself locked in a battle with the state of Ohio's board of workman's compensation. She was in college, in part, because she was being retrained. To supplement her family's income, she had worked at a factory for nearly ten years, a job that ended when she developed carpal-tunnel syndrome. She was entitled, by law, to workman's compensation and a retraining program. However, when she went before the review board at the end of her first year, the committee wanted to discontinue funding her tuition. The excuse (one we heard applied to at least one more working-class non-traditional student) was straightforward enough: factory workers, in the opinion of the board, didn't have the inherent intellectual ability to get or benefit from a college education. They offered to fund some kind of vocational training, but threatened to terminate her benefits if she insisted upon continuing in a four-year college. In the writing campaign that followed, Anita found that Rose served her well. In her arguments to the board and in her discussions with them at hearing after hearing, she quoted from Rose to make her case. She won, temporarily; later problems at home forced her to put her education on hold again.

Students like Anita have, unconsciously or consciously, felt excluded from the learning community because they haven't been able to articulate their problems with learning in a manner that can stand up against the educational traditions and experiences advocated by their high school teachers, families, and outside judges such as the workman's compensation board. However, as they read from Rose, Sizer, Tracy, and Wigginton, they get a sense of what education could be, as opposed to what it tends to be. This recognition, however, is not enough. Like Sondheim says, "Having just the vision's no solution/Everything depends on execution." In order to use their understanding, students must be able to articulate what they've learned.

By the end of the sequence, they've read about and discussed several excellent examples of hands-on and independent learning practices and made claims in their papers that this sort of approach to learning is superior to the practices found in most high schools. Therefore, to test whether they've really absorbed their newly found theories, we ask the students to develop interactive lessons for each other on *Lives on the Boundary.* Just as in graduate seminars, where graduate students must decide what to present about a work they have never seen before, or just as in high school classes where teachers must introduce material that they know the students aren't eager to learn, our novice teachers/writers must make decisions about what their classmates need to know and what will create an effective learning situation. At first glance, this assignment appears a bit overwhelming. Protests of "You're the teacher! How do I know what's important about this stuff!" arise from every corner. We don't back off; however, we show a little mercy by dividing the reading and teaching responsibilities among class groups, rather than individuals. All class members read each chapter of *Lives*— which is particularly well suited for this type of exercise—not just the material their group has to present. If one group does a poor job of teaching its chapter, their peers (in theory) should be ready to jump in and assist them.

They weren't all thrilled with Rose's story; we still heard the obligatory "Who cares about this guy?" complaint. However, we also heard, without coaching,

> Yeah, yeah, I see what he's doing: he tells us his story and the sto-
> ries of all these other students so that we can understand how his
> theories evolved. But I don't understand how the stories of the
> Vietnam veterans fit in with the rest of the examples, so could we
> talk about it?

The student who made this comment began to generate open-ended questions about the book, conversational and investigative ones rather than closed and right answer questions. These new questions become the source of our class discussion. More and more students ask, "Isn't this what Sizer meant about a "conspiracy for the least?" instead of, "Are you going to test us on this?" "Do you think Rose would approve of this class?" instead of "What's this got to do with writing?" And practically no belligerent-toned voice asks: "Will the bookstore take this book back?"

References to other books begin to surface in their discussions, as do more sophisticated issues of education. Students, for instance, recognize that the type of curriculum Rose advocates bears great resemblance to the classical education described by Tracy, but that Sizer claims such curricula will not serve students in today's problematic schools. The idea of an argument between experts fascinates them and creates quite a debate. Together we look for similarities between the four author's educational philosophies, discovering that the one constant in the manuscripts is a belief that effective learning, in both practical and classical curricula, not only prepares students for life, it also enriches that life.

I don't wish to imply that merely taking over the responsibility for teaching will solve all problems of understanding. In the beginning, the groups rarely manage to touch on all the important points of a chapter, and other members of the class need to help them out.

We *professional* instructors intercede when necessary. Like most experienced teachers, we have a sixth sense about who has read and who hasn't, and it only takes calling on the unprepared once or twice to encourage reading. This practice does not have to be the humiliating or degrading one that sometimes passes for motivating students by embarrassing them. If teachers recognize that people quit reading for reasons other than dereliction of duty, they can start a conversation that reveals the problems readers face and determine why understanding proved difficult.

Students themselves do not realize why they can't finish reading. They know that it's not the vocabulary; they understand and can identify most of the words in the passages of our books. In previous experiences with difficult reading, the students have blamed themselves for not reading: they're lazy; they're not interested; they have other things on their minds. A lot of self-degradation builds up because student failure has been the only rationale the students have ever been offered for their problems. However, when the reading of the text as well as the content of the text becomes the subject of class discussion, the students begin to recognize that their problems could result from a lack of understanding about how to approach the text. After a few attempts at teaching, students usually become willing to discuss what they didn't understand as well as what they comprehended immediately. This sense of community learning, where teachers and students alike participate in the problem solving, creates an atmosphere where students can laugh at problems and learn from others. In a classroom where winning is the goal or where students compete for attention or grades, correcting a peer could be devastating, but in a class devoted to mutual learning, this practice rarely takes the form of hostility or one-upmanship competition. Everyone in the class has occasionally missed the point of a passage. Presenters only receive or merit a hard time when it becomes obvious that they haven't read the assigned passages because they don't intend to carry their weight in the discussion.

As they prepare their lessons, students begin to sense what it means to be a teacher and how difficult that role can be. Because they remain so vocal about the failures of their high school teachers, we encourage them to find innovative ways to present their material, ways that they think will be more effective than the old *lecture-then-go-over-the-material-again* process. And as you might guess, they initially fail to find alternatives to the ways they have always been taught. Hardly fired up with the opportunity to expose what they don't know to their classmates, the novice teachers fall back on the familiar. When first we turn the classroom over to the groups, they inevitably cluster together, notebooks or note cards in hand, and begin to list fact after fact, or quote from the book as if the quotation alone could carry the point the author is trying to make. As the teaching process continues, they begin to incorporate into their teaching efforts some of the new ideas from the reading and from the modeling we do in class. Suddenly, a group will take over the blackboard, requesting that the other members of the class help them set up categories. They will ask the class to formulate questions that will lead into the discussion instead of setting their own agenda so that they can control the direction of the conversation. Some students go so far as to ask their classmates to freewrite about a problem before they open the dialogue.

These teaching experiences begin to affect them in ways we had not anticipated; regardless of whether we study education or work or the American Dream, as students become aware of the difficulties of teaching, they start to examine their experiences in other courses. Other instructors become the focus of discussion, not in the derogatory way that so often marks frustration brought about by differences in learning styles, but as the subject of additional inquiry. Questions arise: What does the history professor want when he lectures on one thing and asks the students to write about another? How does the reading in philosophy connect with the lecture and the writing that students must do? What assumptions about learning does the biology instructor use when he sets up the lab? Why are so many college classes set up as lecture classes? What do the instructors know about teaching? Where did they learn to teach? What do they think students should be learning?

All of this metadiscourse about teaching and learning opens up the students' experiences and conceptions of the educational community. Teachers become approachable, subjects less difficult to understand, students less disconnected from their own learning. No longer intimidated by the sheer weight of knowledge the professor possesses, the students learn to pose questions for teachers in ways that will create interaction with the subject and the person. And this connection is important, even necessary in the development of their learning process.

Some Thoughts about Other Research Topics

Because our students initially depend upon emotion and empathy to connect with texts, we chose research topics that have been written about in both personal and academic ways. If the text consists of the sort of dense abstraction and sophisticated language that characterizes most academic endeavors, the students will abandon the reading almost immediately; if the topic doesn't address some issue in the students' lives, they are equally likely to abandon it. My experiences with the tension created between texts and topics led me to come up with a few general rules for selecting texts:

- **Pick a topic with which everyone has experience.** Bartholomae and Petrosky picked adolescence and coming of age because everyone who has lived past the age of 18 or 19 has either experienced or is in the midst of their own rites of passage. We've selected our topics for the course—education, work, censorship, and the American Dream—with the same criteria in mind. Nearly everyone in college has had some experience with high school. Even students who dropped out and later finished GEDs have an opinion on high school as do older students whose children are now in the educational system. Most of our students have worked (or plan to work in the future), and a surprising number of them have been censored in some way. The last topic may seem more abstract and a bit removed from their experience. However, while students might not initially have identified their belief or interest in the American Dream, the very fact that they so often begin and conclude arguments with "We, as American citizens . . ." opens up the topic of what a person should expect as a member of American society.

- **Pick a topic whose experts are numerous, accessible, and willing to talk.** School teachers are legion, and they are articulate; administrators are almost as numerous as teachers, and most adults have had some experience with and some opinion about the education work, censorship, or the American way of life. Our students have interviewed everyone from educators to social workers in their search for people who can bring expertise to their investigations. (I'll discuss finding and interviewing experts in Chapter 5.)

- **Pick a topic that appears in the media.** This doesn't mean front-page headlines or lead stories on the eleven o'clock news. Choose topics that appear on the editorial page, PBS, white-paper or documentary programs. Education rarely makes it to either the front page or occupies the most prominent spot in the TV news; however, many of the "white-paper" reports on television and the "special" reports in newspapers and magazines provide interesting material that will supplement the reading in our classes.

- **Pick a topic that has been written about in lively, interesting, but responsible ways by authors with strong personal voices.**

Our students identify with people, and we need to give them involved people who talk about human experience rather than objective writers who talk about "subjects."

- **Pick a topic that you are interested in and enthusiastic about—and change topics when you are no longer interested or enthusiastic.** I have a tendency to want to preach here, but I'll let it go at one or two truisms. If you don't find the subject interesting, they won't. If you pick a narrow topic that only you find interesting (a former colleague of mine who taught an entire freshman composition course around *Moby Dick* comes to mind), you will lose their attention and respect.

- **Pick a topic that is socially relevant (not just sensational).** Many of our students did not understand that they could play a role in changing the educational system, or indeed that they had the right to expect school educators and state legislators to respond to informed criticism. They have the tendency to believe that teachers know best. They negate their own experience, attributing institutional failure to personal failure, blaming themselves for the failures of the system. Likewise, they were equally unaware that they had the potential to make changes in the workplace. Whenever we discuss any of the topics, we attempt to demonstrate that the students have choices and that the choices they make will shape both their own lives and the lives of others.

Hazardous Topics

Oh, dear reader, would that it were easy to find a topic that is interesting and safe. You will no doubt remember that I began this project as a reaction to my students' insistence that Gail Sheehy's *Passages* did not reflect their experience and as an attempt to capitalize on their willingness to investigate the experiences of family and friends. The topic that fascinated the students the most that quarter was divorce. At least half of them had parents who were divorced, their friends had parents who were divorced, and everyone had relatives who were divorced. Therefore, flushed with success and eager to please, I devised a course that studied the effects of divorce. As reading material, I selected chapters from *Second Chances: Men, Women, and Children a Decade After Divorce,* Judith Wallerstein and Sandra Blakeslee's excellent book. Basing their data on a ten-year study of the effects of divorce on people from all classes and education, Wallerstein and Blakeslee discuss the emotional and economic effects and after-effects of divorce on women, men, and children. Therefore, the students could choose practically any approach to the subject of divorce that they wanted and compare the results of interviews with their own family and friends to Wallerstein and Blakeslee's study.

Initially the topic seemed to meet all my expectations. We read excerpts from the book that excited the students immediately. They engaged actively in discussion, kept up with the reading, and speculated endlessly about the lives of the people in the study. Above all, their writing was lively and insightful. This from a group of students who were just about as underprepared as novices can get. I was ecstatic. I'd found the perfect topic to engage the students: personal yet part of the academic world of research.

Then I assigned the interviews. Immediately, the resistance began. As far as developing projects was concerned, they had little trouble narrowing their topics. Cathy wanted to talk about the effects of divorce on men. Bill was interested in the effects of divorce on children. John wanted to know why men wouldn't pay child support, and Susan wanted to find out why battered women stayed in bad marriages. But Susan, who in writing ability was the most remedial but whose insight was the most advanced, tentatively raised the first objection.

"How do I ask these women such personal questions?" she queried. "I can't just go in there and say, 'Why are you doing these stupid things?' They have feelings."

Cathy also had hesitations. "We're going to write about our friends. Do we have to use their real names?"

"If I tell this guy's story," John offered, "everyone in this room will know who I'm talking about. He's not going to be happy about that."

Once again we were back to the problems brought on by writing autobiographical or personal essays. But I had inadvertently added another dimension: the students would have to ask other people to reveal painful (extremely painful) facts about themselves, knowing that the student would then use the information in an essay for public consumption. This topic spared neither students nor the subjects of their interviews.

In part, I salvaged this class by deliberately discussing and experimenting with objectivity and personal distance. To make the questioning easier for both the student and the respondent, I encouraged the students to carefully review questions to make sure that they were not offensive, to figure out how to involve the interview subjects in disguising their stories and names, and to discuss and re-discuss issues of integrity. In a way, we teamed together to protect thier sources, and that very effort made the problem easier. I agreed that they would not publish this report outside the classroom and did not pressure them into discussing their relationships with the people that they interviewed. As a class, we decided to use pseudonyms for all the people in the study and to find ways to disguise identities without changing the facts about the respondents. This made the whole process somewhat easier to bear.

Then a second problem appeared, one which I should have been expecting from the first: the topic got depressing.

Studying the lives of people in pain becomes painful. Trained professionals can readily cut off the problem of others (or at least claim that they can) and go on with their real lives. As researchers, our frustration with the hopelessness of many of the people interviewed for the study weighted upon us as we discussed the issues of divorce and transcribed the interviews. Our "objective conclusions" became anything but objective. Studying the topic actually helped at least one student, who used the information she gathered to make important decisions about her life. "I'm not going to live this way," she told me right after she asked me to help her contact the local battered women's shelter. The majority of us, however, began to avoid thinking about divorce or marriage altogether. Mostly we wanted the semester to end—soon.

I had to do something to relieve the distress that the topic was causing, so I developed a number of ways to refocus. To make the subject less depressing overall, we talked in class about ways to separate our experience from that of the respondents. We said a lot of positive things about marriage, found cases where the divorce led to survival rather than defeat, and shared stories of children who were not completely destroyed by their parents' divorce. In short, we employed the kind of self-comforting strategies that families and friends engage in—we put the matter into perspective. And I promised and swore never to do such a depressing topic again.

Handling Emotional Fallout from a Topic

Chances are that you will find that no topic is pain free. For instance, I discovered that some older students, and a few of our more traditional ones, had very painful associations with high school. For the majority of students' high school represented a period of marking time (the illusion that high school is a peak time of adolescence ranks high among illusions). Many of these students, placed in remedial tracks and labeled stupid, were given courses of study that presented little intellectual challenge. A number of students had undiagnosed learning disabilities that caused problems with self-confidence and esteem. And some students were on family and social roller coasters that bled into their lives at school and made learning more painful than purposeful. For a few of the older students, high school happened so long ago that they had little memory of what went on educationally. The strongest memories tended to concern the social delights and horrors of being young rather than the subjects they studied and the teachers they encountered.

Working as we do within the affective domain, asking students to push harder than they ever have at thinking, causes us to stumble into emotional quandaries. However, we discovered that if a topic opens up areas that best would have been avoided, the voice of emotion can be replaced with one that is a little more rational with careful coaching:

- **Try not to pick a topic that is inherently painful:** Divorce causes pain; there's no way around it. And no matter how interesting studies are on divorce, AIDS, child abuse, or rape, when students have to study the topic for ten weeks or more and talk to real people about what can only be termed disaster topics, it violates aesthetic distance and everyone's sense of propriety.

- **Redefine the topic for the student:** Many of our older students write about their younger colleagues, rather than about their own experience. This allows them to draw upon their own knowledge and apply it to someone else.

- **Allow the student to work out a means of handling the material:** In other words, talk to students about ways they can make the topic less painful. Often all students want is acknowledgment that they have a legitimate concern. They usually know how to make the topic manageable and want not only to be heard but also to be in control of the topic. Negotiate so that both of you get what you want.

- **Acknowledge that academia tries to make the human (and subjective) into the scientific (and objective):** Then talk about why. Above all, teachers need to situate themselves as humanists, not scientists. The students are studying and writing about people, not subjects. Either type of writing demands adherence to a difficult process, a fact that should be kept in mind when assigning a topic or a writing activity.

Chapter Five

A Sense of Place
Interviewing as
a Meaning-Making Process

We recommend that English Studies be based in
practices—the activities of engaged reading, writing,
speaking, and listening, followed by extensive reflection
on those practices.
> —Andrea Lunsford and Richard Lloyd-Jones
> *The English Coalition Conference:*
> *Democracy Through Language*

The value of ethnography inheres in neither analysis nor
interpretation, but in the researcher's decision to exam-
ine lived cultural experience—to conceptualize it, reflect
on it, narrate it, and evaluate it.
> —Linda Brodkey
> "Writing Ethnographic Narratives"

The research activities proposed in the previous chapter were designed to acquaint our students with the connection between textual and experiential knowledge—and largely consisted of methods
of teaching students how to read and write about various existing
texts. In this chapter I'd like to outline activities designed to continue that process—this time demonstrating how our students

gather and convert the experiences of community members into textual knowledge. The reading serves as a foundation on which to build a context for study and for moving the students away from writing as storytelling to writing as analysis. The work we do as part of classroom investigation extends the art of reading to a new level and integrates it with the arts of speaking, listening, and, above all, writing. As always, I'd like to remind readers that these are not discrete and separate tasks. You don't teach the students to read, then teach them to write; the reading, writing, speaking, and listening activities are integrated and recursive. The ethnographic techniques that we've adopted for our pedagogy give our students practice in bringing together disparate pieces of information in order to make meaning. Making meaning, in this context, can be thought of as creating something useful, in the broadest sense of that word, out of what the students have learned. What students glean from their research should give them theories with which to explain and, if they see the need, change the various communities to which they belong.

Interviewing and Distanced/Personal Research

Expanding the Context for Research

The students conduct one interview each quarter. In the first quarter they transcribe the interviews word for word and assemble a clasbook of these records that we study as a class, a process that takes approximately three weeks. In the second quarter they do not transcribe the tapes; they write a synopsis of their interviews, which we print so that students can pick and choose the tapes they want to review for their research. The interviews, when read against the texts and against student essays about education at the local level, complete the triangulation process for each quarter's project.[1] These particular researchers only have ten weeks for their initial research activities, and during that time, they have to create a theoretical/textual context, interview and observe subjects in a real-life context, and evaluate a myriad of research data. So we reconstruct the ethnographer's task a bit: we help them construct narrowed topics, formulate several tentative theories about educational practices, and assist them in setting up some questions that will help them learn more about both topic and theory. The student remains in charge of the topic, which may begin as something quite vague, such as "Motivation."

"What about motivation?" we inquire.

"You know. How it works?" they respond.

We assure them that we don't know and ask them to "tell us more" (a phrase that soon begins to produce groans). Through careful inquiry on our part and careful thinking on their part, the students will go to the interview with a set of questions that address some version of the following theories:

"Students who aren't motivated won't learn."

"Students who see a practical reason to study a subject are more motivated that those who think of the course as useless."

"Internal motivation is better than external motivation."

"Teachers can't motivate students who don't want to be motivated."

"Motivation has to come from home rather than from school."

Only after completing these initial focusing discussions can we work on developing questions that will bring out pertinent data about their subject of concern. Although the above statements still sound extremely vague, they offer a chance to formulate real questions that the informant has a chance of answering. The final questions may still be broad—"Do you think internal motivation is better than external motivation?"—but the students will feel easier asking them, and the informant will be able to give solid answers instead of spending thirty minutes or more trying to figure out what the students want and need to know about motivation.

Choosing an Informant

In *The Cultural Experience: Ethnography in Complex Society,* Spradley and McCurdy make the point that our definition of knowledge will affect the way ethnographers see the people they study. Using the example of an alien researcher who comes to earth to study checkers players, they describe three ways that the researcher could view people playing checkers: as subjects, respondents, or informants. If the object is strictly to classify behavior of checkers players, people become *subjects.* The researcher observes them at play, then identifies and classifies certain of their actions and behaviors. To complete the research, this scholarly observer proposes relationships between action and behavior and formulates a hypothesis (which could be tested) in order to confirm the nature of checkers and checkers playing. The researcher's descriptions and explanations of the world of checkers playing would probably have little meaning to the ordinary checkers player, but it would have a great deal of meaning to the researcher's culture, the culture of "scientific knowledge" (10).

Another approach the researcher might take would define the people observed as *respondents.* While the researcher would create categories and classify the activities witnessed, a new element of research would be added. The researcher would interview the players and ask them to respond to questions that would confirm or change the researcher's perceptions of the game and its players. Again, Spradley and McCurdy would argue, the researcher's conclusions would not necessarily represent the average checkers player's view of the activity (11).

The third way to look at people in a research project, as *informants,* allows for a greater interaction between the researcher and the people who populate the culture under study. The researcher starts out learning what motivates and activates the actions of the checkers players. Instead of categorizing these behaviors, the researcher tries to discover the categories that the informants create. This requires learning the "language" of the informants: how they talk about what they do, the meanings of words and terms that are specific to the cultural activities. Hypotheses are generated from what the researcher learns from the informant, and the research has limited goals: "To enable the researcher to anticipate behaviors and actions his informants would judge as appropriate" (11–12). An informant teaches the participant-observer. As Spradley and McCurdy claim:

> When people are merely studied, observed, and questioned as subjects or respondents, the investigator may be detached. When "subjects" become teachers who are experts in understanding their own culture, the relationship between investigator and informant becomes quite different. The investigator will ask those he studies to become his teachers and instruct him in the ways of life they find meaningful. . . . He will learn to speak and understand the language of those he studies. Field work for the ethnographer is a *cultural experience.* (12)

Interaction with an informant creates an atmosphere for learning and reflecting upon that knowledge.

Preparing for the Interview

The first-quarter interview is particularly important because it sets the tone for the rest of the study. The time spent on interviewing, in my opinion, is well worth the hard work necessary to introduce the students to field research. During the first quarter, we spend at least a week preparing students for their interviews and allow a week for them to complete the process. Selecting an informant, introducing the idea of a speculative inner dialogue between self and informant, and preparing questions for interviews occupies at least a week before the interview itself. The week for actually completing the interview is necessary not only because of the logistics involved in arranging and conducting interviews but also because students often have to go back to reinterview an informant. The interview assignment often puts students into close contact with authority figures, and sometimes that proximity causes them to cut short the inquiry process.

Initially, we ask the students to pick three people who could shed light on the topic. Although each student will only interview one person, we want them to compare several possible informants so that they can decide which person would best provide the information they need. Once the students have listed three people they might interview, they must justify their choices to us, explaining how the people that they selected can provide help in their investigations. Because we want to maximize the interactions within a cultural context, we insist that the students interview people who are actively involved with the topic under study. For instance, when we study high school education, the informants usually come from local area schools: former teachers, high school administrators, and other types of educators. The important factor in selecting informants is that they speak the same language and use the same terms that the authors of the course texts use.

We also ask the students to explain their previous association with the person they wish to interview and why this person might be willing to talk to a student about a research project. At first, as any of us would, the students tend to pick people they know well as informants. Unfortunately, they often choose people who do not have any special knowledge or authority to speak to the question: their mothers or their uncles, their sisters and their next-door neighbors. Often these decisions are based on convenience. It's not hard to contact these people; they're non-threatening. The fact that the sister has no authoritative experience with the topic seems beside the point to the beginning researcher. "Everyone," they argue, "is entitled to an opinion." We do not automatically rule out sisters, uncles, mothers, and next-door neighbors on general principle. Professionals have to live somewhere and be related to someone; it's not inconceivable that they might just end up next-door or related to our novice writers. In order to use these particular informants, however, the students have to provide credentials to prove they have more than just a passing knowledge of the topic. This means that the students have to figure out what constitutes adequate credentials.

Fortunately, this is not too difficult. We pose questions that are practical and, in a sense, obvious:

"What qualifies this person to speak knowledgeably on the topic?"

"What makes you feel you can trust the information that this person will give you?"

"What is his or her professional background and experience?"

These rather simple questions eliminate many of the unqualified relatives and next-door neighbors. For instance, in the case of the education topic, the students start to see that their favorite elementary education teacher, while in the general field of education, will not necessarily be able to answer questions about high school education.

Finding reliable and knowledgeable informants for their interviews can be relatively easy compared to the next step: requesting the interview. Consider the education topic again. While the students all generally have a teacher they can interview (you'd be surprised how many people are related to teachers), many of them are hesitant to approach principals, school board members, or even college professors. The initial contact seems to be the hardest. The students experience a great deal of trepidation at the thought of calling up a stranger and asking for an interview. What do they say? What would make a person give up time to a student?

Although students initially find the idea a little silly, mock telephone discussion helps them decide what to say to a prospective informant. Practicing their spiel out loud lets them test it without anguish. Before they even practice, we have them write out notes to use in the conversation—who they are, the nature of the project they're engaged in, the topic that they want to discuss, the reasons that they chose the informant. The novice researchers resent what they think of as a *Micky Mouse* exercise; however, their notes provide us with a sense of whether or not the students really understand what they're investigating. Then, with all of us sitting around the table, the students use their notes to make mock phone calls: practicing the ways in which they phrase requests, getting past hesitations on the part of the potential informants, and being clear and straightforward so that persons won't hang up before the students can explain what they want from them.

Hazards lurk between that initial phone call and the first meeting with the informant. Frequently, the hesitant interviewer will be content to leave a messages and wait for a reply rather than call again. It's not uncommon for an interview to evaporate because the students or their informants have to cancel one appointment and never get around to scheduling another one. In either case, the students fall behind. To help the students move forward at a reason-

able pace, we set deadlines for arranging and conducting interviews. If the deadlines are fairly short, we can head off potential
problems by convincing students to let go of informants who aren't
responding to requests for interviews or who can't be interviewed in
time for the students to complete the rest of the tasks associated
with this assignment. Since most of our students have never interviewed anyone before, they have no idea how complex the process
can be. They'd like to put the project off but find that such procras-
tination leads to disaster. They can't just "let things happen" with
interviews—they have to play an active part in order to complete
their research. And this is the easy part.

Often, a more complex matter also becomes evident in the
mock telephone conversations—the students' tendency to think
that the informants will know what the students have in mind as
far as information goes. In the interests of helping them realize
that they will conduct the interviews from a particular, and not
necessarily obvious, context, we introduce the idea of speculating
about what their informants' will say about the topic. Objections
ring out immediately. Some students claim that it's a waste of time
to speculate about outcomes of interviews: people are too unpredictable; one person can't read another's mind. Some claim that
they know exactly what the informant will say, so why bother
speculating? Still others don't wish to be presumptuous, feeling
that it's rude to assume that one person can know someone else's
state of mind. Speculating about an upcoming event constitutes
useless busy work.

I'd argue that their objections stem from a lack of understanding
about the etiquette of questioning. The types of inquiry we as academics take as normal and almost objective, the novice researcher
sees as impertinent, pushy, and, to some extent, mere fantasy work.
Usually they come around when we appeal to their sense of reality;
they can see that speculating about a response to a topic isn't rude,
nor does such an act mean reading another person's mind.
Speculation merely gives the novice interviewer a focus prior to the
interview. "Think about it," we remind them, "speculation is part of
everyday life." They assume they know the reasons their friends
break up with boyfriends or girlfriends or why parents act the way
that parents do. They even, to a certain extent, theorize about the objectives of teachers when they ask the eternal "What do you want?"
Preliminary speculations merely act as a starting place for inquiry,
solidifying their contextual conception of the problem under investigation. As the interview process goes on, these initial speculations
serve as touchstones for determining the students' accuracy in assessing their own biases and prejudices about the topic. Even when

their ideas prove wrong, preparing a written account of their expectations for the interview provides a record teacher and student can use to determine what caused them to misunderstand the context. This process, when guided by the teacher in group and individual discussion, models thinking about a subject in more than a cursory manner. Having to write down their thoughts causes the students to think more clearly and—except when a student is determined to avoid thinking—prompts a greater understanding of context.

Careful preparation for the interview proves to be the first step in making meaning from field research. Along with actually conducting the interviews and evaluating the material from a collection of interviews, these preinterview activities help place the students' personal experiences more firmly within the context created by the books.[2] These activities require that the researcher/writer engage in an ongoing multilevel dialogue with self, subject, and coinvestigators. Engaging in such a dialogue is what academics would call processing and analyzing data—my grandparents and countless other elders of the community would refer to the inner dialogue as the act of "mulling over" a situation. However, regardless of whether or not the students think of themselves as processing data or mulling over events, the idea of having an inner dialogue seems to them to be a private, and for the most part, emotional rather than rational activity. One reflects about personal relationships, budgets, choosing one course of action over another—all events that have consequences that are anything but unrelated to personal well-being. Few of our students habitually indulge in an inner dialogue about their academic course work. Why should they? If learning is all about gathering information and repeating it on a test, then little dialogue is required other than the classic, "Will this be on the test?" If learning is making meaning, then questioning texts, interviewing, and reading student and teacher texts involves interacting with multiple and sometimes contradictory sorts of information about a topic. The inability to speculate and question proves an immense barrier when the final object is a *new,* more substantive text created by triangulating the results of these interactions.

Learning To Ask Questions

In addition to helping select informants and introducing the act of speculation, we must prepare the students to ask straightforward and provocative questions so that their inquiry becomes a self-reflexive activity and questioning becomes a search for meaning rather than an affront to authority. Unfortunately, despite our coaching, many novice writers will go forth to find and interview a person without the vaguest idea (or maybe only a glimmer) of what they're doing. They are, as my great-aunt Helen would say, "hoping that Divine Providence will guide them." Equally problematic are the unquestioning students who seek out informants, knowing with rock-solid conviction what they expect to find. (Such students work in attack mode rather than in an inquiring one and expect to "blow this whole thing open.") In either case, the questioning process is incomplete and damaging to the final paper.

It's almost a given in scientific circles that the key to knowledge is knowing what questions to ask. Novice readers and writers seldom know what questions to ask; in fact, they often fail to realize that questions can and should be asked—not only about the information found in texts but also about the conflicting points of view and contradictions that can be found in almost any conversation with an informant. Interviews can fail because the interviewer finds it difficult to question personal friends and acquaintances. This difficulty is similar to the problems students have when asked to question texts, a problem that, in at least one way, has an easier solution. If a reader disagrees with an idea, the reader can close the book and ignore the author's arguments; however, it's hard to question lived experience when you privilege it and when you respect the source from which it comes. Before they enter the field and actually conduct interviews, the general reaction to any questioning activity is straightforward—a *personal* opinion, stated as evidence, constitutes a sort of final word on the subject. All experience is individual; therefore, few interpretations of lived experiences can be wrong. To question interpretations of experience is to negate the actions that inspired or resulted from the experience. Partially, this stance reflects the attitude that questioning should somehow serve as a prelude to action. If the action is in the past, it cannot be changed, so why question? If the action is to be in the future, there is more point to the questioning, but the questions tend to be practical rather than reflexive. In either case, the critical questioning that the academy demands seems unwarranted.

Questioning is not necessarily a simple process. The students are not sure what questions are appropriate, or what follow-up questions should be developed to get at ideas or concepts that don't surface immediately in the interview. If students don't understand how to construct questions early on, they also fail to understand what they should be accomplishing in their interviews and how the questions they ask will determine the answers that they will get. Therefore, in addition to discussing such matters as constructing closed, open, and leading questions, we try to distinguish between the *functions* of various types of questions: questions illicit information, questions that challenge existing or received ideas, questions that propose other possible ways of looking at a topic or a series of events, and (of course) the ever-elusive rhetorical question. We also talk a great deal about the reasons we should question everything, from the information we receive to the motives of the people who provide that information. Our motto—"Question everything"—is often difficult for the students to accept. To them, some things and some people seem beyond question.

Formulating Questions

Inexperienced interviewers tend to ask vague questions and take extremely indirect (some might even say off-base) approaches to getting information. What has been an inability to express their thoughts results in an equally frustrating inability to ask specific questions. We've all been witness to these bouts of inarticulation; many novice researchers punctuate their conversations with phrases like, "Do you know what I mean?" and "Do you understand what I'm saying?" and "I just can't put it into words." Strangely enough, these inarticulate comments sometimes function as strategies for learning. Those of us who interact with this muddled and confusing pattern of speech—filling in the blanks, asking questions that begin with "Do you mean . . .?"—not only answer the questions the students put to us but also do the work the students should be doing. We come up with the statement; the students merely agree or keep disagreeing until we refine what *they* want to say and lack the language skills to express. While a student will blame his or her inarticulation on a lack of vocabulary, the problem is less one of word usage and more one of not knowing how to identify and express the main point of a problem or a theory. Think back to the student who wants to interview an informant on "Motivation." The problem is not that the student doesn't know the word, nor is the problem not knowing the distinction between internal and external motivation—the reading has taken care of that. The core of the difficulty rests in the student's inability to discuss the aspects of motivation that brought about the student's original concern.

This inability to articulate salient points has serious consequences in interview situations: the students often do not make clear the reason they want to interview their informants, and, therefore, the questions that they ask cause the person to volunteer unwanted and unexpected information. While we cannot completely circumvent the tendency to move their informants away from the topic rather than toward it, careful previewing of an individual student's questions and the reasons the student wants to ask certain questions proves extremely useful. When explaining the thoughts behind a question to us, the student often develops a better insight about the nature of inquiry. In the long run, this insight will shape questions whose answers will add to the discussion at hand.

Let me illustrate.

If I wanted to know if today's high school students really can't read and write as well as students from the past, I would begin the interview with a question somewhat like this one:

> "Do you feel that reading and writing skills have deteriorated in the past twenty years?"

Furthermore, to get a valid and reliable opinion, I would interview someone who has been teaching English for twenty years or more. And if, after the initial question, I did not get a satisfactory or complete answer, I would approach the topic from a different point of view, probably following up the original question with additional questions along this line:

> "You say nothing has changed. Then how do you account for the public outcry for proficiency testing and the constant lament that students can't read or function as critical thinkers?"

> "What do you think accounts for the changes you see? Where is the breakdown in our system?"

> "Can you, as a teacher, be held responsible for any deterioration of standardized test scores?"

Our students rarely ask such direct questions. For example, several of our students, tired of hearing how unprepared they were, decided to find out if students from twenty years ago were, in fact, better writers than students today. We required them to submit a list of questions before the interview and all of the following questions surfaced. The questions seemed completely off-base, and yet if questioned, the novice researchers could explain why they chose to ask these questions and not more direct ones. The logic behind the questions might not be sound in academic circles, but a form of logic was in operation.

"Why did you decide to become a teacher?" is a question designed to give the teacher's subsequent answers credibility. How can a teacher speak to the issue of students without first establishing an interest in teaching for the *right* reasons?

"Do you have your students read Shakespeare?" is a means of determining whether or not the teacher adheres to a standard curriculum or if kids are just too dumb nowadays to read Shakespeare.

"Why do you think we have proficiency tests?" seems a valid question to a novice researcher, especially if he wants to give the teacher an opportunity to open up the discussion rather than putting words in the teacher's mouth.

"Should the members of the community vote for levies?" has to do with the success of education. If students were being adequately prepared to read and write, then the community would support the levies.

The students' failure to understand that these questions will not get the results intended is not a matter of stupidity; faulty logic and misconceptions about the boundaries of academic discourse may be more to blame. For our students, questions that seem rather standard in an academic inquiry can be interpreted as insulting. Our rather direct, "Are student reading and writing skills declining?" for instance, was rejected by a majority of our students because they were afraid that the question would imply that they thought there had been a decline and that the teacher was responsible for it. Reading all of this negative meaning into a rather simple question is not unusual and, in a rather admirable way, shows a concern for the feelings of others. But it doesn't push past storytelling, equated with a sort of inviolate truth, and enter into academic inquiry, which can (and often does) seem to exceed the bounds of polite conversation.

I'm not suggesting that novice writers are fragile flowers who can't survive controversy and disagreement. On their own turf, the students often engage in the sort of battles Simic describes. The academic disagreement becomes problematic when it occurs in the classroom. Novice academics need to know that argument is not necessarily bad, nor is disagreeing with someone tantamount to defying them or calling them stupid. Our students also need to understand that questions, especially those that bring out points of disagreement, can make us think about what we believe and why we believe it.

In many cases, the students' hesitancy to question their informants aggressively demonstrates the residual effects of what has traditionally been a power play between two of the subgroups in educational communities: children/students versus adults/teachers. While power issues never completely disappear—most students are still younger than their adult teachers—the balance of power has changed somewhat. Being in school by choice raises the student to a new level of interaction within the educational system—that of being an inquirer rather than a passive learner. The rules of play in academic discourse encourage disagreement; in fact, they are built upon it, and the sooner the students learn this, the better. Failure to confront can lead to failure to understand, which can result in an incomplete context for study.

Tom, for instance, wanted to know why so much of his high school English instruction consisted of doing grammar exercises: filling in blanks in workbooks and taking tests on the parts of speech. Since entering college, he had not only read Wigginton's suggestions for active learning in the classroom but also discovered from working in our classroom that he could learn a lot more about grammar from discussing his own writing than from working with other people's sentences. He had come to believe that the years of high school grammar instruction had been useless. But it seemed too abrasive to question the methods of a teacher who had been working in the classroom for twenty years, who was known as an advocate for students on many levels, and who had been kind enough to grant him an interview. Tom finally posed his question indirectly so that the teacher wouldn't have to be placed in a defensive position: "What do you think of the new idea that students don't need workbook activities?" he asked.

The teacher, who did not have the same context for the question that Tom did, assumed that Tom had fallen into the hands of some archliberal university professor who knew nothing of teaching in the real world. She launched into what can only be described as a tirade against people who neglected the basics when teaching English, implying that to neglect grammar exercises was to be guilty of malfeasance. Intimidated by this outburst, and caught between one teacher's obvious outrage and his successes with the new approach to grammar used in the college classroom, Tom went on to another question rather than risk what he perceived to be further offending questions. The conversation he might have had was cut short because he would not venture to anger the teacher further nor place her in a position that might show she was misinformed either about grammar pedagogy or the nature of his college professors.

I don't know if the interview would have had a different outcome if Tom had started his questioning in a different manner, but listening to the tape, it became obvious that he had given the teacher little to work with—a vague question, no sense of why the matter was of concern to him, and no contextual reference to situate his ideas. It did not occur to him to use his own experience to open up a conversation about alternative ways of teaching grammar. Another problem became evident as I listened to the tape: he was still the student; she was still the teacher. Her teaching style was anything but Socratic. The authority in her voice left no room for an exploratory academic discussion.

During the interview sessions, more than one student discovers that questioning the actions or objectives of an authority figure from the schools, especially teachers, can bring the interview to a swift halt. To varying degrees, the power structure that has dominated the students' educational years continues to affect their ability to cross-examine or confront. While I don't like it, I don't find it particularly surprising. Those who return to their parents' home or to a place where they were formerly students knows that only a word or two, properly intoned, will turn otherwise confident and mature adults into children. Insecure adults and children recently promoted to adult status are even easier to intimidate—they practically intimidate themselves.

Not everyone feels intimidated by their old teachers. Occasionally students, taking their new exposure to educational theory a bit far, act the role of punk kid. The first year of this project, one of my friends from the local vocational college approached me hesitantly about a second-quarter student who had requested and been granted an interview. We'd just finished reading *Horace's Compromise* and this interview was supposed to provide the student with information on the difference between vocational and liberal arts education. True to form, instead of asking that question directly, the student began the interview with the following questioning strategy:

"Have you read any of the following books—*Higher Ground, Sometimes a Shining Moment,* or *Horace's Compromise?*"

"No," replied the puzzled faculty member.

"Why not?" asked the student, hostility lurking just at the edge of her voice.

Luckily, this professor was an old hand at dealing with students and did not take offense. She recognized that something was amiss and gently led the student through the interview without crushing student spirit or ego. But she rightly sought me out to express her concern. If the student had encountered anyone other than a seasoned and compassionate veteran, the "Why not?" would have been characterized as belligerent rather than naive, and the student could have been in for a tongue-lashing of the first order. Why did the student start with such a strange question? As it turned out, the question served the same purpose as the question, "Why did you decide to become a teacher?" that I discussed earlier. The student was testing the teacher's credibility. Usually I can figure out why students ask the questions they do, but this case had me puzzled.

"Why ask if she'd read our texts?" I asked. "How would having read those books mean that she was qualified to give good answers about vocational education?"

"At first I wanted to make sure she knew what I was talking about," the student replied. "My next question was supposed to be about students like the ones in the books. But I was just stunned that she hadn't read what she was supposed to."

This student *had* attempted to create a context for her questions, but her awkwardness with interviewing had been further complicated by her lack of understanding about how college instructors plan their courses and select the material that they want to use. She thought our books were part of the same sort of general curriculum that had existed at her high school—that every college student, by extension, every college-trained teacher, had read the books that she was reading. Her question was one of genuine curiosity—how had this teacher managed to escape the assignment? Our texts, as often happens in other classes, became *The Texts* merely by their inclusion in the course. The diversity of material and points of view that encompass knowledge and thought in the academy was beyond the student's grasp, and so she seemed rude, and her question seemed more belligerent than exploratory.

Fear of offending authority figures and inappropriate confrontation are not the only reasons that interviews sometimes come to an early and unproductive halt. As we listen to the tapes, many an interesting discussion suddenly falters and ends, even when the informant seems willing to go on with the topic. When we first began reviewing tapes, we thought that most of these stunted interchanges resulted from the students' inability to pose follow-up questions; the informants generally seemed willing and even eager to discuss the issues at length. Quizzing students about what we heard on the interview tapes and encouraging them to explain their reasons for asking one question rather than another revealed another explanation for the abbreviated conversations. More than one interview proved short and nonproductive because *the students* assumed that the extended conversation would be unproductive and boring for everyone involved: their informants, their potential readers, and especially their teachers.

For example, Tami suspected that a school district's educational success could be directly connected with its wealth. To confirm her suspicions, she interviewed a vice-principal from her old school district, located in a residential neighborhood, which depended exclusively upon homes for its tax base. The surrounding districts, which she felt provided better education, were supported by several commercial tax sources. When the vice-principal started to compare his current experiences with his past experience, an expert listener could hear him warming up to the topic and (of course this is speculation based on listening to the tape) preparing to offer concrete examples of differences between poor and wealthy school district services. He paused, expecting a follow-up question to guide him, but Tami went on to a completely different question. Although taken aback, he went with her train of thought. A chance for him to make his additional comments never arose again. When asked why she did not follow up on his statements, Tami replied that it was getting late, he had talked a long time, and she was afraid that he was getting bored.

A bit puzzled at her perceptions, I thought perhaps the vice-principal had been giving body language signals that hadn't shown up on the tape.

"Did he act impatient?" I inquired. "Look at the clock frequently?"

"No," she replied, "but we'd been in there a long time."

"Were other people waiting to see him? Did he seem preoccupied with other, more important, matters?"

"No," she answered, "but he'd been talking for twenty minutes."

Far from being bored, her accommodating informant had pressured Tami to stay. He even offered more time and another interview if she wanted, but Tami couldn't imagine that anyone might want to discuss the economics of education at any length. Besides, she confided, she figured that I wouldn't really want to read all of the stuff he had to say.

"Did you find what he had to say interesting?" I asked.

"Oh, yes," she answered. "He explained a lot of things so they made sense. Like how the money's divided between school districts, and how you need big industrial complexes or malls in your district if you want to have a lot of money for buildings and services."

"Why did you think that I wouldn't want to read about it?"

Stunned for a moment, she finally answered truthfully, "I don't know. . . . I just thought it would bore you."

Practicing Interview Conversations

Overcoming these social as well as educational obstacles to gathering information requires a great deal of conversation about matters of cultural hegemony as well as matters of rhetorical strategies. Whole-class role-playing exercises and individual discussions once again provide an excellent means of changing the culturally-instilled attitudes that interfere with gathering information for the thick descriptions. The students generate a list of twelve to twenty questions, arrange them in an order that they think would be effective, and then pose them to the class and then to small peer groups.

The questions have to meet certain requirements: they have to be a mixture of open, closed, and (here their speculations come in again) possible follow-up questions. The students also have to be prepared to justify the questions. Since we can't test every student's questions as a group, we begin by asking for volunteers who are willing to risk subjecting their questions to group scrutiny. The teacher plays the role of the interviewer's informant and the students act as rather noisy and intruding observers. As the questioning proceeds, any of us can stop the action if we think the interviewer student misses an opportunity to expand upon an important issue. Any of us can ask why a certain question appears, or we can suggest a better way to phrase a question. Not only do peers tell each other why the questions might be difficult or simple to answer, they also discuss whether or not the questions seem inappropriate. The object is not ridicule, but saving face. This dry run of the interview questions nearly always leads to revision.

This kind of discussion of the phrasing of questions serves the same purpose as a search for patterns of textual error. Just as writing instructors use conversation to discover the logic behind comma misuse or spelling oddities, we use conversation as a mean of ferreting out problems in logic that interfere with verbal communication. The role-playing activities help us identify where the students will most likely run into problems with the interviews and, therefore, with the resulting papers. It also makes it obvious when students are about to overstep the bounds of polite inquiry. While we do not want our students to become remote interviewers, checking off questions and avoiding personal exchanges, we definitely do not want them on the attack. If we discover that a student has an axe to grind or a preconceived notion of how the interview "must" go, we model ways to ask questions that are indicative of a "concerned citizen" (one adult to another) rather than questions that will be perceived as those of a "punk kid" (one child to one adult).

In spite of all our preparations, students always have qualms about questioning their informants, especially before they venture out for the first time.

"What do I say if I really disagree with someone?" they ask. "How do I tell them they're full of it without making them mad?"

We once again do a bit of social-consciousness raising beginning with reality testing.

"What are you afraid of?" we ask. "Disagreeing with your informant won't hurt your grade or earn you an afternoon in detention."

No, they admit. But they might hurt the informant's feelings or appear to be rude. After all, the informant's the expert; as researchers, the students are still just students.

First, we talk about etiquette in general: being rude involves *how* you say something as often as it involves *what* you say. To question educational practice under specific conditions doesn't necessarily imply right or wrong. A question can be just a question. Negative remarks about someone's profession don't have to be couched in terms that hold that person responsible for all negative educational practices in the entire United States. We recommend that they use information from the books that they have read in our classes to ask intelligent questions.

It's characteristic of most students, but especially of novice researchers, that they never think of prefacing their questions with quotations from the books and articles they have read. It's also characteristic that they don't realize that this rhetorical shift from asking about personal practice (storytelling) to asking about theories (discourse narratives) will often diffuse the personal nature of questions. We point out that there is a world of difference between Tom's problem question: "Why did we have to do so many worthless grammar worksheets in your class?" and the following one, "Mike Rose has suggested that getting remedial students to do extended writing pieces rather than concentrating on grammar worksheets will help them to see the necessity for correct grammar. They want to be clear and informative, so they learn the rules they need. What do you think? Why do you feel grammar exercises are so important?"

Okay, yet another confession. I'm not always completely concerned with being nice. My colleagues and I ask our students to explore their world in both indirect and direct manners. Take the matter of their educations. Indirectly, the reading and discussion in our classrooms serve to demystify the educational process. We reveal to the students what we know about how decisions are made about curricula, how much control individual teachers do (or don't) have over the subjects they teach, and how local interest groups may or may not influence educational practices. We don't deliver information to be swallowed whole. I've been known to rabble-rouse in order to get students to ask the hard questions.

"Listen," I announce. "Most of you had twelve years of training in a carefully thought-out curriculum, and you still ended up in remedial [I call it like it is] English in college. Half of you have children who will go through the same system. You pay taxes to finance the schools. You've got a right to question the way you were educated!" This appeal to the pocketbook/power-of-the-people argument usually works to get them started.

Even I can't escape my upbringing, however. Gilligan's theories apply to me—concern for the feelings and rights of others causes me to temper my call to action, and I caution them about the limits of their rights: while entitled to information, they aren't guaranteed the right to badger anyone. They're not investigative reporters— muckraking or ferreting out the "truth about education." They're researchers, who seek multiple answers to complex questions. It's not their job to reform or condemn their informants.

From Conversation to Written Text

Transcribing the Interviews

Although I do sometimes think of tape recorders as inventions of either the devil or a vengeful god, taping the interviews and transcribing them leads to a great deal of discovery on the students' part that I would not do without.[3] What students learn from listening to their own conversations and converting those conversations into material for study makes up for all the tape recorders that quit in the middle of the interview and all the conversations reduced to scratchy mumbling. Transcribing recorded conversations, a week-long process in the first quarter, gives us the chance to work one-on-one with the students on specific language problems—both written and oral; moreover, the interpretation of the interview data requires that students pay close attention not only to what was said but also to what was meant.[4]

Equally important in the transcription exercise is the revelation that important differences exist between spoken language and the novice researcher's concept of written language. I'm not referring to the usual sophisticated distinctions between written and spoken language found in the composition literature. The discoveries our students make concern far more basic concepts: the actual number of words it takes to transcribe a lengthy conversation, the amount of text needed to explain an idea thoroughly, and the verbal intricacy involved in forming *simple* statements. Just as the students originally think that two hand-written pages of text amounts to a long essay, they think that any idea can be explained in ten minutes . . . and that any ten minutes' worth of conversation should translate into about a page of typewritten text. This belief grows from their lack of experience with written language and exploratory discourse. The conversations that their interviews bring about open up new perspectives about everything from how *much* they really say when they speak to how *effective* the brief statements they value really are. All this happens—after they get over the resentment of having to transcribe the interview.

We repeatedly hear two comments, usually posed as questions, throughout the transcription process: "How come he's so long-winded?" "She's off topic here. Do I have to put *everything* down?" The long-winded complaint is seldom justified. Being stuck at the computer for hours, listening and writing, writing and listening, gives the students a firsthand portrait of the spoken word. Transcripts often reach lengths of eight to ten pages. The class record was fifteen pages, the horrified student in tears by the time she finished the transcription. "I didn't know," she kept lamenting after the fifth page. "I didn't know he said so much!"

Fortunately, by the time they transcribe their interviews and watch their classmates go through an equally frustrating process, they realize, at some level, that the informant was neither rambling nor unnecessarily verbose. Their complaints merely mark their first perceptions of how many *words* complex explanations require. This realization transfers to their own writing. They begin to see that ideas, especially when they're theories of learning, can't be dashed off in a few sentences.

Transcribing the interviews also gives students a chance to hear how they express themselves. And it isn't always a welcome revelation. One of the painful aspects of this interview can be the groping about for language in which to ask questions. Hearing themselves stumble (despite their preprepared questions) makes some students angry and others defensive. But that's nothing compared to the pain others feel when they realize, by virtue of hindsight, that the questions they ask don't elicit the answers that they expect. That they all groan when listening to tapes reveals that they have to restate their questions in order for the correspondent to understand what they mean.

Analyzing the Class Book

A single interview on an isolated subject will not necessarily broaden the students' senses of either the academic or nonacademic community. The supporting material will be not only limited but also skewed. This is not a problem exclusive to the writing class alone. One of the problems with ethnographies in general, points out Paul Diesing, is that they tend to have limited perspectives—one ethnographer can see only one version of experience even if he or she interviews and collects data from multiple sources. The answer, of course, is multiple observers. After all, Diesing reminds us, ethnography should be a team method, with enough observers to locate in each of the main roles of the community . . . [the single ethnographer] can cultivate informants from other locations, or shift one's location slightly. However, both of these strategies take a long time, and multiple observers can provide multiple focus pictures in a much shorter time. (5)

The next step in the student research could perhaps be called comparative studies—since they compare the results of their research to the results of the other students as a system of triangulation and general information gathering. We have two steps in this process: Students prepare abstracts of their interview data, complete with relevant material about the person interviewed, the questions the students are interested in exploring, and some key ideas that might be helpful to others. Then they write up their observation notes so that they are in a coherent essay form and attach it to a clean copy of their corrected transcripts. We duplicate the information so that it forms the sort of class booklet described in *Facts, Artifacts, and Counterfacts.*

Each class book will typically consist of forty-five to fifty single-spaced pages. Since we usually run at least two and sometimes three sections of 052 or 053 each quarter, this can amount to a lot of reading for the students and a huge photocopying bill. Producing the book also amounts to a great deal of work for the instructor—*someone* has to copy and collate all those individual interviews. The first year we went all out: We made enough copies so that each student could have a copy of each section's class book. Our administration suggested—in a kindly manner—that we find a way to conserve paper. Subsequently, we have resorted to preparing seven class books from each course section. One set stays on reserve in the library and the rest are used in class. Since we have only fifteen students in each class, all twenty-one copies keep everybody reading.

As they read, the students begin processing the information that they find. Instead of creating a theory of change from individual stories told in the literature and in the essays of their peers, our students must sort out a series of statements about practices, theories, and beliefs, and come up with an explanation for the ideas they see common to the interviews. The material consists of far less "storytelling" than their previous encounters with peer-generated texts. Our novice researchers have, in other words, a considerable collection of data from which to create a thick description.

The students take notes on individual interviews and list those that seem particularly related to their own research topics. While ex-

amining education, we discuss patterns that appear in the interviews—categorizing teachers, discourse, methods, and anything else
the students find relevant. Then we ask them to give us an impression, based on the interviews and their own experiences, of education
in central Ohio. What can they say is characteristic of the educational
process? What can they say is similar or different between the education they have received in central Ohio and the education offered at
HCI in Maine and at Rabun Gap in Georgia? The process works the
same when we explore other topics.

Reading the class books together has several advantages in creating a rich discussion. The topics of conversation range from comments about the findings to remarks about the discourse strategies
of the informants. Nearly all of the students begin to recognize
where the failure to be articulate begins. Students who rely heavily
on the "You know what I mean?" strategy of expressing themselves—hoping the informant will fill in the blanks so that everyone
will know—can hear on the tape, and then see on paper, how inef-
fectual their discourse is. As one student said, "My whole conversation was a guessing game—I'd say, 'You know?' and she'd say, 'Do
you mean?' until we got it all out, sort of. It's pretty lame."

As they compare interview transcriptions, students also begin
to notice differences in their informants' discourse strategies; this
proves especially enlightening when they talk with teachers and
then begin to compare notes. The categories remain fairly stable:
one group of informants always answers questions with questions;
another type essentially lectures—not letting the students get a
word in edgewise; and still another group just sits and waits for a
question, answers it briefly and waits for the next question. Some of
their informants act as storytellers—every lesson embedded in a
anecdote; some constantly make points by referring to information
they read or saw on television. The *how* of the interviews—how the
informants express themselves, how they treat the students, and
how well they defend various educational practices—becomes one
of the most controversial topics of conversation.

Interpreting Interview Data

Students have different levels of ability when it comes to making
use of the data from their interviews. While they seldom misunderstand the comments the teachers make, they frequently fail to understand how the data from the interview can be used in a paper—
especially when the comments don't seem to support the biases
they harbor. We find that we must teach them to analyze remarks in

more than one fashion, to change a thesis rather than reject evidence that does not support it, and sometimes to go back to the informant for more information. Simply reading the results of a transcript will not yield enough information for us to be really helpful to the students. Therefore, we read the transcripts while listening to the tapes. This process, which might at first seem to be an additional burden to the grading and responding labors of the teachers, actually moves much faster than reading the transcripts *without* listening to the tapes. The teachers don't have to guess at what's being said and the strangeness of punctuation and spelling disappear as the teachers hear what they're supposed to be reading.

Reading the transcriptions against the tapes has other advantages also. Following the transcript as we listen allows us to pick up nuances of speech that the students miss and therefore misinterpret. Some students demonstrate a complete lack of awareness about irony, for instance, and, therefore, take an ironic statement at face value. More than once, listening to the tape helped clear up a "mystery" statement, one completely out of character or context, that the student attributed to a teacher. In addition to helping us understand the text the student has created out of the interview, we also discover something about what the student thinks constitutes important or relevant information. Invariably, we discover that they find it convenient to leave out what they deem to be "unnecessary" information.

With careful analysis and interpretation of these seemingly irrelevant comments, the students can develop the content of their essays. This fact never ceases to amaze them. Kevin, for instance, interviewed his coach about the relationship of sports to learning. Like many of our students, he believed students learn more on the football field (or in other extracurricula activities) than in the classroom. Reading the interview as Kevin transcribed it made his informant sound like a stereotypical coach, one who lauded *teamwork* and who taught his students that sports were more important than the academic curriculum. When I listened to the interview, however, I discovered the coach had given a number of excellent explanations of how teamwork could translate into collaborative efforts in academic classrooms and that his praise of sports was qualified rather than glorified. He even gave Kevin a hard time about neglecting his studies for sports. Kevin's transcription had done the coach an injustice even though it had reinforced Kevin's rather limited perspective of what sports should do. There was intellectual dishonesty going on as well as laziness.

Dishonesty and laziness, however, are not the primary cause of student misinterpretation of data. Often we have to help discouraged students find meaning in an interview that did not go the way they expected. Usually this type of disappointment occurs when students think they have "the answer" before they go to the interview. Their original speculations didn't work out; the informant doesn't readily agree with them. Generally this comes as a great disappointment as well as an immense surprise. One particular case comes to mind: Doug, who interviewed a principal expecting to find backup for his contention that athletes received special attention.

Doug had been a star football player at a local high school, and he wanted to write a paper that would show that granting special favors to athletes in order to keep them on teams affected their learning in the classroom. He'd been excused from class to attend practice, given passing grades that he knew he didn't deserve, and generally given every reason to believe that he would do well in college. But after his college orientation placement exams, he found himself in both remedial math and remedial English. Doug was anything but dumb, and he wanted to know why he suddenly wasn't as smart as his high school teachers had assured him he was.

After being in college for a few weeks, talking to teachers and fellow students, and reading the books for our class, he decided that he was underprepared for college because he was a successful jock. Teachers cared more about keeping him happy and on the football field than teaching him to understand the subjects he was having trouble with. Deciding that teachers wouldn't give him a straight answer about these practices, he decided to go straight to the top— he'd interview the principal who constantly reminded students that *academics* came first. Much to his amazement, the principal didn't see the teachers' actions as a problem; the principal became almost hostile in his denial of favoritism.

Doug wasn't quite sure what to do with his interview. At first he decided to go out and seek evidence to prove that the principal was wrong—he was building up to a personal battle. It took a number of group and private conferences to convince him that proving the principal wrong would be a waste of time and that there were ways of using the information he had to his advantage. Doug had presented the principal with a number of very specific examples that the principal recognized as current practice. The principal's denial that these practices constituted a problem only reinforced Doug's claim that the school didn't realize how harmful rather than helpful "giving the athletes a break" could be. Doug was right, but he had to learn how to use the results of his interview to argue his point rather than to fight with authority in an "I got ya" manner. He also had to learn a bit about human egos. As he said in his paper, it was naive to think that the principal would side with him: the principal's belief in the teachers and the school and his own personal sense of integrity would not let him admit that actions he knew about and condoned would interfere with student education.

Doug's responses to his interview and to his informant were not unusual, and, as frustrating as the process was, making meaning from data from multiple interviews presented an almost perfect opportunity to broaden the students' ability to see events in context. Creating a thick description from all the interviews, grappling with ways to use pieces of it to make a point, moves students from the rather narrow perspective of life held by the uninformed into a wider perspective that looks at events and people as participants in a constructed community.

Constructing an Essay from Thick Description

By the seventh week of their first quarter, the students have read at least one book, decided upon a topic that their reading has prompted interest in, chosen an informant, created questions for the interview, conducted the interview, and transcribed it. (All this during ten weeks. Oh, what we could do with a semester!) They have also, as part of the process of writing, written up observation notes that include a description of the informant and the conditions under which the interview took place. This collection of written material (the essence of thick description), together with the group discussions and reading of the class books and the texts, has formed a general context for writing an informed paper. But the work of getting elements of this thick description into the student papers, of connecting the journal entries with the in-class writing, with the interviews, with the academic texts, has just begun. The students have many layers of research data, but they tend to view what they have collected as discrete bits of information rather than as part of a whole.

As they learn to process and analyze the data collected from the community, the students' "It's not like that here" comments begin to have some validity because they become very specific as to the designation of the terms *it* and *here*. An individual student's experience may not be "like" that of another. However, through reading the various accounts of the student's peers, the student's individual experience becomes part of an overall experience. Total confusion results—but only temporarily. Now the students are ready to write their versions of experience in context—the grappling with diverse and divergent views of how "here" is has begun the process of analysis: what doesn't fit, why doesn't it fit, how can it be connected with other bits of information—especially bits that seemingly disagree with the premise that the student wants supported?

At the end of the first quarter, using the material they have gathered as a class, the students start to write their first draft of the last essay and discover that writing about their personal experiences, which at the beginning of the quarter they thought of as difficult, seems a rather easy and uncomplicated activity. That essay occupied only about two weeks of their time. No outside sources were required. Even though, as teachers, we would take issue with their conclusions and force them to be more specific about "why," "how," and "what," the final conclusions couldn't be disputed. The students' perceptions controlled the *truth* of the matter because they alone knew what really happened. These new essays called for manipulation of much more complicated (though not necessarily more objective) data.

The final essay assignment is purposely open. While studying high school education it looked like this:

> By now you have probably read and written more about education than you thought was possible, much less desirable. This last essay assignment asks you to make some coherent sense out of your reading and writing. Pick some aspect of your reading and writing (any and all of the material we wrote or read in class) and write an essay that expresses your concern over that matter. Here are a few examples:
> 1. The conflict between social and academic life
> 2. The importance of good teachers
> 3. The relevancy of what we learn in high school to daily life
> 4. The ways that high school prepares people to work in the outside world
>
> These are only examples; you need to develop a topic that addresses matters that truly concern you. Once you have decided upon your topic, use your class book, *Sometimes a Shining Moment* and *Higher Ground* to prove your point. We will talk about developing evidence from sources as we draft the essay.

They begin working on this more complex essay by reviewing their original tentative thesis and deciding whether or not it applies anymore. The next step becomes adjusting their premises to better represent their interpretation of the data. This very process is illuminating and hard. The writing task far exceeds the type of research they've done before. Remember the high school essay on cheese: "Cheese Is an Excellent Substitute for Meat"? No one doubted that premise in the first place, and the proof the student had to produce was informational. He didn't have to sort out the implications and consequences of switching a community from a diet of birds and mammal flesh to one of cheddar and Jarlsberg Swiss. The student didn't even have to work out the various complexities that separate Velveeta from ripened and aged cheeses.

The difficulty involved in the cheese paper varies considerably from the difficulty involved in proving the following premise: "Students in wealthier schools receive a better education than students in poorer schools." This paper topic, which appeared in the first year of the class, might serve as a typical example. Mike and Tami (who worked on the essay collaboratively) discussed not only their original feelings but what they learned as they gathered information:

> As we wrote this essay, we tended to use our personal beliefs more than anything. We felt we could have gotten a better education at a wealthier school. . . . I guess we learned that it is just not the school but where you live and the influence your family has on you. . . . Wealthy schools have everything they need to give a student a better education. We think the biggest factors were, class room size, student teacher ratio, better teachers, and new materials.

It is an understatement to say that they relied on their "personal beliefs." To our shock, the first draft of the essay consisted almost completely of complaints about a lack of bleachers for the football games, extracurricular activities that had been cancelled, and, almost as a side thought, lack of "materials." Where was the insight we thought they'd almost naturally absorb from the research, the reading, and the class discussion? Mike and Tami were not the exception to the rule. Despite our hopes for essays full of insightful analysis, most of the students ignored the thick description when they began to write and went back to surface-level detail. The information gathered from the interviews and the reading disappeared. Rather than fight this return to the obvious, we decided to exploit it. We had already planned to have the students write at least three drafts of papers, and we expected to see substantial difference in the content and development of each draft. Since the students obviously didn't automatically know what needed to be done, we structured the next two drafts so that they had to include more analysis. In Mike and Tami's case, the first draft told us *what* seemed to be the problem. We asked them to show us in the second draft *why* these outward signs of a poor district constituted a problem. When they finished the second draft, we insisted that the third draft address *how* their school came to be poor.

In the "What-went-wrong-here" analysis that we do every time an assignment doesn't accomplish what we had hoped, we decided that our expectations for these novice writers were unrealistic. How could they know exactly what we wanted without practicing the new skills? Telling them wasn't enough. Fortunately, this insight on our part led to a more reasonable approach. Although tempted to formulate and announce in advance all the "steps" we would require in drafts *before* the students began writing, we resisted, asking instead for changes *while* the students worked.

Building the essay bit by bit has several advantages. Breaking down the process of constructing an argument (in the broadest sense of the term) by reconstructing original drafts models the thinking process. In the first draft, the students identify a phenomenon, then attempt to explain (depending on the final task) how and why it exists. As the second and third drafts develop, we show them how to integrate the material they have collected into the argument. We also ask them to search for new or missing information, pose questions that will send them back to the data, question their assumptions and the assumptions of their sources. For example, in order to explain why the physical appearance of the school was so discouraging, Mike went back to his interview and discovered a section where the teacher discussed the visible deterioration of morale that took place in the community after a tax levee failed. Tami interviewed her informant again to learn more about the manner in which overcrowded classrooms affected a student's chance of learning. During this second interview, she discovered that Ohio had a senate bill that would allow students to transfer to better school districts, carrying along with them their tax dollars. After discussing some of the ramifications of the bill with other enthusiastic informants, she and Mike decided that this bill might solve some of the problems poorer districts faced. If students didn't like their district they could transfer to one with better facilities. "Does that mean that poor districts would become even poorer as they lose students?" we queried. They had to go back to rethink this solution to their problems.

Workshops and Conferencing

This sort of confrontational pedagogy works only under workshop conditions. Unless we spend a good deal of time in individual and group conference, the students don't take advantage of the material they collected. Reworking drafts helps emphasize not only that drafts can be fertile ground for working out ideas but also that no exploration of a topic is ever complete. We try to instill in them the wisdom of the writer who said, "You don't finish a work; you abandon it." Of course, they want to abandon the work much sooner than we're willing to find it on our doorsteps. Therefore, we keep refusing to accept the writing until it can stand on its own, without being explained or excused verbally.

Our refusal to accept papers full of garbled and undeveloped ideas frustrates the students. They argue, quite sincerely, that we *know* what they mean, and to a certain extent, they're right. As readers who have talked to them in class, conferenced about everything from descriptive detail to overall organization, we *do* understand what their essays hint at. Our knowledge is particular and associated with the fact that we are acquainted with them as students and as people rather than merely as writers.

The students are not altogether naive in taking this position. Teachers have often been their only readers; they seldom have written for an audience who did not know them and who would not credit them with knowing and understanding more than they have actually said on paper. Their teachers probably considered themselves to be generous readers, readers who help make up for writing deficiencies. In reality, these forgiving practices encourage sloppy and incomplete writing and thinking. In order to counteract the years of generous readers, we play the role of the slightly skeptical reader who has not had the students in class, who insists upon questioning everything, and who, in general, throws monkey wrenches into their arguments.

This one-to-one or small-group endeavor, less adversarial and more advisory, leads to what students come to refer to as "ripping apart" the essay, an activity they come to joke about rather than dread. The conferences follow the general pattern that teacher/ student and peer conferences take. We read, ask questions, show each other where new description can be added or a claim validated. Sometimes we use guidelines for feedback; sometimes we merely play the believing and doubting game. But one thing never changes, even the weakest of peer editors can find something to ask for in the manner of clarification. As teachers, we find scads of places where we want more information.

At first, shocked that peers and teachers can find so many things to talk about and so many questions to answer, novice writers teeter on the brink of being overwhelmed. By the second quarter, however, the questioning of assertions, the push for further explanations become almost secondhand. They discover that a series of unexamined statements, incorporated piecemeal into their writing, will not create a lucid document; the statements have to make sense as part of a whole. From the far corner of the room, we'll hear one group member say to another: "I'd buy it, but Marcia won't. She'll want to know." "What you're saying sounds like Sizer. Where's that section on teachers?"

Issues other than content come up in an atmosphere where students share data. The technical end of writing presents new problems and issues. How does one quote properly? When does one quote and when does one paraphrase? Is it okay to use material from someone else's interview? How do you reference interviews? If you want to contrast the statement of one person against the statements of another, how do you make it clear who's speaking? When do you do block quotations? How do you make sure the audience sees the relationship between the comments made in the interview and the comments you're making now? Such matters can be, as the King of Siam would say, "a puzzlement."

The results of this first-quarter enterprise are still somewhat stilted and flawed pieces of discourse. But they are *conscious* pieces of discourse in most cases because the students are not only studying an academic topic, they are studying their own experiences. Since we have another quarter to practice the skills they learned in the first half of the sequence, I do not worry about the faults of these early papers. Once they find a critical voice and a means of arguing with evidence, they start to make observations on every aspect of writing for college, figuring out what their current teachers want, why they want it, and how to give it to them. And gradually we start to get reports about successes in their other classes: competent and impressive observations made in class, papers with A across the top, praise for being insightful. And while I would hesitate to claim that everyone gains great respect for the academy, the students at least no longer feel at the mercy of people whose expectations they do not understand.

Chapter Six

The Horror, The Horror
Assessment and Grading

Face it: if our goal is to get students to exercise their own judgment, that means exercising an immature and undeveloped judgment and making choices that are obviously wrong to us.

—Peter Elbow
"Ranking, Evaluating, and Liking:
Sorting Out Three Forms of Judgment"

If the process takes up most of the semester, and the products are few, teachers must grade the process itself. What the norm is for evaluating process, we don't know, but it looks as though it would be moral rather than intellectual.

—Marie Ponsot and Rosemary Deem
Beat Not the Poor Desk

Testing and grading sometimes seem to be at the heart of composition darkness, buried under a rather general desire, as Mina Shaughnessy suggested, to "bring culture to the natives." Teachers somehow find themselves placed in the position of judging whether or not the natives learned their lessons and must assign a grade that indicates how well the natives learned. Because most English teachers (and I suspect other types of teachers) would rather teach students than fit them on to a bell-shaped curve, grading tends to be a most distasteful and somewhat problematic task. Cherryl Armstrong-Smith sums it up for me:

> At the end of the semester, when I review portfolios of selected papers from students in my writing and literature courses, I usually feel that my system of assessment is fair; yet when I assign the grades I feel sick at heart. It seems almost embarrassing, after the work of the course and the spirit of inquiry and collaboration, to end the semester on what always feels to me an awkward note, a note that may be necessary, but is beside the point for everyone, a duty like paying taxes, or sending overdue thank-you cards. (279)

In theory, grading should be easy. We should know an *A* from an *F,* good writing from bad, shouldn't we? And shouldn't we feel comfortable assigning those grades? Our education and experience as teachers and readers surely qualify us to make simple judgments on undergraduate papers. Behind those judgments rests our training, the same training that allows us to think of ourselves as critics capable of making competent judgments about the works of every canonical writer from Geoffrey Chaucer to Toni Morrison. Nonetheless, grading and evaluating student work haunts the end of the quarter (and places in between) for all but the most stone-hearted or numerically fixated of composition teachers.

Assessing those students that I call *novice* writers, that others call *basic* writers, and that still others call *developmental* writers, can be particularly problematic. Most of these students have made their way to college despite their obviously poor writing skills, and they need inspiration as well as instruction if they're going to remain in college. As we teach, we ask the following questions: How do we fairly test students we know are going to fail (placement, midterms, finals, proficiency exams)? How can we fail them and still encourage them to stay in school? How do we grade students whose thoughts are compromised by the way they express themselves? Perhaps there are more important questions to ask:

- Why do we feel compelled to test and grade these students?
- What are we measuring?
- What does it mean to them and to us when the assessment process is over?

If I had to answer these "important questions" off the top of my head, I guess I'd answer the first two in the following way:

- I test and grade my students because my university requires me to test my students.

- In my class, both tests and grades measure progress toward mature writing habits and individual endeavor as much as overall competence and improvement of skills.

That's my immediate and wildly general answer; the contemplative one will follow. I can't answer the third question by myself, obviously. I can only guess what the grades for tests and for classroom performance mean to my students. Sometimes I have what one might call "really strong indications" of what these marks mean to students: notes of thanks, phone calls of outrage, smiles in the halls, frowns at a distance.

As I've indicated, I feel much as Armstrong-Smith and others feel about final grades in the composition classroom. Uncomfortable. Not myself. I suddenly become the good witch or the bad witch—depending on which end of the grading spectrum the student falls on—dispensing rewards or punishment as if such an action really made the students' efforts visible for the world to see. Such a one-sided balance of power defeats the main purpose of my teaching. When the assessment is done, I want the students to feel that they learned something about writing and themselves as writers, not that they've been given compensation for giving me what *I* want.

Judgment, Learning, and Grading

Types of Judgment

Assessment in the composition classroom usually falls under two judgment tasks—testing and grading—which generally involve either ranking, evaluating, or a combination of both activities. How teachers handle these judgment calls reflects their theories of student learning and is manifest in their assessment practices. I use the terms ranking and evaluating as Peter Elbow defines them in "Ranking, Evaluating, and Liking: Sorting Out Three Forms of Judgment." *Ranking* student performance means "summing up one's judgment of a performance or person into a single, holistic number or score. . . . Ranking implies a single scale or continuum or dimension along which all performances are hung" (187). Ranking occurs most obviously at the end of a project, a course, or after a test. When teachers apply that final *B* or *D*, or even the more ambiguous *S* or *U*, they rank student writing, and, sometimes, the students. Where a student writer appears on the ranking scale depends upon context—who is testing whom for what. And while ranking procedures, especially those in large-scale testing, may seem to be objective, any ranking scale grows from a set of criteria that reflects the subjective values of the person or people who create the test.

Evaluating, Elbow argues, implies "the act of expressing one's judgment of a performance or person by pointing out the strengths and weaknesses of different features or dimensions. . . . Evaluation goes *beyond* a first response that may be nothing but a kind of ranking . . . and instead look[s] carefully at the performance or person to make distinctions between parts or features or criteria" (188). Evaluation occurs before, during, and between writing tasks and can vary in form from written comments on a paper to workshop conferences. Students can evaluate—and should evaluate—as well as teachers. Evaluation, while no less subjective than ranking, can open conversation between students or between other students and teachers about writing; it offers an opportunity to make suggestions rather than pronouncements—discuss the relationship between strengths and weaknesses rather than just point them out. Because of its ongoing interaction between writer, text, and readers, evaluating makes more sense in teaching than ranking. When inspired by a genuine desire to help, evaluating can be far more productive to learning and far less devastating to egos than mere ranking.

Elbow adds a third judgment task that affects teaching and learning—*liking.* Good teachers, he argues, genuinely like student writing and serve as "readers" of student work, not just as evaluators. A living, breathing, nonobjective reader serves a definite purpose in assessing writing. Friendly readers, Elbow maintains, encourage good writing:

> The way writers *learn* to like their writing is by the grace of having a reader or two who likes it—even though it's not good. Having at least a few appreciative readers is probably indispensable to getting better. (200)

Certainly, saying "I like it" or "I hate it" has dramatic results in a writing class. Students listen much more carefully to these emotional responses than to our carefully worded neutral ones. Reacting to a piece of writing as a reader builds trust in the novice (or expert) writer—as long as the emotional reaction isn't purposefully derogatory. Saying "I really hate this idea because . . ." and discussing the problems of varying worldviews and experiences can be helpful to students and teachers alike. Saying, "This is a stupid (dumb, ridiculous, obnoxious, insufferable) idea," is quite another matter. The first opens discussion without implying a complete failure of student knowledge or integrity; it invites the student and teacher to articulate difference, to discuss whys and wherefores. The second pronounces complete judgment of the ideas in the student writing.

Such pronouncements close conversation; the student is on the defensive because the teacher has already passed judgment on the student's ability, ideas, and, often, virtue. There is a narrow tightrope to walk, but one worth balancing on. Most of the time we *do* like what we read.

Another type of judgment affects the grades we eventually assign to student work, a type of judgment hard to define because it's based on what Ponsot and Deem would term moral rather than intellectual judgments (3). Most of the time, these moral judgments translate into grading criteria as "participation," "effort," or "preparation." Whatever we call this "fudge factor," we can't escape the fact that our opinion of the students' performance can be affected by our opinion of the students' behaviors and involvement with the class. Like it or not, these moral judgments often slip in and start operating when we must evaluate those we teach. In extreme cases, the assigning of a grade starts sounding like evaluating students' worth as human beings rather than as writers. The most serious personal "faults" that find their way into grading schemes might be summed up as the following: missing deadlines, not "living up to potential," and not spending enough time on revision. The students' virtues come into play also: working exceptionally hard, opening themselves to new ideas, and always meeting assignment deadlines.

On occasion, these moral judgments make assigning that final grade to a paper easy: students don't turn in or revise drafts, meet deadlines, or respond directly to the assignment. The students' behaviors and *intentions* (as we may see them) make it easy to fill in an *F* or *D* bubble on the grade sheets. If we think students don't try hard enough, it's easier to convince ourselves that they deserve to fail—or at least to be given a B+ instead of an A. On the other hand, such moral judgments can make grading incredibly difficult when the teacher must assess conscientiously prepared but nonetheless borderline writing. The students who turn in this sort of work try hard—turning out twice as many drafts, handing in papers early, seeking extra conferences in an attempt to make their writing "better." There's little question that they warrant special consideration. BUT—sometimes, despite the effort, the writing remains below the institution's standards for competency. Never mind that the student may have to contend with interference from learning disabilities, family problems, and years of undereducation. The paper is bad under any criteria applied to it. Under traditional assessment procedures, the teacher is left with two impossible choices, both of which can have negative consequences.

Failing skills-deficient students discourage them immensely (to state the obvious), especially when they have worked diligently.

But to pass them is no favor, either. If they choose to stay in the academy, they must go on to write in freshman composition, in the classes of professors in other disciplines, and for future employers. "Social passing" hardworking students with obvious flaws in their writing is giving them a gift; we know it and, most of the time, they know it. The ones who realize that they've been given a gift will continue to worry about whether or not they actually improved. The ones who do not realize the limits of their skills will develop a false sense of their writing abilities.

In addition to worrying about how prepared students might be for the next level of writing, teachers have to worry about other consequences of grading. A lot of things depend upon that final grade. Chief among these outside influences are the financial implications inherent in being placed and perhaps retained in a so-called *remedial* course. Remedial courses often do not count toward graduation, but they certainly cost as much. Additionally, being placed in remedial courses can mean students must postpone graduating as much as an additional year. More rides upon the grade than the abstract future of the English language, and although most teachers are more committed to the students than to the retention of the past-perfect tense (being a gatekeeper disagrees with the imperative to educate), this commitment doesn't make grading any easier.

The solution may not be to stop grading according to various hidden agenda, but to acknowledge, defend, and be consistent about them. These nonwriting elements affect writing assessment. There's no escaping it. Receiving a hastily written and ill-conceived paper affects my judgment of both student and ideas. In fact, writerly negligence sways my appraisal of a student's work as surely as misspelled words and sentence fragments govern others' judgments. Why not simply acknowledge these prejudices to the students? Why not teach them coping strategies, not only for my course but for other courses as well? It's not enough to alert students to the idiosyncrasies of teachers or to simply evaluate the reasons students fail to perform. Equally important is a self-evaluation of grading practices and a constant recognition that the type of assessment measures that I apply to student writing must take into account interferences in the learning process.

Types of Learning

But to back-track a bit. Perhaps the most important point of Elbow's article is not the definition of types of judgment, but the reminder that assessment is inexorably locked into current theories of learning that inform current teaching practice. Teachers are nearly always required to rank (though not always required to evaluate) the students who take their classes. What teachers decide to test reflects their teaching objectives and affects what their students learn. Here, then, are two versions of how students learn that inform current theories of assessment.

Developmentally based learning. Many teachers believe that learning occurs in a developmentally anticipated sequence, one that is orderly, predictable, and controllable. Many of our current models of writing assessment also assume that students will move, step by step, from being novice writers to being expert writers. One almost gets the impression that writing follows a natural order similar to the one we imagine controls the development of children: children should crawl, toddle, walk, and finally run. Writers should move from simple to more difficult tasks: mastering words, then sentences, paragraphs, and finally whole essays. Growth, an interior process, can be interrupted or accelerated by virtue of talent, interest, environment, and parent/teacher/peer influence. This is only a partial list. However, the process by which the writer develops remains fairly consistent. This orderly vision of the learning process allows for continual and progressive testing of what student writers have learned.

To meet demands for responsibility in teaching, proponents of developmental models have developed innumerable versions of proficiency tests, which vary only according to the tester's view of what writing tasks students should be developmentally able to perform. Students in the ninth grade, for example, supposedly can write "coherent paragraphs" (whatever those are—in the real world they vary according to genre and artistic inclination). If ninth graders can write carefully constructed paragraphs (complete with topic sentences), they have proved themselves competent at their developmental level, and subsequently, they will be passed on to a "higher" writing task—the five-paragraph essay. During their high school years, students find themselves subjected to massive state and national testing, that supposedly will determine whether students can produce these supposedly more developmentally difficult essays. Even in college, they do not escape. Many universities have constructed exit exams that test a variety of developmentally defined writing skills: critical thinking, organizational competence, discourse styles. And so it continues, far beyond the freshman year. Many schools now push undergraduate assessment to its final frontier, requiring a "culminating experience" test that certifies that juniors and seniors—future teachers and accountants alike—can think and write professionally even before they are active in their professions.

Even if students avoid schools that place undue emphasis on testing, grading systems may reinforce the same developmental sequence. What does an *A* mean, in most cases, other than that an *A* student has developmentally progressed far beyond a *C* student? To apply my "children's-progress-toward-running-proficiency" analogy, this sort of testing and grading—which is ultimately based on ranking—implies that knowledge has clear-cut milestones with predictable and identifiable final goals: walking and running well. It also implies that educated people abandon all but walking and running as they mature into knowledgeable adults.[1]

Unpredictable Learning

I support another model of learning with very different premises and very different levels of expectations, which naturally requires a different kind of assessment. Just as no one can really predict exactly when a child will move from one level of locomotion to another, it's impossible to predict the rate at which their writing skills will develop. We should abandon the "children's-progress-toward-running-proficiency" model of learning and adapt a "children-learning-to-move-appropriately" model. In this learning model, some children sit and watch while others crawl, toddle, and so forth—then, after a year or two of engaging in various forms of locomotion, all the children will be able to perform whatever locomotion task they happen to need—they will know when to walk, when to run, and when, if necessary, to revert to crawling.

Most writers develop irrationally and erratically. For every writer who finds the linear process from outline to finished product a comfortable way to create an essay, there are four or five students for whom the process is irregular. These novice writers learn paragraph structure *after* they've written whole essays, come to grips with sentence structure *because* they have something complex and slightly wonderful to say, and master grammar and usage at age thirty-two, when threatened with the loss of a job. Such unpredictable learning patterns cannot be measured easily because what the writers learn is often obscured by the unevenness of achievements. One student may make great leaps and bounds in descriptive writing, creating characters that both please and delight. Yet the beauty of the description may be buried under the misspelled words and the effort it takes to ignore punctuation mistakes. Another student may spell carefully and create correct but rather simple sentences yet be completely unable to explain how an event has shaped her life. And as I have been arguing all through this book, many students may be able to break down and work through the issues in a problematic conflict during class discussion, yet only produce a short, stunted, and undeveloped explanation in writing of what had been a rather sophisticated oral argument. A small minority simply can't keep up with their classmates; another minority sometimes willfully abandons writing convention in order to flaunt their disdain of teachers who grade for spelling and sentence-level errors.

All of these students are at different levels of writing experience, responding to different stimuli, and no series of evaluations based on development of skills will contain or describe them as writers. Testing will not measure improvement in any concrete way because, and here I quote C. H. Knoblauck and Lil Brannon, "The growth of students as writers is not the same as the improvement of texts" (151).

Assessment That Supports Instruction: Portfolios

Portfolio assessment serves my theories and practice for a number of reasons: it fits my own particular theories of learning to write better than any other form of grading I've yet encountered; it enables me to function better as a teacher and as a grader; and it allows my students greater latitude to prove themselves as writers. My beliefs about the ways students learn, combined with our class design, almost necessitates portfolio assessment. Evaluation of process rather than ranking of performance is at the center of assessment, and my students' processes are anything but linear. Working on the theory that students learn from writing in ways that may seem chaotic to us but that have rhyme and reason, the portfolio offers the students multiple writing experiences and flexible learning conditions. Having both a quantity of writing and a variety of writing permits students to demonstrate everything from their abilities to work through complex problems to their abilities to eliminate surface errors and patterns of errors. Students generally fail at the writing/reading tasks during the first weeks of class and often do not pull together the various reading and writing skills until the second half of the two-quarter sequence. However, by the end of the first quarter, and certainly by the end of the second quarter, they are handling logic, organization and general writing skills with something akin to style. I'm not even sure how they do it, so it's impossible to measure what they do—or their growth—and measuring texts isn't enough. It's necessary, perhaps, but not sufficient. To average those beginning papers in with their final papers is to ignore what they have learned and to fail to give them credit for their progress. The portfolio allows me to put off grading until the students have had a chance to pull together some of the chaos into a recognizable order.

At the Marion campus, teachers come together at the end of each quarter to read problem portfolios and to discuss assessment issues. Although we seek each other's advice, we don't always take it. We may come to agreement about a grade, but we don't necessarily come to an agreement about what we value in student writing. Since this is true, and since grading is almost as private an act as one can commit in academe—the classroom teacher holds the final responsibility for assigning student grades. However, our conversations prove invaluable because my colleagues help me put into perspective the following problems:

- I'm vulnerable to the "she tried so hard" and "she didn't try at all" syndromes.
- I want more than a final written product when I'm trying to determine if a novice writer is proficient because novice writers can be proficient in some areas while remaining less than proficient in others.
- I fear that I will send students on to freshman composition unprepared, so I want to check my grading against others.
- I just plain need support and conversation about student writing.
- I want to give the students the opportunity to succeed by making revision and self-evaluation of their writing a natural process rather than a teacher-imposed process.

I believe that portfolios present better opportunities for students to demonstrate their abilities as writers because portfolios allow a respite from grading. During this "evaluation-free zone" (Elbow, *Judging* 197) students can

- make preliminary mistakes without penalty;
- learn to integrate pieces of writing into longer and more comprehensive essays;
- learn to think of writing as a recursive activity rather than as a one-time effort;
- see how journals, freewriting, and other activities contribute to the learning, thinking, and essay-writing process;
- have a ready body of material for teacher review and conference;
- learn to evaluate their own writing;
- review their progress as writers.

A Sample Portfolio

After several quarters of experimentation, I discovered that for my purposes the following system for generating and grading portfolios works, so I intend to continue it with only minor modifications. The following is a simplified version of the process. At the beginning of the course, I hand students a course packet that contains the following:

- a course syllabus and description complete with grading scales, a working schedule of due dates, and reading assignments;
- weekly journal assignments that explore the reading assignments and provide material for the essays;
- prompts for all major essays;
- prompts for the midterm and final exams (yes, prompts for the exams—bear with me);
- a portfolio criteria sheet that explains the portfolio, the final student self-evaluation, and the grading scale for portfolios as well as instructions for preparing and turning in the final portfolio (see Figure 3).

To counteract the students' desire for a grade on everything that they write, I provide ongoing evaluation and discussion of what's good about the student writing as well as what's wrong with it. In my portfolio, I establish deadlines for journals, essays, and exams. During the quarter, I collect journals once a week and read them to see if the students can generate material in response to a text, to determine whether students are getting the point of the books they read, and to offer comments that will build a dialogue between the students and myself. I do not comment on journals in the way that I would on papers—expecting them to be changed. However, I do give each week's journals one of four possible grade indicators: checks (with +, ++, or − marks attached). This acts more as an indication that the student is doing a good job or a poor one than as a grade. The only time their journal check marks come into consideration is at the end of the quarter, when they indicate either a steady improvement of journal entries or give me an indication that students have made no attempt to improve the content of their journals.

I do not put grades on individual essays; instead, I comment extensively on the content. Acting as a reader with questions rather than a grader, my task is to evaluate the text rather than pass judgment on it. Evaluative comments vary: requests for more information, indications that a passage is particularly effective, questions about generalizations (and about particular statements), and suggestions for obtaining or integrating examples and illustrations. In other words, I make comments on strengths as well as weaknesses. At the end of the essay, I offer general comments of my own and append a list of grammar errors that seem to be part of a pattern of error.

At the end of the quarter, the student revises selected pieces of work and submits the portfolio for a final grade. The portfolio usually constitutes eighty percent of the student grade; the remaining twenty percent falls under class participation. While I make the final determination of the students' grades, I do seek help with the portfolios. The Marion campus teaching faculty has agreed to read sample portfolios at midterm and during finals weeks. Originally we had planned only to read "problem" portfolios—those that we had trouble assigning grades to—but eventually we read a wider range of portfolios and have plans next year for revising the portfolio criteria so that it fits all our classes, making it easier (at least in theory) to exchange portfolios.

But let's discuss a real portfolio so that I can bring a little concrete evidence into the discussion. (A copy of the English 053 packet can be found in the appendix.) In our second-quarter course, English 053, we read two books—*Horace's Compromise* and *Lives on the Boundary.* The students write a minimum of four journal entries a week (all of the journal entries for *Horace's Compromise* are focused entries that address and reinforce reading strategies; the students use a suggestion list to create their own journal entries on *Lives on the Boundary*). They write a total of five essays—three *miniessays* (2–3 pages) and a comprehensive essay (7–10 pages) on problems associated with *Horace's Compromise* and a discussion of their own educational experiences (4–6 pages) after reading *Lives on the Boundary.* In addition, they write two short in-class essays (2–3 pages) that serve as midterm and final exams.

There is no lack of writing here, and by the time you count revisions, the students are writing daily both in class and out of class. The three miniessays are brief and meant to focus on reading sections of Sizer's book and are due at the end of each section. The comprehensive essay, due just before midterm, grows out of those three miniessays—the student can revise and use any or all material for the comprehensive essay. Often the student does not revise all of the miniessays, but I read each one and comment upon it. I also hold individual conferences with those who have particular problems with the assignments. When a number of students have similar problems, I hold group conferences as well.

Figure 3
Requirements for the Portfolio

DUE DATE: [The day of the final exam]

TURN IN THE FOLLOWING ITEMS IN A FOLDER WITH POCKETS:

1. Essay 1, **with the drafts attached to each essay and everything clearly marked.** NO DRAFTS, NO GRADE!!
2. Essay 2 : *include all drafts.* NO DRAFTS, NO GRADE!!
3. ALL journal entries.
4. Your midterm exam.
5. A carefully written evaluation of the work that you have done this quarter. Answer the following questions *in detail:*
    a. Which essay represents your best writing? Discuss a few of the qualities that make this essay better than the other one.
    b. Which essay gave you the most trouble? Compare it to the others. Why was it more difficult to write than the others?
    c. Which book was the most helpful as you wrote your essays? The least helpful? Which book appealed to you the most? Why?

Grading Criteria:

A/B: All of the above material is in place.
Essays 1 and 2 show significant revision (content, not just grammar).
The journal entries are substantial: full of description, analysis, ideas for drafts, and rhetorical questions.
The evaluation sheet directly responds to the questions, is informative, and carefully edited so that there are few mistakes.

C: All of the above material is in place.
Essays 1 and 2 have been corrected (grammar, not content).
The journal entries are adequate: they address the prompts, answer the questions, and explore some ideas for drafts.
The evaluation sheet answers the questions and has no serious errors.

C–: All of the above material is in place.
All essays are present but uncorrected. No attempts at revision have been made.
The journal entries are poorly done: simple one-sentence answers to questions, few ideas for drafts, no analysis.
The evaluation sheet answers the questions and has no serious errors.

D or lower: Material on the list above is missing. This means drafts.
No corrections or revisions on any work. Remember, a revision IS NOT merely a printout of a previous draft.
Journal entries are missing and/or inadequate.
The evaluation sheet is hurriedly written and devoid of explanation. It has not been proofread.

Grading Portfolios

Take a look at the criteria for portfolios that is attached to both my first- and second-semester portfolio assignments (see Figure 3). I have broken down the various aspects of the portfolio in order to discuss what I look for and value in a portfolio.

Evaluating Essays

Students appear to be somewhat distressed when they first discover that I believe that the perfect paper—one that needs no revision—is a myth. But, as I tell them, professional writers seldom let themselves be satisfied with one draft, why should novice writers? Each essay assignment presents a multitude of opportunities to revise, to come closer to "perfect" than the previous draft. After I read and comment on the first draft, they revise for their peers, then as a group we work on proofreading the final product. The essays have to go through at least one more revision before they become part of the final portfolio. I tend to let students choose what they want to revise and when they want to revise it. This means that they often spend more time on one essay rather than an equal effort on all pieces. I'm not particularly upset by this asymmetrical effort. Essays seldom present the same problems and seldom require the exact same effort. For some students, the learning that takes place by working out difficult problems in a text is more important to learning to write than the time-management strategies that set deadlines teach them. My lack of participation as an overseer has its drawbacks. Not everyone will take my advice. And it's true, some students attempt to revise everything at the last minute. They must take the consequences for this action, but the consequences are clear from the beginning. As we work, we have conversations about what they must write not only in my class but for their other classes. I try to help them figure out what the stresses are during the quarter and how best they can adjust their particular schedules to meet all final deadlines.

At the end of the quarter, the student essays must show significant revision of content. This means that I can see distinct development of the ideas and clarification of the generalizations the students make in first drafts. To me, development means several things: that the students go beyond their immediate reactions to a topic; that papers contain references from the reading that prove or disprove the students' theories; and that the essays contain quotations from the text that illustrate the writer's points in significant ways. Significant revision means the final copy of an essay should be noticeably different from the drafts in other ways also.

Paragraphs should be moved around to make points stronger, active verbs found to replace passive ones.

The only way to check this sort of writing progress is to ask to see *all* the writing that students do for a course. As Jeffrey Sommers has suggested, in "Bringing Practice in Line with Theory: Using Portfolio Grading in the Composition Classroom," a portfolio complete with drafts, journal entries, all scraps of writing "closely resembles an archivist's collection of a writer's entire *oeuvre.* Instructors do not deal with selected writings but evaluate the entire output of the student writer" (160). Having access to this *oeuvre* helps a teacher understand how the activities the students do in journals, for instance, make it (or don't make it) into drafts of papers and how much of the interview data is brought to bear on the final conclusions that the students reach. These extraneous bits of material, carefully fit into the drafts and polished until that rough draft becomes a final product, provide real indicators of what the students have been doing throughout the quarter.[2]

The emphasis on revision and the acknowledgment that revision alone does not constitute grounds for high grades confuses them at first. When they turn in their first essays, I always ask for their perception of the grade they should receive. During that first quarter, even the weakest writers assign at least a *B* to their papers. The comments are revealing:

> I worked real hard and put in my perceptions of the assignment. This is more work than I ever did in high school, but I'm clear in my ideas so I thimk at least an B+ should be given.

By the time the students hand in their portfolios at the end of the second quarter, they are more likely to place value on the writing rather than on "effort."

> As I think about what we have been doing, it becomes obvious to me that this class deals with the root of communication. That is communicating the whole message, not just enough so the audience has a basic understanding of the idea. As we read each others writings, I was surprized that my fellow students didn't understand some of the things I had written. To me, the idea was crystal clear. I had to really read what I had written, and it was then, that I saw how vague my message was. I guess, I just expected the reader to think the same way as I.

Evaluating Exams

Most of the time, teachers inherit assessment systems that they must use, regardless of the theories that inform their classroom practices. At the present time, I've inherited a system that demands that I administer both a midterm and a final exam.[3] I abhor (yes, I mean to use this passionate verb) these types of ranking exams, so I compensate by turning them into evaluative activities that might be more useful for instruction and less threatening for the students. Because I employ portfolio assessment, the students do not receive separate paper or exam grades that can be averaged into an overall grade at the end of the quarter. The exams veer sharply away from any sort of ranking scale and exist solely to provide an opportunity for evaluative conversations with students about their writing.

Since the object of instruction is to teach students how to engage in written academic discourse, then any assessment measure should reveal whether or not they are conscious of their own thinking, reading, and writing processes. The students participate in the evaluative process engendered by the midterm and final, assessing their progress toward becoming better writers and researchers. To demystify the tests, both the midterm and the final exam prompts appear in the course packets that the students receive at the beginning of each quarter. This action also reduces the importance of the exams, making them just another writing assignment, while at the same time emphasizing that self-evaluation plays a major role in the course. In essence, the exams all come down to two types: exams in which the students evaluate their growth as writers and exams in which the students evaluate experiential knowledge against what they have learned as readers and researchers in the academy.

Evaluating Growth

Self-evaluation does not start with the midterm exam; it begins on the first day of class. The students write about themselves as readers and writers, defining their strengths and weaknesses. I also have them fill out a modified version of the writer's survey found in Elbow and Belanoff's *A Community of Writers.* These two records of self-evaluation form the foundation for subsequent evaluative exams. The evaluative midterm takes place during both the first and second quarter, almost immediately after the first essay is completed. By midterm, they've been traumatized, to varying extents, by the differences between our demands of them and the demands of high school writing and reading. The shock of college composition usually causes them to rethink their position on the scale or continuum from "Good" to "Bad" writer; a "test" seems as good a way as any to focus their attention on the matter. The first-quarter midterm exam presents a sanctioned opportunity to stop, reflect, and even complain.

Midterm Exam—ENG 052
A Case Study of Myself as a Writer

As teachers, we have tried to introduce you to new methods and processes of writing. It would be helpful for us to know whether or not this introduction has changed the way you write or the way you think about writing. Refer to the survey you filled out at the beginning of the quarter and your early journal entries, then discuss how you have changed (or not changed) as a writer. Do not hesitate to level with us about what has helped and what has hindered your development as a writer, but whatever your position, give us examples that will make your points clear. REMEMBER: You are writing an essay—don't just list assorted facts, create a thesis and develop it.

I do not grade evaluative exams in any traditional form; I use them as texts to study in student conferences. As I read the exams, I compare the students' perceptions of what's happening to their writing process against my own perceptions. To get the exam back, the student must arrange a conference. Not only do we discuss the exam itself, but we discuss the rest of the writing the student is doing in class. It's an excellent chance to examine what the student does well and why. If there is a need for a stern lecture, I give it. Interestingly enough, the students do most of the talking. They know, by and large, what they need to do.

The final exams in both the first and second quarter also provide opportunities for multilevel self-evaluation. We use the first-quarter final as a starting place for self-evaluation during the second quarter. Even though I cannot review the second-quarter final exam with the students—they sometimes come back during the third quarter, but often they've left campus—it still serves a useful purpose. The students need to "come to closure," but as any of us who write constantly can testify, learning to write never really ends. The best I can offer the students is closure on the quarter. They seem to welcome this chance to tell us what they've accomplished not only as writers but also as learners. Ending on this note brings together the personal and the academic a final time, and makes a matter of record their insights about themselves and their place in college.

Final Exam—English 053
The Student as Writer

Using your experience in this class, the experiences of your friends, and any other writing experiences you have had here at OSUM, write an essay that describes the major problems that students face when they enter college. Include a detailed description of the problems, but do not stop there. Offer suggestions to instructors that might help the student overcome the problems (you may not suggest that the instructor assign less writing!) and give advice to students that will help them perform better.

Each year they leave a legacy for the next year's class, a record I think should be preserved. The advice is both personal and practical, covering everything from how to study to how to manage family and friends. I expect it to be the best work they've done yet, so they can work on it outside of class. They proofread and print up the final copies during the exam period. Exhausted as they are, they generally do a good job on this essay. The improvment in sentence skills and other surface-level errors is quite noticeable. While the papers are not by any means perfect, the students' writing now demonstrates the sort of general proficiency we have come to expect in *entering* freshman composition students. Here are two examples I'm particularly fond of:

Michael

Dear Freshmen

I'm writing this letter to let you know what to expect out of college. Your first week or even maybe your first day you will say; what the hell am I doing in remedial classes! Good question, but do not let it bother you. It is not that you are stupid, it's just that you are under prepared. Somewhere in high school, you lost your focus on what you had to do to be prepared for college. Our whole class decided that we had to find someone to blame for not being prepared for college. We blamed people in three categories: teachers, guidance counselors, and parents. In my case it was the guidance counselors that were useless to me, it seemed like they took no interest in my college career. They were only interested in students with good grades. This is why I blame them for being under prepared. With my lack of intuition, I was satisfied with what I was doing and not what I should have been doing. I should have been taking classes that would enable me to be prepared for college. I am talking about college prep classes. I did not track myself into them until my senior year; by then it was too late, but a good start. If my guidance counselor would have pushed me into the right direction at the beginning, I would have been all right.

College is unlike high school. You will find college to be more demanding and less forgiving. It will take total concentration and a lot of discipline. Most of you are still very young and have no responsibilities. In college the responsibility is totally on you and no one else. You will have to discipline yourself to make study habits and not excuses. For example, most people are very poor in math. It is a subject that can be understood if you participate in class as well as doing your homework every night. This is where discipline comes into effect. You have to make sure that you do it and do not let anything side track you, like t.v., friends, and extra curricular activities. None of these are wrong, but college work has to come first.

In college you will find that what professors are looking for is not facts and dates; they are looking for reasons why things happen. If any of you has the pleasure of taking 151 history, you will find this out. History in college is not memorizing facts, and dates, but learning why things happened the way they did. It seems confusing, but you will figure it out in time. We call it "entering the conversation." Let me explain what I mean. Pretend you are invited to a ball where you know there are going to be a lot of rich people that are well-dressed in tuxes and maybe driving up in liemos. You are not going to go to the ball in a pair of blue jeans and a flannel shirt. To fit into the "conversation", the ball of college, you are going to rent a tux and maybe even a liemo to make yourself fit in as well as look good. This will happen in your school work as well. You will need to look for the right answer and not just one that is half right. Entering the conversation is expected of you, if not it will make you look stupid.

One way to enter into the college scheme is to find the way that you learn best. Whether it is being competitive or being aggressive like me. Do not let your emotions get in your way, like anger. Most of you are feeling anger as you read this letter because you have been placed into this remedial English class. I believe that anger will only hurt you in your work. Being competitive is the way that I learn best. Competition is a good way to get ahead. Try to out do your fellow classmates. You will have different ways of learning, but you have to find the way you learn best, and focus on it. Use it to your advantage to find the right answer. That is what college is all about.

You will find college at O.S.U.M. to be a good experience if you are here to learn. The professors here have good student-to-teachers relationships. They will help you and show you what needs to be done if you are interested in your college career. College is fast moving and it will be easy to get behind if you are not dedicated to your school work. You will find college much easier if you do not fight what has to be done. Do what is expected, enter the conversation, and you will be able to give the right answer in all your classes.

Good luck!

Tambra

Dear incoming freshmen,

I am writing this letter in hopes that you will find out a little sooner than I did, what college expects from you and how to go about delivering what they want. This letter in essence is a survival manual to college, something I wished I would have had access to before I entered their realm of learning in college.

What should you do before coming to college? When I was in high school, I figured college was a long way off and when the time came I would just go; yeah that sounds simple and when you're in high school, that is the way things often seem, especially your senior year. Some of you will have had brothers and sisters to tell you what to beware of, but some of us are first generation college students and don't have the inside scoop as to what to expect from college or what it will expect from you. If I were a high school senior again I would suggest that you listen to those teachers that lean toward the fact that what you are doing now is nothing to what you will do in college; they know what they are talking about. You should also get as much information upon deciding and entering a college as you can. I did the wrong thing by accepting the fact that I had to go to the college my parents wanted me to, not the one that I wanted to go to, so definitely sit down with your parents and have a good long mature chat about your life in college. I would go and talk to college advisors, visit campuses—actually visit the campus, not take the day off school to fish or something like that. If you know of someone that is attending the college you are visiting, contact them for a possible tour of the college, this way you get the social and academic perspective from someone that has experienced it first hand. This is a definite plus, sometimes colleges will tell you anything in order to get you to attend their college, kinda like the army, but at least you can change schools. You should also talk to college personnel to find out the inner workings of the college, and what the college expects.

You may be wondering how much different can college be from high school. If their is anything more different than high school it is college. It is amazing that we spend twelve years in an institution that when all is said and done will have very little bearing as to what we become. You can be the most academically successful student your high school has ever had, but most likely it will not have much relevance on the kind of student you will be in college. I was an above average student in high school; I regurgitated what the teachers wanted on tests and homework. I was part of the group included in the "conspiracy for the least"; maybe I didn't learn anything but I could tell them what they wanted. In college you try to do that and you have sealed your fate of an unsuccessful college career. You must be able to critically think, this is the most important key to college success.

If you think English classes are rough in high school, think again. In my high school English classes we wrote a few papers and the rest was literature. You can memorize facts from reading but when it came to writing a paper everyone was lost; you could tell especially around term paper time. We were not taught to think on our own, but to give the teacher facts not opinions supported by facts. In college you more than likely will find yourself underprepared in the areas of math and English. You may be surprised at the low level of course work that you will possibly be placed in. I know without having taken 052/053 that I wouldn't have been a good enough writer to survive 110 English; I wouldn't have had the critical thinking skills necessary for English as well as my other classes.

In high school I could never figure out how anything fit together or applied to my life much less someone else, how does English and history fit together? In college you begin for the first time to realize the correlation between the variety of courses you are taking and when this realization comes about, the things you have learned all these years can be applied. A friend of mine that I attended high school with made the comment that this quarter it finally clicked as to how her math classes actually had something to do with each other; it made sense, which it never did in high school. The teachers go out of their way to allow you to see the correlation.

The goals of college are pretty straight forward. They want the best education money can buy and you will master what you learn. In high school it is memorization; in college it is learning. They won't baby you, you are on your own schedule, if you want to learn then you will but if you're there to goof-off you won't stay long.

How can you survive the rigorous schedule, the teachers, course work involved, working and having any social life at all? The obvious key to this is time management. You absolutely must keep up with your course work; if you get behind, it is almost if not impossible to catch up. Last quarter I got bogged down toward the end and my English grade suffered for it; it was hard to get caught up and so I did a slop up job on my last paper and it showed; college teachers don't take half-assed work. The teachers in college expect one-hundred and one percent from their students and if you can't handle it get out. The teachers will go out of their way to assist you in your educational goals. Most colleges have a tutorial center, my experience hasn't been too good in that area. It is somewhat easier to receive help one-on-one, but in order to get it done around your schedule and the teachers' is hard. If I had a choice when it comes to working and going to college at the same time, I wouldn't work at all. It seems for me at least, that the times you have to work are the days that you need to write a paper or study for a test. The days and times the labs are open are the times you are working. If you want to have fun in college, that can happen too, but you must remember that it gets to be easier to skip class and have fun than go to class and be bored. This is a rut that many students have: they must choose between fun and receiving an education; it is pretty obvious which is more tempting. If you are going to college to have fun and that is the only reason, it isn't for you; it requires a lot of hard work.

I wish you luck in your educational endeavors in college!

Evaluating Research Against Experience

The second type of evaluative exam (usually administered in the second quarter) asks students to apply the knowledge they have gathered in their research to a real-life situation. Many of the students have begun to write or speak of a desire to return to educational basics or to the type of education that "older" people supposedly experienced. However, most of the time, their ideas on this topic are generalizations, addressed to some rather phantom situation. Curriculum design remains the domain of professional educators. The conversation isn't really personal. To show that parents and community members have a right and a responsibility to speak out about education, I give them all copies of a rather long letter, written by my father while he was in France during World War II. Why bring my family into the novice writers' class instruction? For several reasons. Not only to build trust—I've asked them to write about their lives, they're entitled to know a little about mine—but once again it brings the nonacademic into the classroom.

My father, Ray Dickson, resembles our students in many respects. He grew up in a small rural area, did not finish college, and lacked the credentials that professional educators bandy about. Although a more experienced reader and writer than most of our novice writers, he had similar experiences in the public schools. As readers will discover, he graduated from high school more by virtue of his personality and ability to come up with quick and clever answers to questions than by diligent study. After high school, he rather willfully flunked out of Texas A & M. He worked at various jobs my grandfather helped him find until he married my mother. When it became obvious that World War II was inevitable, he, like many other men during that period, joined the Army. The letter that has become known in our family as "The Education Letter" was written just before he began serving as a forward scout in Patton's army, about a month before he was killed by a sniper.

The students are quick to recognize the similarity between his life and their own. And because we have been studying the educational system so intently, they are also quick to recognize that much of the educational reform he proposes for his children's schools echoes the reforms that Sizer proposes nearly fifty years later. Not only do they see the relationship between a parent's concern for the educational system and the academy's concern, our discussion leads them to see how this particular letter played a part in my own desire to become an academic. Not insignificantly, they discover that I intend to use this letter and other personal family letters in my research. We talk at length about my plans to write a book that explores the way in which letters, newspaper articles, and other written documents helped create an aura of optimism and expectation in my father's small Texas hometown during the Depression and World War II.

Midterm Exam—ENG 053
An Open Letter About Education

Read the Dickson Letter and, using its format, write your own letter to your relatives explaining the type of education that you want for your children and how you want their teachers to prepare them for the future. Use your own ideas, but back them up with information from the books you've read, class discussions, last quarter's interviews, conversations with friends or relatives, or any other source you can so that these people will be able to help you meet your goals. Remember, Ray Dickson was not a teacher, nor was he a college graduate; he was just an ordinary twenty-eight-year-old man who had goals for his children. If he could write a letter like this, so can you.

When the students compose their own letters, they speak of today's educational practices—vocational tracks, hands-on learning—and discuss the difference between the dream of an education that gives everyone what they need and the reality of an education that slots students into what has become a fixed curriculum. They contrast the past, the present, and the future, drawing from the past two quarters' work and reading. As with the evaluative exam, the students discuss their own perceptions of their abilities during conferences. In the case of the Dickson Letter exam, where the text acts as a model for their own ideas, I go over the similarities and differences in rhetorical and discourse strategies between the students' and my father's texts, as well as review such fundamentals as organization and use of examples and illustrations. The object here is not to hold up my father's letter as perfect, but rather to discuss where the students' letters can be more specific or descriptive.

Evaluating Grammar

As most novice writing instructors know, correcting papers in the traditional manner doesn't teach grammar, and tracing the students' progress as practitioners of Standard English Diction can't be done with workbook sheets or sentence-level quizzes. The students simply don't make the connections between the red marks on the papers and the problems with their grammar skills. John F. Butler, in "Remedial Writers: The Teacher's Job as Corrector of Papers," talks rather clearly about the problems of marking or correcting grammar errors:

> As a method of evaluation, a grade is exactly like any other nota-
> tion I make on a student's paper: behind it, in my head, are all
> kinds of complex thoughts which would take me ten to thirty or
> more minutes to write out. As a student looks at his grade, I am
> hoping he will see it as standing for all of the thoughts in my
> head. . . . But the student can only stare at the grade, not look in-
> side my mind, and make up whatever kind of story he is disposed
> to about what it is supposed to mean. If he is a remedial student,
> and the grade is poor, there will be no chance in the world the
> story he constructs about its meaning will bear the slightest re-
> semblance to the story I had in mind. (559)

The only effective way that I've found to acquaint novice writers with their errors and my comments is to forgo correcting mistakes. However, I don't forgo my responsibility as teacher. I mark
problem areas rather than specific problems, then talk with the students individually about their particular pattern of error. Rather
heartlessly, I refuse to label or correct the errors on the papers, and
if the students don't seek me out to discuss the problems, I don't
work with them on grammar. This policy may sound harsh; as one
critic said, it's hardly an example of positive reinforcement. But the
actual process is not as unforgiving as it might seem, and once the
students understand that correcting grammar is their responsibility,
not mine, they accept it fairly readily; they have no particular desire
to sit through lectures on grammar. I'm always willing to discuss
marks I place on a student's paper, and since all drafts of papers are
in the portfolio, I have an opportunity to discuss with them their
progress toward erradicating their particular grammar demons.

When I mark the student papers, a simple code indicates the
general problem:

- *Brackets around a sentence*[4] mean there is a punctuation or sentence error: faulty end punctuation, comma splices, incorrectly
  joined dependent and independent clauses, run-on sentences,
  and sentence fragments.

- *A squiggly line under a passage* indicates a syntax problem—
  what I call a train-wreck sentence, one that becomes nonsense
  because the student switches from one thought to another or
  one in which the wording doesn't resemble standard English in
  any of its varieties.

- *A squiggly line under a word (or a short phrase)* indicates incorrect usage or, in some cases, incorrect verb tense.

- *A circle around a word* means it's incorrectly spelled.
- *The words "Ask Me"* indicate that there's a problem that can't be explained by the markings above—parallel structure, for instance.

These proofreading marks are simple to remember and give an indication where to start when the student starts asking, "What's wrong with this?" However, with the exception of the circle to indicate a misspelled word, they don't exactly point out what's wrong. This process makes it hard for the student to correct the problems. First, they have to figure out what's wrong; then they have to figure out how to fix the mistake. But having to grapple with hard problems actually improves their grammar and mechanics in the long run.

When they want to know why I don't correct the mistakes, my answer is simple and from the heart—I know how to correct the mistakes. If I correct the papers, the students don't learn anything. However, if we correct them together, identifying patterns of error, talking about why the sentence is wrong, learning the rules that apply, and finally correcting all instances of the problem, then the students have a real opportunity to learn. Usually working through one or two error conferences serves to make the students aware of their particular pattern of errors. In the case of multiple error interference, we can progress from the most grievous to the simpler. If students have particular problems in common, I will have them work in groups after our initial one-to-one sessions. The one cardinal rule in these peer-group grammar sessions is that no one can suggest a change to a paper without justifying that change with a rule that covers the situation. As I tell them, "If you can't explain it, you don't know it."

At the end of the quarter, when I review portfolios, it's easy to see if students have learned to correct surface error because all drafts of the papers from the quarter provide a record of the students' progress. Reading the final product against the drafts shows the extent of the individual student's progress in amending errors. The consequences for leaving proofreading undone and grammar problems uncorrected are severe. In my class students must demonstrate a reasonable competency with grammar to complete 053 successfully. They do not have to prove that they can write error-free texts. After all, I have students in regular freshman English who still mistake *affect* for *effect,* who dangle modifiers about in the most unlikely (and sometimes unfortunate) places, and who do not know how to manipulate the elements of a sentence so that they produce flawless parallel structure.

I expect the novice writers to reach a certain level of competency. Therefore, from the beginning I establish a hierarchy of error that governs my instruction. I expect students to address the problems that will make them look uneducated, and—given the cultural biases of the academy and other institutions—stupid. In my mind, students are marked as poor thinkers (whether they are or not) by blatant errors; faulty sentence structure, especially sentence fragments; incorrect verb tense; problems in subject-verb agreement; inappropriate word usage; and simple spelling errors obscure their thinking process. These are the errors that I push the students to correct, and if they expect to go on to ENG 110, they must make serious headway in removing them from their final copy. Should we come across other problems as well, we talk about them; however, I try to watch for that glazed look in the students' eyes that indicates they're trying to learn too much too quickly. When they try to operate at overload, even the simple problems reappear. The students must finish my class with the following skills:

- They must be able to recognize sentence boundaries and straighten up the most egregious syntactical errors in their own prose.
- They have to learn the difference between the following words: *there, their* and *they're; you're* and *your; its* and *it's;* and *then* and *than.*
- They must be able to edit out most errors in verb tense and subject-verb agreement.
- They must learn to use the speller on the computer to correct their spelling *and* learn to compensate for the words that the speller can't check as well.

While I consider grammar important, I do not consider it so important that it can make up for lack of critical thinking. I do not give significant grade increases for merely cleaning up grammar errors. As important as correctness may be, turning out presentable text is the smallest factor in the students' job. It is a minimum requirement of the course, and if it is all they do, then they get a minimum grade.

Final Portfolio

For the final ENG 053 portfolio, the students revise the major essays once more for final presentation. Most of the revision still consists of rethinking content. Usually this means expanding upon statements and making the transitions between ideas apparent. The students also revise sentence structure, word usage, grammar, and the mechanics as well as content; in fact, at this time the greatest concentration of effort on correctness occurs. In my classes, the portfolio contains more than final products. The rest of the writing from the quarter must also be in the portfolio—journals, essays the students do not want graded, drafts of everything, and the midterm exam, too. Such a variety of material allows evaluation of both process and product. The two revised essays represent the best the students can do over a period of time. I know that they have had plenty of opportunity to conference with me about these papers, revise them, and proofread. The exams show me how the students react under pressure, and how, when asked, they can pull together their thinking about a topic of study. The other pieces of writing indicate how much effort the students put into the course. All of this material allows me to trace the students' efforts over the quarter.

In addition, I have as a resource a portfolio cover letter, that serves as the students' final self-evaluations of their writing ability. In this letter, they discuss how they have changed as writers and learners and what (if anything) they have learned about education and writing. They also discuss the process of creating individual papers and the reading for the course. "Which was the hardest assignment?" I ask. "Why?" "Which was the easiest writing task? Why?" "What reading was the most complicated? What the most useful?"

This letter, written in an informal manner, reveals more about the students and their writing than teachers could gather if the teachers relied strictly on observations and the students' grades as they appear in the columns of her grade book. For me, the cover letter acts as a guide to the portfolios. As I make my final evaluation, I look for the strengths that the students attribute to themselves as writers and for work that they're particularly proud of. If, at the beginning of the quarter or in the midterm, the students have set goals for themselves, the letter attests to the successes or failures the student has experienced. The remarkable thing about these letters is the honesty with which the students evaluate themselves as writers. I rarely find myself in the position of "bursting someone's bubble" in this final reckoning of ability, which makes it infinitely easier to assign the final grade. In fact, I often find myself pointing out strengths that students have not given themselves credit for, strengths that deserve rewards.

The final portfolio is not the first time the students receive a grade. Havoc would reign if I denied them some sort of indication of their grade before that point, and it would be as unkind as it is unfair to withhold a grade in a university system that places such value on ranking. Novice writers are as grade conscious as any other set of students, perhaps even more so since they have real reason to fear that they will not succeed in college. Therefore, after midterm, when they want to know what their "grade" is or "how they're doing," I give them a current ranking. I base this decision on my judgment of the problems they confronted when they began the course (both first and second quarter) and the quality of the work they are currently producing, but I always follow that judgment with a discussion of the strategies that will lead to further improvement.

I rank their progress in the terms they want: A-E. (E is, of course, the popular euphemism for F). However, I always caution them that this grade is not set, and that they cannot average what they think of as "the midterm grade" with subsequent grades they may wrestle from me on individual papers and come up with a firm numerical value. Everything is in flux; final grades aren't set until the final portfolio is assessed. An essay that might initially place somewhere in the *B* range but never changes from draft to draft sinks in my estimation of its worth. Not attempting to struggle with difficult material affects overall grades negatively. If students do not revise substantially, they do not receive more than a *C* as a final grade. As indicated earlier, significant revision means rethinking content rather than merely correcting grammar mistakes or adding a sentence to respond to a question that indicates that significant development of a point is necessary. I do not consider this insistence upon revision unreasonable because I don't necessarily expect that revision always leads to improvement. In the attempt to work out new ideas, the papers sometimes become more confused, but the novice writer has a right, perhaps even an obligation, to work through the subject and the expression of ideas. The effort is worth a great deal of credit.

However, I'm also very forthcoming about the role of effort in a final grade. All the effort in the world cannot guarantee an A. The students must demonstrate a certain level of competency not only to pass but also to receive a grade somewhere along the continuum from *C*– to *A*. Behind this judgment is, of course, yet another set of criteria set by our particular academic community. While I do have a standard that derives from my knowledge of novice student performances from past classes, I also try to keep in mind the goals of ENG 052/053: preparing the students for ENG 110. It would be unfair to grade novice writers according to the 110 rubric, but those standards can't help but influence my judgment. I do point out what will be expected of writers in 110 and urge individual students to work on those particular skills where they're deficient.

And here we approach the heart of darkness once again. Sometimes a student continually refuses to hand in drafts, participates only nominally in teacher and peer-group conferences, and corrects only surface errors. This portfolio is easy to grade: it fails. I'm clear about this, almost righteous. Because of the highly structured criteria for the portfolio and the lack of development such an individual's work has demonstrated, even an outside reader could see that this student did not fulfill the requirements of the course.

Other portfolios are a bit more difficult to handle, and "what's right" a bit more difficult to ascertain. Sometimes I read a portfolio and discover that questions about content have been answered with an additional sentence rather than with an exploration of ideas, or I find that, despite the class discussion, the only revisions are periods and commas. I'd sincerely like to fail this portfolio. However, what if it's *reasonably competent?* The student has learned to make a thesis statement, organize ideas so that a reader can follow them, and "pretty up" the final copy. The student expects to receive a B, reasoning that completing the assignments was always enough to earn a B in high school and the student's done more than that here. I expect to see a portfolio that reflects progress, more than surface thinking and surface-level corrections. The student's portfolio simply does not meet the minimum standards for my classes, which include evidence of revision, peer editing, and constant consultation. Do I grade the student on the intellectual or the moral standard? Intellectual, it turns out, but I don't reward the student with a B. Comparing the final portfolio to the portfolio criteria sheet indicates that the student has merely done satisfactory work, a C perhaps, perhaps a C–, no more.

Other final judgment calls become even more complicated. A student works really hard, revises many times, shows up to conferences with valid questions about writing, and asks questions until the teacher wants to say "do it yourself!" This student wants an A. But what if the final portfolio remains far below my standards of minimal competency even though the student has displayed A effort? Such is often the case with novice writers. In open-admissions schools, such as ours, some students come to college so poorly prepared that even after a quarter or sometimes two quarters of instruction, they only make minimal progress toward standard English skills. Their ideas are still unclear and sentence-level errors still interfere with understanding. To pass this student, much less give the student a B or A, would send the wrong message. In the long run, effort isn't enough. Working hard is the student's job; I expect it as a minimum effort.

The portfolio can't remove the problems of grading; it can only make them a bit less grievous for me and sometimes for the students, too. I wish I could swear that all students like portfolio assessment, that they appreciate my efforts to move toward an evaluative assessment system and away from one that merely ranks. It's not always true, and given the fact that school systems have seldom relied upon any other form of assessment, it's hardly surprising. A few students object to this system, insisting that they need to know how they're doing in the course at all times. These students operate on agendas of their own. So much depends upon a red *A*, graced with a +, in the middle of the white paper. It represents very real success and very real progress in a system that values "the best."

The majority of my students (I'm happy to report without stretching the truth) are relieved to be free of a grading system that puts them back in the lowest percentile of writers. They were never particularly happy with the grades they received in high school. But they are only free of a grading system for a while. I don't suspend grading, I merely delay it a bit. And not *grading* papers doesn't mean not *commenting* on them. Student drafts are read, marked for surface errors, and commented on. Extensively. The delay in grading allows the focus to shift to the writing process. The grade conscious students know where they stand; those who are discouraged by grades have a bit of breathing space. Those who want to fight about grades will have to supply evidence that details their efforts and changes, and those who don't care will continue not to care.

Afterword

Assessment may be the last official contact I have with my students, but I find it difficult to end this book by discussing how I assess and grade them. To let evaluation, the sole prerogative of the teacher, be the last word in this text seems to negate, at least in my mind, the value of the knowledge that is created in dual communities: the academic and the nonacademic. It might be more appropriate to tell you a bit about what's happened to some of our students—where they are, what they're doing. While I can't provide personal anecdotes about everyone, I do have a few statistics. The research studies my colleagues and I have conducted reveal that approximately fifty percent of the students from our original two-year study are still at Ohio State, progressing toward their degrees. They haven't all made steady progress, but they're progressing just the same. Another twenty-five percent have gone on to different schools—both liberal arts and vocational colleges—and are completing degrees and programs. The rest are alive and well, working at jobs they like and having families. Despite academic lore, which posits that dropping out of college is tantamount to failure, they do not seem to suffer from having made the decision to leave our hallowed halls.

Since Lynda Barry, my coresearcher, and I both live in Marion, we run into a number of our former students at the grocery store, the movies as well as in the campus halls and in advanced-level composition and literature courses. They contact us, too.

> —Laura, whose learning disabilities so plagued her, sent us a note two years ago. She was going to beauty school and working full-time, but wanted us to know that all the study and writing strategies she learned in our classes still served her well. Her teachers constantly praised her ability to handle the essay questions on tests. This year I learned that she'd completed her beautician's training and was working at a local shop; she plans to start her own business in a couple of years.

> —Anita, who once ran crying from the classroom on a regular basis, had to give up school for financial reasons—but she's participating in a home-schooling program in her neighborhood. She's using

methods she learned in class to supplement the back-to-basics approach found in the textbooks, slipping in process writing techniques to help her children understand that writing about a subject helps develop an understanding of it. Anita would like to be back in school, but like other students who can't handle the tuition debt, she won't be back until she can save some more tuition dollars. Looking at the economy, she sometimes fears she won't be back at all.

—Brad, one of the group of students who left OSUM and enrolled in four-year liberal arts colleges, confesses that he couldn't get the type of undergraduate education he wanted from OSU. He, like other OSUM students, had gone off eagerly to study at the Columbus campus, expecting the independence of on-campus living and studying to be exciting and challenging. Although his grades did not suffer—he held his own admirably—he discovered that he liked the attention he received on the Marion campus much better than the anonymity he experienced in the huge classes on the Columbus campus. Therefore, he sought out a school where the atmosphere more highly resembled the interactive education he received at OSUM.

—Michael and Tami, whose collaborative paper on school districts and wealth is quoted in Chapter 5, appear from time to time. I see Tami fairly often because she's completing a degree in early childhood education, the only four-year degree we offer at OSUM. Michael dropped in to show us his uniform and visit a bit before he left for training as an army Warrant Officer. He's going to be a pilot—accepted to the program, he told us rather proudly, partly because his letter of application was the best his CO had ever read.

—Tambra, who graduates this year in History Education and plans to attend graduate school, evolved from a disinterested adolescent to a competent and responsible adult during the years she monitored the writing lab. She honed her teaching skills as she coached new novice writers and readers through the system.

—Jeff, who worked full-time as a guard at a juvenile detention center as well as part-time for us while he finished his first two years of college, has moved on to main campus. He's preparing to apply to law school, given his 3.8 grade average, and his willingness to tackle difficult problems, I have no doubt that he'll make it.

I'm aware, because these students and others have taught me, that my account of the Distanced/Personal pedagogy reflects my own personal construction of learning and teaching. This book is my version of "What It's Like Here." The student/teacher dialogues we engage in over Chinese food or in front of the computers in the Writing Center have revealed as much. Happily for me, the students tend to agree more often than disagree with my perceptions about what happens in class. Still, the ethnographic "historic present" that Brodkey warns against has haunted me throughout the writing of this book. While I believe that I have been faithful to the Marion experience with novice writers—who they are, how they respond to the Distanced/Personal pedagogy—I always search for verification of my ideas and perceptions. As Brodkey suggests, I try to interrupt my own voice with the voices of others. This year, while teaching an advanced writing class, I received an unexpected boon: A student wrote about his experience as a novice writer.

The class—Intermediate Essay Writing: English in the United States—was designed for sophomores to fulfill the university's second-level writing requirements. In my course, the text was Dennis Baron's *Declining Grammar,* a choice that was not universally popular with the students. As part of the ongoing extended writing, I had the students write about language and literacy issues in their own backgrounds, especially their views of themselves as novice or expert writers. They wrote in journals; they wrote in class; they talked to each other about English, English teachers, and the insecurity they felt each time they had to write. I found out a lot about what it was like to be a student in an English class—on practically every level of education.

One of the quietest, but most observant, students in that class was Lewis Columber, a former ENG 052/053 graduate who works with Lynda as a tutor in the Writing Center. Lewis has an interesting history. The first time I saw him, fear had him literally moving in slow motion. Lewis hunkered over a computer key board, almost in shock. It took a full thirty seconds for him to respond to simple instructions. A nontraditional student returning to school to find a new career after an accident placed him in a wheelchair, he had been gainfully employed in the real world and had children of his own. His behavior, however, didn't fit his biography. Somehow we felt that he shouldn't be quite *this* intimidated by technology. It didn't look good for Lewis, because, as his teacher, Carole Kirkton, confirmed, his hesitancy on the computer matched his hesitancy in class. I didn't see him again that quarter, but I was happy to learn that despite our concern, Lewis survived the rigors of ENG 052 and made it to the second quarter. He'd been in my ENG 053 class for only a few days before medical problems sent him to the hospital, and because he missed so much time, he had to drop out for the rest of the quarter. When he returned, the next quarter, Lewis was assigned to Carole Kirkton's section of ENG 053, so I missed having him as a novice writing student.

The next time I became aware of Lewis, he was taking my Introduction to Shakespeare course and tutoring students in writing and math. He'd done quite well in ENG 110, decided to major in Computer Science, and settled into his other college courses to the extent that learning seemed to come easily to him. Indeed, his personality had undergone an amazing change. No more panic, no more fear. Although his sentence-level skills still needed enough work that we wouldn't let him tutor the students in grammar, he excelled as a reader and coach for almost any 052 or 110 student. Lynda and I would listen with fascination as he guided unsure and sometimes resistant students through the process of critical thinking. Asking questions, urging them to think for themselves, his quiet manner and unflappable demeanor enabled him to reach the panic-stricken novice writers in a way that few of the other student tutors could. He understood. He also understood students who didn't care about English and could talk with them when the rest of us lost patience and wanted to throw them out of the lab and possibly out of school. Frequently, he found a way past the disinterest; sometimes he just shook his head.

Lewis's literacy autobiography, an eleven-page document written for the intermediate writing course, explored the problems of being a novice writer. There, in black and white, was proof for me that our course of study had actually had an effect. He discussed his literacy history in terms of what he'd learned from Rose, Sizer, and even Baron. He didn't lose sight of how his family history and public school training had affected his performance in school. In fact, he wove these two elements together in such a way that it was obvious that he had learned what we had hoped he'd learn—how to make meaning out of disparate ideas, events, and theories. Here are some passages from that literacy autobiography; the first describes the event that marked him as an "average" student:

> Under the windows was a three foot tall bookcase that stretched the full length of the wall. In one end of this bookcase were books that all the "average" students would read and then give oral reports to tell the other students what the books were about. On the other end of this bookcase were "special" books that only the "smart" kids were allowed to read. They were *Hardy Boys* and *The Nancy Drew Mysteries*. As the students who were allowed to read these "special" books gave their reports to the class, the "special" books started to intrigue me. I decided that I would like to read them too. When I asked the teacher if I could read one of them she said, "No, they are too hard for you. You won't understand what you're reading. You continue reading the books that you have been reading because they are easier and more on your level." I was stunned! This was the first time since I had started to school that I had ever had a teacher or anybody for that matter tell me that I wasn't smart enough to do something. Until this point in time I had accomplished everything that I had tried with better success on some things than on others.

When I heard those words my whole attitude about school changed. I thought, "If I'm not smart enough while I'm trying, why try?" If a student is told he's not smart enough to do something by a teacher or by someone else he looks up to, chances are he will start to believe they are right. He won't put any effort into doing the task or worse yet he won't even try at all. As Mike Rose pointed out in *Lives On The Boundary,* "Students will float to the mark you set" (26). If the student is told, "yes, you can do it; I believe in you," the student will try harder. With this little encouragement the student may succeed. If the student doesn't succeed, at least he tried; failure is also part of the learning process. As Theodore Sizer explained in *Horace's Compromise,* "Learning involves exposure—the exhibition of things not known, skills poorly developed, ideas ill formed. One learns to get things right by revealing where one is wrong" (174).

The next passage I'd like to quote concerns Lewis's experiences with English as a rigid system not connected with critical thinking and his subsequent discovery that grammar is only part of what it means to write well:

> Eighth grade English was taught by a tall, thin, imposing figure of a woman who seemed to take great pride in the fact that she could make our lives miserable. Maybe she really didn't, but it sure seemed so at the time. She would assign us the retched chore of diagramming or labeling the parts of speech in sentences. The day the work was to be done, she would call each of us up to the blackboard one by one to show our work and explain why we diagrammed the sentences this way. As we waited for our turn, it felt like we were lambs in a slaughter house waiting for our time to go down the shoot to our impending doom. If the sentences weren't correct, she would make the student break the sentence down correctly. When she would come up to my sentences, they were never broken down correctly—they were always wrong. As I would stand in front of the class, all red-faced from the embarrassment because of my "crime," it seemed to take hours to correct my mistakes.
>
> Who cares about diagramming sentences? English teachers. I wasn't going to be an English teacher; I saw no use for diagramming sentences; I felt "why learn?" But does being able to diagram a sentence show real literacy? No! As Mike Rose stated in *Lives on the Boundary,*
>
>> grammatical analysis [is a] subskill . . . The real stuff of literacy [is] conveying something meaningful, communicating information, creating narratives, shaping what we see and feel and believe into written language . . . The curriculum [of diagramming sentences] drained the life out of all this, reduced literacy to the dry dismembering of language—not alive, not communicative at all. (109)

We can almost see Lewis's eighth-grade teachers in his essay as he describes what the very word *grammar* conjured up each time he heard it:

Mike Rose described The Goddess of Grammar in this way:

The Middle Ages envisioned the goddess of grammar, Grammatica, as an old women. In one later incarnation, she is depicted as severe, with a scalpel and a large pair of pincers. Her right hand, which is at her side, grasps a bird by its neck, its mouth open as if in a gasp or a squawk (1).

I don't see this as a complete description of her. Grammar has always terrified me so I have a more sinister description of her. I see her as a haughty woman with a cold stare. As she looks at you, you feel as if you are under a microscope, expected to perform as she sees fit. Her skin is as cold as her icy glare as she stares down upon those that dare confront her. Her spine is ram-rod straight with no bending or yielding just as her rules for grammar demonstrate. There is only one way—the correct way—her way. Grammatica has many arms protruding from her body which she uses to keep her attackers off guard—totally confused. When they think they have her weakened and ready to concede defeat, she hits them with another arm. She is all powerful and is able to defeat any foe whenever she sees fit because they are unsure of her all-powerful forces. Of these many arms extending from her body, half end with scalpels, used to cut off any ideas that are not to her liking. She likes to demonstrate her power by confusing all who confront her with the many angles in which she can attack those who offer her tribute. Large pinchers protrude from the rest of her arms, used to squeeze the life out of any ideas that are not correctly presented to her.

This is my idea as to what Grammatica looks like. I feel she is a little more sinister and deceiving than the description that Mike Rose gave in *Lives on the Boundary.* Things of the unknown awaken images that are dark and terrifying. Anything that is unfamiliar to a person scares them into conjuring up mental blocks that cripple, slow, or stop the learning process. This is how I feel about grammar. To this day, grammar still has the power to petrify me.

The trauma Lewis experienced in these classes affected the way in which he thought about school in general and about himself as a student. When he entered college after his accident, he met with an unexpected ghost from his past:

Talking to the admissions counselor about what I wanted to major in was exciting. I felt like I was getting a new start on life—a new career. I was given the choice to do anything that I wanted to do, but before I could start I had to get my grade transcripts from high school. After I saw my transcripts I thought "who am I kidding? I don't belong in college." Looking at my transcripts brought back memories of me sitting in English class trying to diagram a sentence. I also recalled how difficult it was for me to read a passage in a book and figure out what it meant. The memories scared me to death but I wanted to try anyway. I decided the one class that scared me the most was English so I might as well start my college experience there. My thoughts were "If I'm going to flunk out because of English, it might as well be early—why waste time?" When I was told by my academic advisor that I had to take a placement test to be placed in the correct English course, I told her "Why waste our time having me take a placement test for English?" I knew I belonged in the remedial English class—This is where I had belonged all my life. English just wasn't my subject. Through twelve years of school I had a C average in English—I knew I needed help.

As my introduction to Lewis indicated, he did need help, and he sought it. But he needed more than tutoring in grammar. He needed to rediscover that excited learner who had been squashed back in the fifth grade and associate his success in the business world with his potential as a learner. Two years later, he had:

> Going through the [public] school system I was hampered from learning by a school system that continually showed me with words and grades that I wasn't smart enough to do the things needed to excel within the system. I was told that I couldn't read and understand certain books. I wasn't able to diagram sentences in English class. I wasn't able to analyze why things happened in history. I didn't have any idea what a certain passage in a poem meant. It didn't seem to matter how hard I tried, I always seemed to receive a C. I was just average. After a while I developed a shield—I really didn't care. I seemed to continually fall short from the grades I wanted or hoped for. After a while I started to believe what the system had been telling me for all those years in grade school through high school—I was average and there was nothing that I was going to do to correct the system's thinking.
>
> Now that I have the chance to start over at college . . . I am trying to overcome some of the barriers put in my way through twelve years of training. All those barriers that I have to overcome weren't placed there by the system—the most damaging one of all was placed there by me. Self doubt is a killer of potential.

Lewis's literacy autobiography confirms my beliefs about the way that labeling students "average" (in this case a euphemism for "not college material") affects their chances to succeed in school. They reject those types of education that they cannot master. It also confirms my thoughts about teaching. The teachers who set their agenda or the state's agenda for teaching—diagramming sentences and learning the formula for creating the perfect five-paragraph essay—before the students' agenda for learning—reading and writing about interesting material—create students more interested in getting the commas in the right place than in saying what's on their minds. Lewis's experiences echo those that we've heard about in conversations with other novice students—ones who are traditional and untraditional, ones who range in age from eighteen to forty—as they have described moving through years of English instruction. Lewis is not naive. As you can see, he acknowledges his part in his mediocre high school performance—and when we talk, he rightly gives himself credit for his excellent performance in college. Like many other novice writers who have survived our course, he's an A to B student now. Lewis succeeds because the linking of nonacademic and academic communities helps him to see the different ways in which people can learn as well as the connection between the way people learn and the making of meaning. He's aware that he dwells in two worlds: one in which people can survive quite nicely without analyzing every thought and phrase and another whose inhabitants find analysis a joy rather than a bother. It is in the bringing together of these worlds that novice readers and writers find access to the academy. It is in the bringing together of these worlds that academics will find access to their students.

Appendix

English 053 Course Packet

Many of the assignments for the first quarter of the Education Project are included in the text; however, I felt it would be useful to see them all in order so that teachers could trace the progress from personal to academic to Distanced/Personal that the assignments form.

Assignments for English 052, Basic Reading and Writing I

Essay I

One of the chapters of *Sometimes a Shining Moment* is entitled "So what *Did* I Learn in School, Anyway?" In it Eliot Wigginton presented statements from high school students that detailed what was important in their education at Rabun Gap and discussed what was valuable in his own high school education. From this chapter we began to understand the conflict between what teachers believe they are doing and how students see their efforts. In your essay you will want to answer some of the following questions:

What did you learn in high school? How did you learn it? Which teaching methods were effective and which ones merely created hostility and indifference? Where were the dissonances between what your teachers thought they were doing and what you needed? Where were the shining moments when knowledge and interest came together?

Do not limit yourself to these questions; you may have more important issues you want to address. If you are concerned that what you want to write about will not meet the assignment, discuss it with us; we will decide together how to pursue your interest.

Essay II—Ethnographic Research

Part I: Individual Grade: You must write an essay that focuses on a narrow hypothesis about education, speculates upon what you will find out, and provides proof that either supports or disproves a theory you create from your research. You must interview at least one person and transcribe the interview. (More interviews, better proof, clearer theory—better grade) Interviews should be accompanied by a detailed description of the person you interviewed, a statement that confirms their ability to speak knowledgeably on the topic, a summary of how the information you acquired helped you form your theory, and an explanation of how your interview fits into the paper you will collaborate upon with your group.

The essay must be double-spaced and carefully edited. (If you can't do it yourself, get help!) The interview will be single-spaced in dialogue form and must be identical to the tape you will turn in with it. It will be graded upon accuracy and careful editing as well as how thorough a job you do as an interviewer. The essays and interviews will be reproduced as a class book for all four English 052 classes, so make sure you have the permission of the person you interview to publish the results.

Part II: The Collaborative Paper: This paper will be written with your group and will use as research material the individual essays and the interviews. Each group will form a hypothesis that they will attempt to prove using material from the class book and other reading that they have done in our class and in other classes. (Don't decide in advance that you will follow through with the old topic— you may find some more interesting information in the interviews and essays.) You will be expected to quote from the interviews, from the essays, and from any other sources you discover to prove your point. If you wish, you may illustrate your essays, but only use an illustration if it adds to your point or offers proof that you could not otherwise explain.

These essays, too, must be double-spaced and proofread to the point of perfection. We will publish the results, so work carefully and ask for help when you need it.

Midterm Essay—Case Study of Myself as a Writer

As teachers, we have tried to introduce you to new methods and processes of writing. It would be helpful to us to know whether or not this introduction has changed the way you write or the way you think about writing. Refer to the survey you filled out at the beginning of the quarter and your early journal entries, then discuss how you have changed (or not changed) as a writer. Do not hesitate to level with us about what has helped and what has hindered your development as a writer, but whatever your position, give us examples that will make your points clear. REMEMBER: You are writing an essay—don't just list assorted facts; create a thesis and develop it.

Essay III

By now you have probably read and written more about education than you thought was possible, much less desirable. This last essay assignment asks you to make some coherent sense out of your reading and writing. Pick some aspect of your reading and writing (any and all of the material we wrote or read in class) and write an essay that expresses your concern over that matter. Here are a few examples: (1) the conflict between social and academic life, (2) the importance of good teachers, (3) the relevancy of what we learn in high school to daily life, (4) the ways in which high school prepares people to work in the outside world. These are only examples; you need to develop a topic that addresses matters that truly concern you.

Once you have decided upon your topic, use your class book, *Sometimes a Shining Moment* and *Higher Ground* to prove your point. We will talk about developing evidence from sources as we draft the essay.

This essay will be three-fourths of your final grade. Don't let it slip just because you have a lot of other work to do! The essay should follow the usual format; turn it in the day of the final exam.

Final Exam

Using your experience in this class, the experiences of your friends, and any other writing experiences you have had here at OSUM, write an essay that describes the major problems that student writers face when they enter college. Include a detailed description of the problems, but do not stop there. Offer suggestions to instructors that might help the students overcome the problems (you may not suggest that the instructor assign *less* writing!) and give advice to students that will help them perform better on their writing assignments.

Assignments for English 053:
Basic Reading and Writing II

Assignments for Weeks 1–5

Just as Sizer's book is divided into individual sections that form a whole book (complete with an introduction and conclusion), your first essay will be divided into sections that will be incorporated into a comprehensive essay (with a slightly abbreviated introduction and conclusion). So that you can work at your own pace, we are giving you both your journal assignments and essay assignments now. You can use material from your journals, your reading, and other sources in your essays—most of your revision will consist of finding ways to combine journal entries into miniessays with very narrow topics, and miniessays into one long comprehensive essay. As you write, refer to *Horace's Compromise* (use page numbers) and past essays you have written (or ideas that you've had in connection with reading from last quarter or in another class).

Journal Activities—Week 1: "The Students"

Summarize each chapter (Intro., Prologue, Section I), being sure to note Sizer's main points in each chapter. [This is a week-long activity; summarize each chapter as you read it, and write about it in connection with the prompts below.]

1. On pages 2 and 3, Sizer discusses the ways in which adults apply their knowledge about how they learn to understanding new concepts and to solving problems. We think that you would benefit from analyzing your learning style: Do you have favorite places to study? When encountering a problem to solve, do you approach it piece by piece or do you try to see the "big picture" first? How do you learn to play games? These are just questions to stimulate your thinking about how you learn both inside and outside educational institutions. It may be helpful to describe a situation in which you had to start from scratch and learn something entirely new and then go on to analyze the strategies that worked for you. It may also be helpful to describe what situations prevent you from absorbing new ideas.

2. Sizer claims that Horace Smith represents typical teachers. What about Sizer's description of Smith and his schedule surprised you? In what ways does Smith differ from your perception of "typical" teachers? How does Sizer's composite (if we haven't discussed what a composite is yet in class, you will

need to look this word up in your dictionary) sketch of Horace Smith match your previous perceptions of instructors?

3. Are the "typical adolescents" that Sizer describes in Chapters 1, 2, and 3 of Section I found at your school? Write about the ways in which students at your high school (or freshmen here at OSUM) do and/or do not fit his descriptions.

4. After you have summarized Chapters 4 and 5, Part I, respond to the following comments from teachers. What do you think of these comments? Use the book and tell us what you think Sizer would think about these comments. Would he agree with them or disagree? Take a position in between? (Don't forget the why.)

   a. "Students are docile; they just sit in class, never answering questions, never fully engaged in the ideas."

   b. "Nothing will get kids to work if they don't see a purpose for it. The only point in giving grades is to motivate students; you need something to hold over their heads . . . something to make them take responsibility for their education."

Miniessay I: "The Students"

Using your journal entries, write a careful comparison/contrast essay that details the similarities and differences of students in your high school and the students whom Sizer describes. Remember, you must start out with a summary of Sizer's findings and make your descriptions detailed enough so that your readers can picture how your school differs or is the same. Leave nothing undone—student clothing, attitudes toward studies and teachers, personalities, work experiences, socioeconomic status, family backgrounds, and involvement in extracurricular activities. Use Sizer's writing as your model in this paper; try to be as detailed and as "reader friendly" as he is.

Journal Activities—Week 2: "The Program"

Summarize each chapter (1–7 in Part II) being sure to note Sizer's main points in each chapter. [This is a week-long activity; summarize each chapter as you read it and write about it in connection with the prompts below.]

1. Did your day differ greatly from Mark's [Chapter 1, Part II]? Which part of his day seemed the most like yours? Do you think

that the "goals" Sizer attributes to high schools are being met by the schedule in Mark's school? Why or why not? What do you think the goals of high school (or its schedule) should be? (If you choose, you can write about your day at OSUM in comparison to Mark's day. HOWEVER, if you do, you must talk about what you believe to be the goals of a college and how those goals are met by the schedule at OSUM.)

2. Do you agree or disagree with Sizer's assertion in Chapter 2 that "less is more"? Cite evidence for your position from your own educational experience. What do *you* remember from learning experiences you had five years ago?

3. In Chapter 4, Sizer outlines four principles to guide choice of subject matter in high schools. Comment on your perception of the effectiveness of these principles, and then go on to offer specific choices for curricula, taking into account either Sizer's guidelines or the ones you have suggested might be better.

4. Write about your reaction to Sizer's discussion in Chapter 6 of the complex ways in which morals and religion affect education.

Miniessay II: "The Program"

This essay focuses upon the goals of high school. Compare the common goals that Sizer says control most of the high school programs in the U.S.A. with the goals of your high school (or OSUM). Sizer suggests ways to improve education by setting more reasonable goals for today's students. How does Sizer suggest these goals could be accomplished? Which ones did (or does) your school impart and which ones were (or are) neglected? Would Sizer's recommendations work at your high school? If not, what do you suggest?

Journal Assignments—Week 3: "The Teachers"

Summarize Section III, being sure to note Sizer's main points in each chapter. [This is a week-long activity; summarize each chapter as you read it and then write about it in connection with the prompts below.]

1. We'd like to concentrate on the writing strategies that Sizer uses in this section. Review your summaries of Chapters 1–3, noting the clear and logical transitions that Sizer uses to move from one point or example to the next. Explain each example or concept, and then go on to demonstrate how Sizer bridges the gap

between his two significant passages. Here's an example of what we want you to do:

LYNDA'S JOURNAL ENTRY: The main point of this chapter is . . .
(you fill in this part)
First Sizer describes S. Michael as the "stereotypical teacher-nun."
(I'll bet she even carries a ruler.) Although my idea of stereotypical nuns is pejorative, S. Michael is different—she is an example
of someone whom Sizer points to as being an excellent teacher.
Using the Socratic (guiding through posing questions) method, she
engages her students' intellects and as Sizer says, "engages energies" (p. 145). To introduce his next example of good teaching,
Sizer uses the idea of contrast. He contrasts the students in S.
Michael's class who agree "they want to work together," (p. 145)
with the students in Charlie Gross's class who are "demoralized
youngsters" (p. 146). Gross must use completely different incen-
tives to work with students who do not agree that they want to
work together. Instead of the Socratic method, Gross uses . . . (you
finish)

2. After having read Chapter 4, we'd like you to think back to your
   educational experiences (or, if you prefer, experiences here at
   OSUM) and remember conditions which enhanced or detracted
   from learning. After describing specific examples, generalize in
   the same way that Sizer does about the conditions necessary to
   effective learning environments.

3. Sizer devotes two chapters (5 and 6) to discussion about the
   qualities, the training, and the trust teachers need to have in
   order to teach well. Do you agree with his assessment? Write
   about specific areas with which you agree/disagree, being sure
   to develop your arguments with examples and explanations.

4. Discuss your understanding of each of the three types of classrooms that Sizer describes in this section.

Miniessay III: "The Teachers"

Sizer maintains that there are different types of classrooms:

- productive classes where teachers and students interact, making
  learning challenging and important;
- disruptive classes where the teacher exercises little or no control, causing little or no learning to occur;
- calm and orderly classes that are "conspiracies for the least"
  (156), where the teacher and the students do not upset each

other, but where instruction is so mediocre and students so intellectually unchallenged that very little learning takes place.

Which type of classroom was predominant in your experience? Follow Sizer's model for writing by first describing what happens in your class:

- Who is teaching the class? (A composite figure is fine.)
- How do they arrange the room, greet the students?
- What is the teacher's attitude toward the subject?
- How does the teacher present the topic to the students?
- What proves to the teacher that the students have learned what they are being taught?
- How do the students act?
- Who's asking the questions and what kind of questions are being asked?

After your description is complete (and intensely interesting), go on to discuss the effects of this type of instruction on students both during the time they are taking the course and after they have completed it. If you choose to write about a problem classroom, suggest some solutions to increase learning. If you choose to write about a productive class, suggest ways to spread this type of instruction to other teachers and other classes.

Journal Assignments—Week 4: "The Structure"

As usual, summarize (Section IV and Afterword), being sure to note Sizer's main points in each chapter. [This is a week-long activity; summarize each chapter as you read it, and then write about it in connection with the prompts below.]

1. In Chapter 1 Sizer lists six defects common to high schools in America. Think about your high school (or OSUM); which defect stands out to you? Would you agree with Sizer about the importance of the defects he suggests are the most problematic?

2. Are the five imperatives listed in Chapter 2 realistic? Do you agree that these five would produce significantly better education? Why or why not?

3. Respond to Sizer's ideas in Chapter 3. (You know what we want; DO IT!)

4. Frankly, we hated the way Sizer chose to conclude *Horace's Compromise*. Do you agree with us? If so, tell us what you think

Sizer is trying to communicate in this chapter and how you think that he could have written more effectively. If you don't agree with us, provide specific arguments as to why the chapter works.

Comprehensive Essay

Choose one of the following topics for your essay or propose a topic of your own that will explore an idea in Sizer's book that you found particularly interesting and significant. This essay is a summary of your thought on the issue; you can draw from your other essays (as Sizer draws from earlier parts of his book) to make a point—just make sure that you add new insight to what you wrote before rather than merely repeating information. After all, as he wrote the book, Sizer developed his ideas; as you wrote these essays, you should have developed yours.

Topics:

A. Sizer insists that education is based upon a triangle of students, teachers, and educational programs. Which point of the triangle does he claim holds the key to good education and why does he claim this? Who do you think is responsible for providing students with a good education and why do you believe this? How would you suggest encouraging people to take full responsibility for improving education? Discuss those you hold most responsible and any other people you feel need to be concerned: administrators, students, teachers, parents, or legislators.

B. Sizer looks at students, teachers, and programs all over the country and then suggests an overall plan to improve education in America. You have looked at these three elements at your school. Can you suggest a plan to improve education at your high school? Make your plan as detailed and as carefully explained as the plan in Sizer's Afterword.

Essay II—Lives on the Boundary

Sizer says that experienced adults can reflect on their learning or lack of it. That is what we want you to do. We have concentrated upon teachers and systems in our investigation of education. Now we'd like you to analyze yourself as a learner, not just a student. You may choose one or both of the following suggestions to develop your essay.

- Examine your learning history in the same way Mike Rose examines his. He begins his book by talking about what kind of a student he was and what areas affected his ability to learn in high school and college; you should do the same.

- Not all of Rose's reflections about learning involved experiences within the walls of an educational institution; he writes about learning outside school as well. Again, using Rose as a guide, analyze how you learn in environments other than schools.

You might consider using pages two and three of *Horace's Compromise* to aid you in considering how you learn. What kind of experiences have you had outside school where you accomplished a goal or solved a problem or learned a multiple-tasked process (e.g., learning to play an instrument or working on an automobile engine). How do these experiences connect with those you have had inside school? Can you think of any times when you were surprised at how easy learning was? Or, conversely, can you remember times when you had expected something to be easy and instead it turned out to be difficult for you? Remember, the object of this essay is not just to look at yourself as an individual learner, but to see yourself as a representative of typical students in central Ohio. As an expert in this area, you should be able to provide help in recommending change in the local educational system.

Journal Assignments—Weeks 6–9:
Lives on the Boundary
[These assignments appear in Chapter 4 on page 95]

Midterm Exam

For the midterm exam we would like you to write a three to four page essay/letter (double-spaced). You should demonstrate your best thinking and writing; each example should be well thought out and each sentence clear and correct. We'll expect you to check your spelling and word usage carefully. Read the Dickson Letter and, using its format, write your own letter to your relatives explaining the type of education that you want for your children and how you want their teachers to prepare them for the future. Use your own ideas, but back them up with information from the books you've read, class discussions, last quarter's interviews, conversations with friends or relatives, or any other source you can so that these people will be able to help you meet your goals. Remember, Ray Dickson was not a teacher, nor was he a college graduate; he was just an ordinary twenty-nine-year-old-man who had goals for his children. If he could write a letter like this, so can you.

Final Exam

Using Rose and last year's group of letters as models, write a letter to next year's crop of incoming 052/053 students. Tell them what to expect in college (and not just in English) and how to cope with the demands they'll encounter. In effect, you will be writing a survival manual. Give examples, refer to specific classes, your experiences, experiences of friends, details from Sizer, Rose, and whomever. Don't forget tips on dealing with family, work, and fun. The object is to prepare them for the transition from high school to college. You can expect that their experiences will be similar. If you're not an expert on this, no one is.

Notes

Chapter 1

1. While I would agree with Conners about the topics for college papers, I have trouble accepting the notion that high school students are encouraged to write personal essays. Too many high school texts try to teach students to be objective and removed from the topic, to hide their personal feelings in a stilted, impersonal approach to topics—including personal incidents.

2. Lester Faigley, in "Judging Writing, Judging Selves" (*College Composition and Communication,* December 1989), points out that when writing teachers label essays as "honest," "sincere," and "true," they equate good writing with honest writing. Joseph Harris, Faigley tells us, warns that judging an essay by this criterion "reduces writing to a simple test of integrity. Either your guts are out there on the page or they're not" (409). Most teachers avoid demanding guts on the page, but Harris's worst-case scenario for assessing writing is not altogether removed from reality, or from the sort of situation we hear about in freshman composition legend.

Chapter 2

1. Before we judge students and their high school teachers too harshly, we need to admit that we do spend little effort trying to understand nonacademic ways of knowing. For example, Moffett argues rather persuasively that academics, while faulting the conservative for agnosis, ignore the idea of gnosis, knowledge that is based on spiritual or mystical knowing. Thus, the biologist refuses to look at the idea of creationism, the composition teacher refuses to accept religious texts as evidence in an argument.

2. In *Facts, Artifacts, and Counterfacts,* there is a brief description of a class of adult students who were asked to investigate the topic of "Working." This topic, which one of our group tried for a slightly stronger group of remedial students, was much more suitable for our students, 95 percent of whom work full-time while attending college.

3. A number of recent articles discuss a modified use of Wigginton's *Foxfire* model, and a notable few mention using ethnography in the classroom. The reader might want to consult John Lofty's "From Sound to Sign: Using Oral History in the College Composition Class," James M. Deem and Sandra A.

Engel "Developing Literacy Through Transcription," JoAnne Liebman's "Contrastive Rhetoric: Students as Ethnographers," and Sondra Perl's "Reflection on Ethnography and Writing."

Chapter 3

1. Which came first—the reading or the writing? In reality, it's difficult to decide—almost impossible to separate the two activities, I'd have to report. After many attempts to balance the complex elements of reading and writing instruction, I have (in reluctance and frustration) resorted to a traditional linear discussion. How did I decide which problem to start with? I flipped a coin and then, while revising, flipped many a section of the manuscript. Eventually, it seemed most expedient to discuss reading and then writing; however, in practice, I find it impossible to separate the two.

2. Reading out loud can also be informative, but it is initially so painful for some students that it seems hardly justifiable. I also doubt that most students read out loud when doing their homework—the problems of reading are largely silent ones.

3. High school instructors, unfortunately, aren't the only ones who privilege this type of writing; many college instructors value it also because this formulaic, straightforward structure allows for easy testing. If the student can respond in essay form to direct questions designed to demonstrate grasp of information and facts, the instructor will know that the student has been listening and taking notes carefully. At its best, one can say that this form of writing meets the minimal requirements of academic discourse.

4. One note of exception, however. Occasionally, a student will exhibit a different problem: the everlasting, rambling essay that says nothing or does not address the topic in any definable manner. There may be a good essay somewhere in all that text; the trick is figuring out how to get it out of the verbal mire in which it's trapped.

Chapter 4

1. Although this might seem to be a narrow research base, the reading they must do for class is too extensive to require additional sources. Not all of our students have been through the high school research process, but those who have been do not have to abandon the primary skills that they learned. In fact, they often serve as peer resources for those who have no library skills.

2. At this time, Ohio does not have a state-mandated curriculum, only a suggested one. However, in addition to completing the local curriculum requirements, the students must pass a state-wide proficiency exam in order to graduate.

Chapter 5

1. Here I use the term *project* as Simon and Dippo reconstruct Sartre's sense of the term: "an activity determined both by real and present conditions, *and* certain conditions still to come which it is trying to bring into being" (159).

2. Surveys can also prove to be another useful tool for information gathering. However, the problems that the students have with formulating questions for interviews recur when they attempt to formulate questions for surveys. When we decide to include surveys in our data-collecting process, we prepare students to conduct surveys in much the same manner that we prepare them to conduct interviews. They write and test questions in class long before they go public with the survey.

3. Tape recorders are fairly easy to come by; most students have access to one. Since we do so much interviewing, we bought eighteen recorders and two transcription machines with money from an OSU Center for Teaching Excellence Grant. We check them out to the students, who buy their own tapes. If students want to use their own tape recorders, we encourage them to do so.

4. The opportunities to discuss grammar and mechanics should be obvious.

Chapter 6

1. Lest it go unsaid—students aren't the only people being judged in a developmentally structured assessment program. If students are to progress well in their development, then they have to be well taught. Any failure of students to develop may be traced back to the teacher by zealous reformers. Thus, those who analyze proficiency exams may blame what is seen as "poor" student performance on the teachers of a particular district or state.

2. Many people include drafts in the portfolio simply as a mechanical guard against plagiarism—seeing the hand-written draft supposedly proves that the student wrote the paper. However, reviewing the drafts can be, and should be, more than a check against plagiarism. In fact, plagiarism is seldom a problem with portfolio classes since so much of what students write is written in class and reviewed by the teacher as the quarter progresses. Additionally, students in portfolio classes know that I grade portfolios with my colleagues. The chances of getting caught if they plagiarize are immense, so students seldom risk copying a paper. I would just add one cautionary note—if you ask for drafts, read the drafts. Some students look tremendously busy. But the drafts can indicate that they really did little or no revision—some students do not even correct the mechanical errors that the teacher marks. In an indication of how technology may foster deception, I've discovered that if students write on computers, some try to fake the teacher out by printing up several versions of their last draft and marking them draft #1, #2, #3, and so on. The same thing can happen with hand-

written drafts. It's up to the teacher to encourage real revision rather than a collection of paper.

3. As the result of some long-forgotten administrative or pedagogical crisis, OSU—like many other universities—insists students be given a final exam in all courses, regardless of discipline or departmental objectives. They also suggest that instructors administer a midterm exam. The English department has to apply for special dispensation in order to eliminate the test in composition workshops—an action, I'm happy to report, that is now under review.

4. Here I use the term *sentence* rather loosely. If it has a capital at the beginning and closes with a period or some other type of end punctuation, the student thinks it's a sentence, whether a teacher would recognize it as one or not. Therefore, I recognize such a collection of words as a sentence, but insist that they correct whatever faults it might have.

Works Cited

Armstrong-Smith, Cherryl. "Reexamining Basic Writing: Lessons from Harvard's Basic Writers." *Journal of Basic Writing* 7.2 (1988): 68–80.

——. "Writing Without Testing." In *Portfolios: Process and Product*, edited by Pat Belanoff and Marcia Dickson. Portsmouth, NH: Boynton/Cook, 1991.

Baron, Dennis. *Declining Grammar and Other Essays on the English Vocabulary*. Urbana, IL: NCTE, 1989.

Bartholomae, David. "The Study of Error." *College Composition and Communication* 31 (1980): 253–69.

Bartholomae, David. "Inventing the University." In *When a Writer Can't Write: Studies in Writer's Block and Other Composing-Process Problems*, edited by Mike Rose. New York: Guilford, 1985.

Bartholomae, David, and Anthony Petrosky. *Facts, Artifacts and Counterfacts: Theory and Method for a Reading and Writing Course*. Portsmouth, NH: Boynton/Cook, 1986.

Belenky, Mary, Blythe M. Clinchy, Nancy R. Goldberger, and Jill M. Tarule. *Women's Ways of Knowing: The Development of Self, Voice and Mind*. New York: Basic Books, 1986.

Bizzell, Patricia. "Cognition, Convention, and Certainty: What We Need to Know about Writing." *PRE/TEXT* 3.3 (1982): 213–243.

Brandt, Deborah. *Literacy as Involvement: The Acts of Writers, Readers, and Texts*. Carbondale: Southern Illinois University Press, 1990.

——. "The Message Is the Massage: Orality and Literacy Once More." *Written Communication* 6.1 (January 1989): 31–44.

Brodkey, Linda. "Modernism and the Scene(s) of Writing." *College English* 49.4 (April 1987): 396–418.

——. "Writing Critical Ethnographic Narratives." *Anthropology and Education Quarterly* 18.2 (June 1987): 67–76.

——. "Writing Ethnographic Narratives." *Written Communication* 4.1 (January 1987): 25–50.

Bruner, Jerome. *Toward a Theory of Instruction*. New York: W. W. Norton, 1968.

Butler, John F. "Remedial Writers: The Teacher's Job as Corrector of Papers." In *A Sourcebook for Basic Writing Teachers*, edited by Theresa Enos. New York: Random House, 1987.

Conners, Robert J. "Personal Writing Assignments." *College Composition and Communication* 38 (May 1987): 166–183.

Coles, Nicholas, and Susan V. Wall. "Conflict and Power in the Reader-Responses of Adult Basic Writers." *College English* 49.3 (March 1987): 298–314.

Diesing, Paul. "Ethnography." *The English Record* Fourth Quarter (1983): 2–5.

Ede, Lisa, and Andrea Lunsford. *Singular Texts/Plural Authors: Perspectives on Collaborative Writing.* Carbondale: Southern Illinois University Press, 1990.

Elbow, Peter. "Ranking, Evaluating, and Liking: Sorting Out Three Forms of Judgment." *College English* 55.2 (February 1993): 187–206.

———. "Reflections of Academic Discourse: How It Relates to Freshmen and Colleagues." *College English* 53.2 (February 1991): 135–55

Elbow, Peter, and Pat Belanoff. *A Community of Writers.* New York: Random House, 1989.

Faigley, Lester. "Judging Writing, Judging Selves." *College Composition and Communication* 40 (December 1989): 395–412.

Flynn, Elizabeth A. "Gender and Reading." In *Gender and Reading: Essays on Readers, Texts, and Contexts,* edited by Elizabeth A. Flynn and Patrocinio P. Schweickart. Baltimore: Johns Hopkins University Press, 1986.

Fonow, Mary Margaret, and Judith A. Cook. *Beyond Methodology: Feminist Scholarship as Lived Research.* Bloomington: Indiana University Press, 1991.

Hamp-Lyons, Liz, and William Condon. "Questioning Assumptions about Portfolio-Based Assessment." *College Composition and Communication* 44.2 (May 1993): 176–90.

Heath, Shirley Brice. *Ways with Words: Language, Life and Work in Communities and Classrooms.* London/New York: Cambridge University Press, 1983.

Ionesco, Eugene. *Rhinoceros and Other Plays.* New York: Grove Press, 1960.

Kantor, Kenneth, Dan R. Kirby, and Judith P. Goetz. "Research in Context: Ethnographic Studies in English Education." *Research in the Teaching of English* 15.4 (December 1981): 293–309.

Knoblauk, C. H., and Lil Brannon. *Rhetorical Traditions and the Teaching of Writing.* Portsmouth, NH: Boynton/Cook, 1984.

Lauer, Janice M., and J. William Asher. *Composition Research: Empirical Designs.* New York: Oxford Press, 1988.

Lees, Elaine O. "Proofreading as Reading, Errors as Embarrassments." In *A Sourcebook for Basic Writing Teachers,* edited by Theresa Enos. New York: Random House, 1987.

Lloyd-Jones, Richard, and Andrea Lunsford. *The English Coalition Conference: Democracy Through Language.* Urbana: National Council of Teachers of English, 1989.

Moffett, James. *Storm in the Mountains: A Case Study of Censorship, Conflict, and Consciousness.* Carbondale: Southern Illinois University Press, 1988.

North, Stephen. *The Making of Knowledge in Composition: Portrait of and Emerging Field.* Portsmouth, NH: Boynton/Cook, 1987.

Payne, Lucile Vaughan. *The Lively Art of Writing.* Chicago: Follett, 1982.

Perl, Sondra. "Reflections on Ethnography and Writing." *The English Record* Fourth Quarter (1983): 10–11.

Phelps, Louise Wetherbee. "Practical Wisdom and the Geography of Knowledge in Composition." *College English* 53.8 (December 1991): 863–85.

Plato. "The Allegory of the Cave." In *The Norton Reader: An Anthology of Expository Prose,* edited by Authur M. Eastman. 4th edition. New York: W. W. Norton, 1977.

Ponsot, Marie, and Rosemary Deen. *Beat Not the Poor Desk. Writing: What to Teach, How to Teach It, and Why.* Portsmouth, NH: Boynton/Cook, 1982.

Probst, Robert E. "Literature and Literacy." In *On Literacy and Its Teaching,* edited by Gail E. Hawisher and Anna O. Soter. Albany: State University of New York University Press, 1990.

Riley, Philip F. *The Gobal Experience. Vol. 1, Readings in World History to 1500.* Englewood Cliffs, NJ: Prentice Hall, 1987.

Rose, Mike. *Lives on the Boundary: The Struggles and Achievements of America's Underprepared.* New York: The Free Press, 1989.

———. "Remedial Writing Courses: A Critique and a Proposal." In *A Sourcebook for Basic Writing Teachers,* edited by Theresa Enos. New York: Random House, 1987.

Severino, Carol. "Where the Cultures of Basic Writers and Academia Intersect: Cultivating the Common Ground." *Journal of Basic Writing* 11.1 (1992): 4–15.

Sheehy, Gail. *Passages: Predictable Crises of Adult Life.* New York: Bantam Books, 1976.

Simic, Charles. "Reading Philosophy at Night." In *The Best American Essays: 1988,* edited by Annie Dillard. New York: Ticknor and Fields, 1988.

Simon, Roger I., and Donald Dippo. "On Critical Ethnographic Work." *Anthropology and Education Quarterly* 17 (1986): 195–202.

Sizer, Theodore. *Horace's Compromise: The Dilemma of the American High School.* Boston: Houghton Mifflin, 1984.

Sommers, Jeffery. "Bringing Practice in Line with Theory: Using Portfolio Grading in the Composition Classroom." In *Portfolios: Process and Product,* edited by Pat Belanoff and Marcia Dickson. Portsmouth, NH: Boynton/Cook, 1991.

Sondheim, Stephen. *Sunday in the Park with George.* New York: Dodd, Mead, and Co., 1986

Spradley, James P., and David W. McCurdy. *The Cultural Experience: Ethnography in Complex Society.* Prospect Heights, Illinois: Waveland Press, 1972.

Tarbuck, Edward J., and Frederick K. Lutgens. *The Earth: An Introduction to Physical Geology.* Third edition. Columbus: Merrill Publishing Company, 1990.

Tompkins, Jane. "Fighting Words: Unlearning to Write the Critical Essay." *Georgia Review* 42 (1988): 585–90.

Tracy, Ann B. *Higher Ground: A Memoir of Higgins Classical Institute.* Camden, ME: Down East Books, 1988.

Troyka, Lynn Quitman. "Defining Basic Writing in Context." In *A Sourcebook for Basic Writing Teachers,* edited by Theresa Enos. New York: Random House, 1987.

Ulmer, Gregory L. "Textshop for an Experimental Humanities." In *Reorientations: Critical Theories and Pedagogies,* edited by Bruce Henricksen and Thais E. Morgan. Urbana: University of Illinois Press, 1990.

Vygotsky, L. S. *Thought and Language.* Cambridge, MA: MIT University Press, 1962.

Wigginton, Eliot. *Sometimes a Shining Moment: The Foxfire Experience.* Garden City, NY: Doubleday, 1986.

Zinsser, William. *Inventing the Truth: The Art and Craft of Memoir.* Boston: Houghton Mifflin, 1987.

Zitlow, Connie Swartz. "'To Think about What I Think': Inquiry and Involvement." In *On Literacy and Its Teaching,* edited by Gail E. Hawisher and Anna O. Soter. Albany: State University of New York University Press, 1990.